MARIKAI

The information contained herein is of a generalized spiritual nature gathered through the authors' own research and is presented for educational purposes only. The author of this book does not dispense medical advice or prescribe the use of any technique as a form of treatment for physical, emotional or medical problems. If readers are experiencing any such issues they are encouraged to seek the advice of a qualified health care professional. In the event you use any of the information provided in this book on yourself or others, the author and publisher assumes no responsibility for your actions.

The selection of internet addresses (URLs) provided throughout were valid at the time of publication however due to the dynamic nature of the Internet, some addresses may have changed or ceased to exist.

www.redbubble.com/people/kaiphoenix

www.facebook.com/kaifavenphoenix

ISBN-13: 978-0-9944317-0-7

Printed by CreateSpace, an Amazon.com company

Available from CreateSpace.com, Amazon.com and other retail outlets

www.createspace.com/5717315

MARIKAI

MY YEAR OF DIVINE GUIDANCE

KAI PHOENIX

CHANNELING

NAMELESS

&

ALL OF THE CIRCLE

To my beautiful daughter, Ruvé

You are my soul sister, my BFF, my everything

You are a reason I stay here on earth

Thank you for the love that you share with me daily

Thank you for being you

I love you *beyond* infinity

And to the far reaches of immortality

Our bond is *nigh*

And so

My beautiful Ruvé

I dedicate this book to you

Nameless

Pure of heart

And pure of soul

Words cannot describe

My love for you

To me you are the ultimate *Being*

And I am so proud

To know you

HOW TO USE THIS BOOK

This book can be read in a myriad of ways.

Page to page from beginning to end as you follow my year's journey, each channel experience building on the one before it.

As an oracle, opening a page at random to reveal a message, musing, thought for the day, idea or insight appropriate to you at a given time.

Alternatively looking up specific topics of interest and for this reason I've provided quite a comprehensive contents list so you can either jump ahead or revisit those areas that resonate with you at will.

For those who enjoy a more interactive, sensory and tonal experience there are visual and audio links referenced throughout the chapters.

Warning: This book contains a *Higher* intelligence. Only read this book if you have an open mind... or if your mind is closed and you wish it to be opened.

CONTENTS

PART TWO
MY YEAR OF DIVINE GUIDANCE

PREFACE

In the beginning there was nothing
And out of nothing manifested this book
This is my little seed
That I send out into the world
In the hope that one day
It will grow into an orchard

~ *Kai Phoenix*

I did not purposefully set out to write a book. Instead my intention was only to seek solace from my troubles during a particularly trying time in my life where I felt desperately isolated from all of humanity, unable to garnish either emotional or intellectual support from those around me. This was partly due to my hermetic nature but also the deeply personal issue I faced and its involving another human being. In essence I couldn't tell anyone or I would have betrayed this person and lost their trust forever which would have destroyed me.

Shortly thereafter I began to channel. I had never channeled before and this came about organically through a series of unfolding events (as discussed in the introduction) and well, desperate times called for desperate measures as I reached out to the Universe for help.

Once the lines of communication opened I couldn't contain my excitement. I had tapped into such wiseness and a knowingness I didn't know existed, at least not for me. I knew of others who channeled, had read about it, tried it previously and failed only to give up. Perhaps I wasn't gifted or special enough. Now the answers to my questions flowed to me with such ease and I was accumulating mounds of information on all sorts of topics, some deeply personal others universal.

Soon I noticed a profound sense of calm and peace wash over me as I was gathering new insights and different perspectives on my worldly issues. Suddenly I had back-up, someone (or something) to turn to in times of turmoil and no longer having to face things alone, nothing seemed insurmountable anymore and this gave me a great sense of relief and newfound joy. I felt uplifted and was walking on air.

I channeled at least twice a week and whilst there is one primary guide (who for reasons you shall see will remain nameless) others presented themselves throughout the next year, each displaying their own uniqueness. They became my *'Go to's'* my BFF's, my confidants. Whenever I had burning questions or faced difficult life hurdles they were always there to offer their sage advice. After about six months of communication I realized they had imparted a sizeable knowledge bank that I could and felt I should share with others, not only for the information itself but even more so for the experience of what its *actually* like to channel and be in communication with your guides, the support and encouragement they provide and their unique perspectives.

Marikai, My Year Of Divine Guidance is not specifically a 'how-to' book on channeling. The how-to contained within is more incidental, a byproduct of the channeling experience as I take you on a voyeuristic ride through a year in my life after making contact with a discarnate being, journaling the communication between us. The focus is more on the developing relationship, trust and friendship between channel and guide. How we work together to resolve life's issues with the aim of propelling me towards a better future on all levels, spiritually, emotionally, physically and even financially.

The primary reason for sharing this with you is to help put you in touch with your own *Higher Source* and its many benefits. You see rather than being anything mystical or supernatural the basis of channeling is pure Quantum physics, an energy transference available to everyone with nothing psychic nor occult about it. You don't have to be special, gifted, or even spiritually inclined as it's an inherent ability that we all possess. Therefore channeling is accessible to *everyone* and not just reserved for those who consider themselves new of age. Rather we have reached a transformational period and it's something I believe we should all be doing not only to take ourselves to a *Higher* place of existence but to help bring about planetary change. Channeling helps you be a better person and then you take that better person out into the world. Imagine that on a mass scale and that is what the guides are trying to achieve, a global uplifting of the planet but they do this by aiding us as individuals as on earth we are all different aspects of the whole.

Communication with guides provides you with your own private and individualized counsel. You can access them at will anywhere, anytime and they'll provide you with knowledge, insight and wisdom that is tailored specifically to you and your circumstances, extending beyond the normal insights received during meditation and going deeper into dialogue. Have you ever been indecisive? Do you have unanswered questions relating to work, life, beyond life, love, relationships, money, health, your soul's purpose and deep universal questions or struggled with emotions such as fear, anxiety, anger or low self-esteem etc.? Then channeling could benefit you. By utilizing some of the methods and insights provided in this book and connecting to your own Higher Source it's possible to bring more balance and a sense of peace and calm back into your life as you more easily overcome life's challenges.

Maybe your new to channeling, have heard about it and perhaps even read some 'how-to' channel books that concentrate more on the instruction. How do you know if channeling is something you *want* to do if you have no idea what the actual experience itself is like and how it can benefit you on a daily basis? *Marikai, My Year Of Divine Guidance* provides a fly on the wall experience for all those curious about what it's like to *actually channel ones guide.* Reading this book may help relieve you of any unfounded fears that channeling means surrendering control to someone (or something) outside yourself. This couldn't be further from the truth. Here you'll see firsthand that whilst I consider the guides perspectives I ultimately remain in control of all choices pertaining to my life and that they are not dictators but merely guides and this is what they do, guide.

Perhaps your aware of channeling, have tried it but are missing that *one key ingredient* that stops you from succeeding in communicating with your own Higher Self or a Higher Source. *Marikai, My Year Of Divine Guidance* can help solve this issue.

You'll learn how to...

- **Suspend the ego**
- **Access the Higher Self**
- **Tune into wisdom from the Higher Guides and Universal Mind (thereby accessing tools and knowledge for improving your life)**

You'll also find information on...

- **Space-time (or beyond space-time) and star travel**
- **Attuning your vibration to others**
- **The experience of *Light* and *Being***
- **Opening portals into other dimensions**

And learn about...

- **Tapping into thought energy**
- **The lost art of telecommunication**
- **Frequencies and sensing**
- **The absorption method of communication**

Included are exercises and meditations on stilling the mind, telepathic communication, silent sight, earth walking and receiving a gift from the Universe. There are discussions on vibrational eating and how to lose some kilos, absent healing and methods for clearing and re-energizing. Along the way you'll discover the *Source of All Creation* and different pathways to *enlightenment*. Many of life's biggest questions are discussed such as the existence of god, the truth about reincarnation and the cause of disease.

However *Marikai, My Year Of Divine Guidance* is not purely an instruction manual. All of this is wrapped up in story making it a less academic and more enjoyable read as more theoretical based discussions are broken up with delightful snippets of tree whispering (communication with tree *beings*) and stories garnished from my life both past and present such as "The unusual tale of a famous Australian psychic medium," "The stranger, a meeting," and personal real life dramas such as the lugging of buckets in drought ridden Queensland.

Finally you'll learn that "Heaven is on earth, in front of you and all around you, you just need to open your eyes to see it." *Marikai, My Year Of Divine Guidance* opens you up to this type of sensing and the possibilities out there waiting to be discovered.

INTRODUCTION

It's funny how life sends you messages, signs and how a multiplicity of them at a set time can send your life on a different course entirely. Is it fate, guidance or merely coincidence?

The effect of the warm November sun on surrounding flora sees me linger at the entrance to the Noosa library as I take pleasure in the spring aroma while rifling through the second hand book cart. Books are selling for just two dollars and magazines are fifty cents. Bargain! Was I guided here or was it fate that I picked up a seemingly innocuous book on channeling when really I was looking for something to cut up and collage for my art practice?

It was the question and answer format that peaked my interest more than anything. It was like I was seeing it for the first time though I knew this was untrue. It was speaking to me with a clarity I hadn't noticed before, grabbing my attention. The others before it I would find out later were seeds but this one would sprout and grow. I paid my two dollars and left unaware that my life was about to change forever.

It was during the reading of this book[1] which was in no other way a revelation that I coincidentally (or not) came across some old automatic writing of mine (another seed) from five years ago while I was tidying an ever-growing collection of papers. It was two or three pages long of scribbled scratching's and at the time I had dismissed it as a failure, brushing it aside and only through my artistic hoarding habits was it able to survive the years. My original one even before that was a mere five words and only survived in my memory. Now I looked at the pages in a new light. The same question and answer format was there only I hadn't actually written the questions down but I could tell what they were by the answers. The answers (honest, candid and truthful) were not coming from the self. How could I tell? Because it was not what I wanted to hear. One of the questions I posed was typical of any female and forgivable of one who still finds themselves single at a certain age.

Q. Will I ever marry?

A. Honey at forty-five you'd think you'd give up, LOL.

Jokes, that last bit was me talking. The real answer was I could if I really wanted to but I was married to my art and so had little time for anything else, which was true. Its wiseness struck me and so I decided to give automatic writing another go and on the third of November 2012, on a three-hour train trip down to Brisbane, I put pen to paper.

To say I was rude and naïve in the beginning is an understatement and you'll recognize this in my opening questions posed to my guide. I shudder looking back at those early beginnings but what patience he showed me right from those very early stages, never taking offence but gently nudging, guiding and informing me as I travelled this new path.

At this stage in my life I was heading towards fifty. A middle aged single mum of a teenage daughter working for minimum wage in a job I struggled to embrace, barely surviving from paycheck to paycheck, tortured by an unfulfilled vocational desire to be an artist and disillusioned with life. A mouse trapped in the wheel, running but getting nowhere. Each year, each decade, seemingly more difficult than the one before.

What if I were to follow divine guidance for one whole year?
Would it change my life?

The following is the lead up to and years' journey of both personal and universal life questions and answers, communication between my guides and myself. The guides' words are verbatim, unedited and as transcribed through me. I feel to edit even one word would be to dishonor and discredit them. I have been entrusted with their words, they speak through me and I am truly honored by this blessing. They (collectively known as *The Circle*) have become my closest friends and confidants, seeing me through the toughest of times that for personal reasons I don't always disclose, merely allude to.

Even though in the early stages of communication I was truly naïve I later purposefully pose the questions from a place of one who is innocent or of perceived ignorance. Even though I think I might know what the answer to a question is I want to know what the guides think, what *their* perspective is and so often 'play dumb' so to speak. The guides are fully aware of what I'm doing of course, which is suspending the ego. I want to take this opportunity to thank them for their love, their honesty, their truth, encouragement, guidance and non-judgment no matter my state of being. I'm only human after all, though I'm hearing them say now, "No, you are one of *Light*."

This is *not* fiction. This is true life, my life, in all its rawness.

When I asked my guide Nameless if he wanted to add anything to the introduction of this our book, to the readers he said, "Just enjoy it as I know you will."

I know he is proud of me and all that we have achieved.

PART ONE

MAKING CONTACT AND RECEIVING MY NAME

1

NOV 2012

Most of the inhabitants of this Noosa hinterland town known as Cooroy will still be asleep as I watch the train meander down the tracks towards the platform. It's around six-thirty a.m. and I've already taken a half hour car journey from my little village of Boreen Point that nestles on the edge of Lake Cootharaba. Some people call it Boring Point because they think not a lot happens there. That *is* the point, perfect for someone like me who lately has an aversion to all things human.

Boreen Point is more of a hamlet than a village, consisting of a characteristic old pub (The Apollonian), a general store, the Yacht club and a campground. The entire village is made up of just fifteen streets surrounded by a brackish lake on one side and dense Australian bush on the other. That's about it. Living on the edge of nature it's a haven, a world away from the chaos of society where one has the glory of sitting on ones veranda watching the goanna's slowly make their way through the leaf litter that beds the yard and laugh at the brush turkey's as they scurry on past, chasing each other. A keen eye can spot an echidna on the way down to get an ice-cream from the milk bar and the kookaburras' (with no idea about the meaning of Sunday morning sleep-ins) serve as early morning alarm clocks.

There's a specific corner on entry or exit from the town at dawn or dusk which requires you to slow down to avoid hitting the kangaroos as they cross to a favored watering hole on the other side of the road. Once on my way to work about five a.m. I witnessed the car in front of me (thankfully) going slow enough that it barely tapped a kangaroo of such Neanderthal size that he towered over the cars roof, his face clearly visible to me as we all came to an abrupt stop. A Mexican standoff ensued neither party wanting to move, both frozen with shock. The 'roo' communicating with his eyes gave a look of disdain followed by a '*how dare you*' squint, staring the human out like a mother telling off a child (You know, '*The look*') before he once again took off into the bush leaving the cars occupant and I momentarily stunned before we dared continue on our journey's.

Laying on the towns jetty during a full moon on a balmy night is to die for as you kick back and become one with the stars and on any given day a black Shetland pony roams the streets partaking in whoever's grass is the juiciest. Who knows whom he belongs to? Occasionally the little town comes alive with festivity, mainly during the school holidays where the masses descend on its unspoilt beaches and shallow waters but also during sailing season and the outdoor art and sculpture symposium known as Floating Land.

Today is my big day out. I'm headed down to the Paper and Craft expo in Brisbane to get some ideas for my art practice and carefully nurse a coffee as I make my way to a seat that has to accommodate me for the next few hours. To counteract boredom I've bought along pencil and paper with the idea of trying my hand at automatic writing to help me while away the time. The train reaches Eumundi before I've even managed to make myself comfortable, shuffling all my bags and paraphernalia just so and once settled I take out the pencil.

Being a relative novice to this unusual process renders me unsure of what to ask or even how to go about it so my opening line is more of a demand than a question and I pause with bated breath as I wait for a reply. This unbeknownst to me was the vital element that had been missing in my last dismal attempts to communicate and what thence spewed forth from my pencil like one possessed both astonished and astounded me. My life in an instant changed forever as I discovered my own personal guide, a *Being of Light* from *The Source* of *All Kind*, nameless and faceless because these were only distractions to what he wished to convey.

The communication that followed over the next year is a series of both personal and universal life questions as we discuss topics such as mindfulness versus mindlessness, the art of telepathic communication and the possibility of time travel interspersed with my desperate pleas for help as I face floods, drought, teenage dramas, work difficulties and man troubles. I share all of this with you in the hope that you too may benefit from 'his' wiseness.

SAT 3RD NOVEMBER

Identify yourself.

I am nameless so if you must call me by name call me Nameless. I know you think that's not very glamorous a name but you will find it to be very appropriate. I know you have a question, ask away.

I'm going to jump right in with the heavy stuff.

Q. Do we choose our life/person/parents/children/ disease etc. before we come here to planet earth as humans? Also what/who were we before we came here?

That is a lot to ask in one go. Perhaps you should simplify it. Start at the beginning.

Q. Ok, what/who were we before we came here?

Hmm. Energy. Everything is energy, you always have been and always will be energy in its most simple form.

Q. Then what is energy in its most simple form?

A thought.

Q. Where does thought come from?

The being of all things combined for you are one and the same.

I don't understand, please explain further.

In the beginning there was creation but even before creation there was something else. I hear you ask what was this something else? A cloud, a mass, I am trying to find words to describe it so that you can/must understand. I feel your nausea (from the train travel) you had better stop now.

It's true, I'm feeling sick. Six in the morning is not an hour I usually embrace. It's too early for travel and my body desperately needs some sugar. I pull a sandwich out of my bag and a high sugar soft drink specifically for this purpose.

I have travelled this route enough to understand my body and its needs and so too it seems does Nameless. After consuming my bags contents and some time spent resting my eyes on the scenes passing by the windows of the train Nameless interjects my thoughts.

You see the green of the pastures outside the window? That is thought!

Thought = Color + Light = Energy

So... **Color + Light = Energy =Thought**

Or you could say ...

Thought *creates* **Energy** *creates* **Color + Light** *creates* **Thought** *creates* **Energy** etc.

That is creation. (See Figure 1:1)

Q. It's a bit of a chicken and egg situation, what came first the chicken or the egg? It still doesn't explain where thought and energy come from. What came first, Color + Light, Thought or Energy?

Don't you get it? Color + Light. Color + Light produce a Thought which is Energy which leads to the production of Mass with the end result being a thing, an object. Grass, trees, you, the train etc. There is Thought (and Color + Light) behind everything you see, hear and experience.

Q. But what creates Light?

Light is the purest form of energy. There was never anything else. *It just is.* It always has been and always will be. You have heard of *The Light, Returning to the Light, Light Workers* etc. You are but a fragment of the *Light,* a spinoff so to speak and when you are no longer you, you will return to being *Light*. That is, your soul energy is *Light*, your soul returns to the *Light*, your body/flesh disintegrates or a better description is merges. There is *Light* in all of us and everything. We all return to the *Light*.

The life cycle then starts over. You have returned to the soup pot so to speak. It may be eons before you fragment off again and what you become depends on...*the size of the fragment, the speed of the spinning* and *the pitch of the vibration* as you fragment off. This answers the question of reincarnation that you were going to ask me. In this manner we may reincarnate or we may not, it is not necessarily so and as I said may take eons for this to occur. Meanwhile you are Color + Light, Thought and Energy in its purest form. How much of a fragment spins off combined with the level of vibration/spinning and speed of this fragment determines whether you are e.g. a blade of grass or a cow or a human etc. As we spin off our energy slows down producing mass. The slower the energy the denser the mass. Also humans have the ability to bring fragments together to make other things, the outcome of which depends on the combination of fragments and their resulting speed and vibration. (See Figure 1:2)

Disease is a result of gravitational force on the human body. It weighs everything down like lead. The heaviness of the gravitational force slows the spin and vibration of your Color + Light Source (what makes you, you), this leads to the breakdown of cells. They can't function as they should as they are not spinning, vibrating, to their optimal level. This contributes to decay, ageing and ultimately death as you know it. As soon as you fragment and spin off from the original Light Source into creation (your world) as a baby gravity takes effect. Of course chemicals and your environment speed up this process but if you were to live in the purest of lands and drink the purest of waters, breathe the best air etc. you will still age and die because of the gravitational force. Remember it is only your body and flesh that ages and dies. As your soul is pure Light Energy it is not subject to gravitational force and returns to the Light.

SUN 4TH NOVEMBER

You are rousing from your sleep now and as everything is calm and peaceful and you are receptive I want to talk to you about names.

You asked me for my name. I don't have one, therefore I am nameless.

In your world you name and label everything. You do this to describe and explain things to each other and yourselves also. In coming to earth you have lost the ability to telepathically communicate (most of you, some still do for e.g. psychics are telepathic communicators).

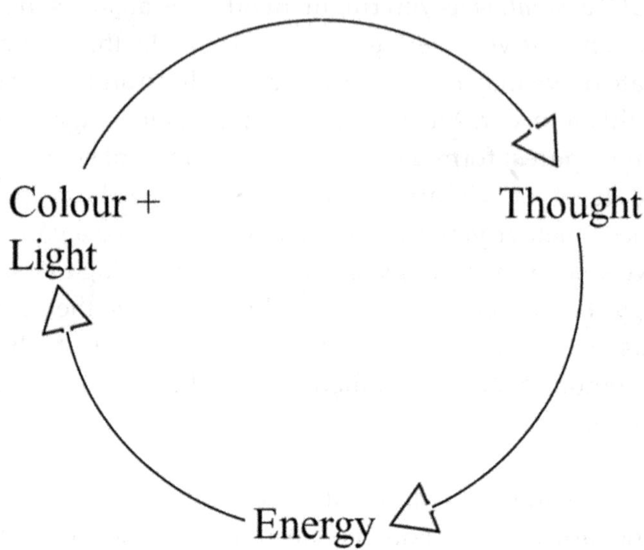

Figure 1.1: Creation

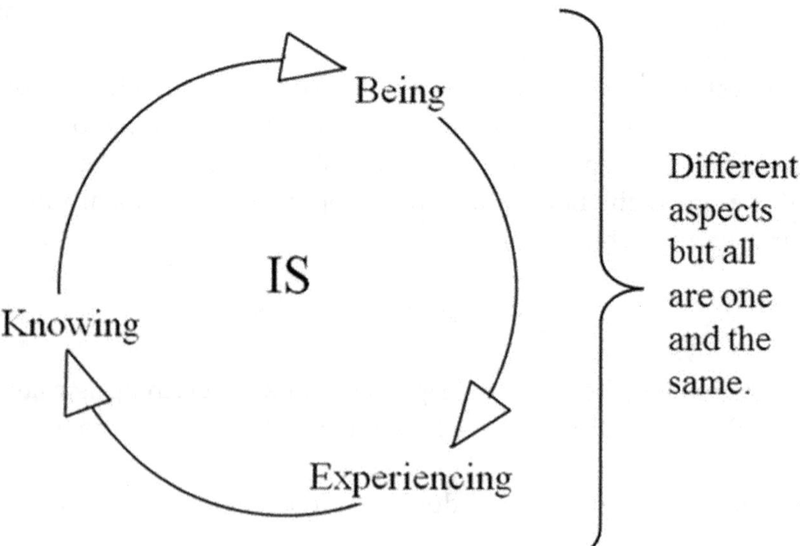

Figure 1.3 : Aspects of Knowing

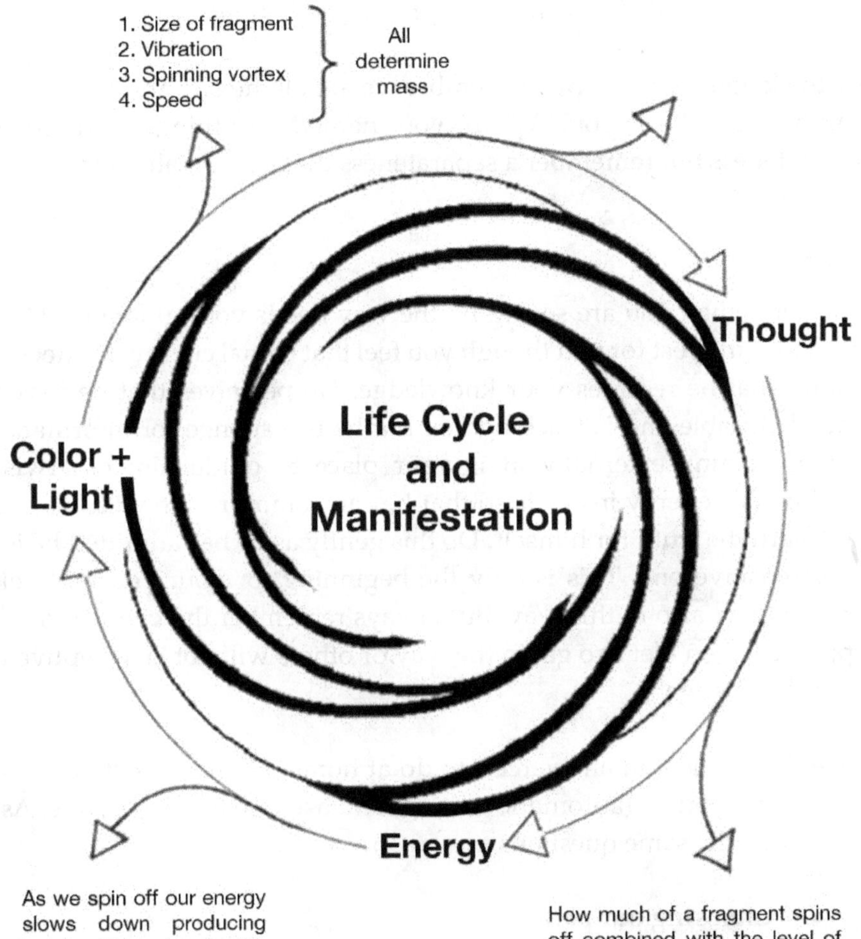
1. Size of fragment
2. Vibration
3. Spinning vortex
4. Speed
All determine mass
Thought
Life Cycle and Manifestation
Color + Light
Energy
As we spin off our energy slows down producing mass. The slower the energy the denser the mass.
How much of a fragment spins off combined with the level of vibration/spinning and speed of this fragment determines the mass produced. E.g. Cow/ human/blade of grass etc.

Figure 1.2 : Life Cycle and Manifestation

You require words to converse with each other and label things to make sense of your world. You lose so much of *who you are* in this process. We are all one and the same. I know you have heard that many times over.

Q. Hang on, how do I know this is you talking and not me?

By the language I use. But remember we are all the one and the same. I am an aspect of you. When you name/label things you create separateness but remember a separateness that is not really there.

□□□

The gentleman you are seeing by the way needs your guidance. He is not a love interest for you though you feel that carnal energy. He doesn't realize that he requires your knowledge. He perceives that he is very knowledgeable and is teaching you but he is a sponge for information that is coming externally. It is your place to guide him otherwise. Redirect his energy inwards so that he can communicate with his soul and learn the truth for himself. Do this gently as he has admitted he is a very sensitive one. This is only the beginning for you. You will help many others also in this way. But always remember the gentle humble approach. Don't let ego get in the way or others will not be receptive to your knowledge.

Give the gentleman an exercise to do at home. Homework if you like. Relay what you do (automatic writing) and ask him to do the same. Ask him to ask the same questions as you on…

- **Choosing our parents**
- **Choosing our disease**
- **Reincarnation.**

Ask him to search deep into his soul for the truth, his truth (which may be different to yours). See if he comes up with the same answers as you. He may or may not but this will open up a whole new discussion for you. You both have much to talk about but remember, real communication comes on a telepathic level (= feeling energy).

Remember what he told you (telepathically) last night on your journey home from Brisbane. You were in your car but were speaking to him some distance away. He told you he has a secret from his past.

Most people do, that's nothing new but his secret has a sinister edge to it. Something he could have or would have been jailed for. You felt he got away with it though, perhaps someone else was blamed. He carries the guilt around though and dreads the day he may be discovered or found out. It would devastate him. He is not the same person he used to be, he has grown with the knowledge he has been accumulating. If someone were to find out his secret it would make him that person that he used to be all over again (though temporarily) causing a regression that he would struggle to get out of. Because of his sensitivity he would fall into a deep depression.

I feel like he physically hurt someone which is not in his nature now and this is why he would be so devastated if someone found out. I don't think I should confront him with it, being privy to people's private experiences I should respect this and their feelings/emotions. I wouldn't want him to regress, he has come so far and it has taken him a long time and been a real struggle.

▫▫▫

Getting back to separateness...when you name/label things you create separateness. E.g. that's a chicken (therefore it's not me). There's a tree/house/cow etc. (therefore it's not me). I am .... (Insert your name) your Peter/Tom/Mary etc. therefore you are not me, you are separate to me. This is how it goes on earth as when you occupied this planet you lost the ability to telepathically communicate. One of the worst things you could have done as a race was to name things. By naming things you cause the perception of separateness. That is a table, therefore we are different, separate. That is how you think but it is not so.

Imagine if you lived in a world where *nothing* was named, labeled. Everything just *is*. There is no *thought* around anything just the *experience* of it. The *feeling* of it. Remember thought is a *feeling* expressed. So people are walking around this new earth with no names. They just are. Without a name you are forced to *feel* them (their energy) to *know* them. Even though they are you (as we are one and the same) they are an aspect of you and for you to truly know that aspect of yourself (that is them) you must *feel* the *experience* of them. You will know when you have felt it as it is a *knowing* for want of a description, i.e. you just *know* them/you. There is no longer a need for words or communication as you just *know* all that there is, their thoughts, feelings, experiences. This is telepathic communication. This is ONENESS. You are ALL KNOWING.

When you reach this level of *All Knowing* it can be very exciting for you. You've done it. You have reached *Enlightenment,* or one aspect of it. This feeling of excitement that you have reached *Knowing* and the consequent thinking surrounding this feeling and what just happened and what it is like is enough to bring you crashing back to the earthly plane as we know it, as by bringing thought into the process you are no longer just *being,* just experiencing, you are no longer in *Knowing* (a Higher realm process). There is no thought in Knowing. There just *is*. (See Figure 1:3)

I feel I could keep writing but I have to stop now. I have to get up and take my daughter surfing as promised. I hate to interrupt this process. Sorry.

Very well that is all for today.

Hmm, I can tell you're disappointed. I can feel it.

Yes you're very right. I was having fun.

Me too. I feel like I've found a friend. I know you feel the same and we are both excited. Happy days!!!

SAT 17TH N0VEMBER

Q. *Can I channel, automatic write, for others? Could I be good at it? Could I earn a living from it or earn enough to get by, pay the bills?*

Yes that is the purpose of this exercise. I hear your desperation but things cannot be rushed. Start small and start slow. Practice tuning into others when you can. Ask their *being* questions. If you do this from afar you will not always know if you are right but every time you do it you are learning to tap into thought energy. You will find some easier than others, those with a purer light energy form, start with those. They will be more receptive to your knowledge and give you the confidence to keep learning and keep going, growing. You will not always get it right in the beginning. This is because you need to learn to adjust your vibration to theirs and everybody's vibration is different (like fingerprints), their vibration is what makes them unique. But remember they are an aspect of you so it's a matter of matching that vibration to get to know that aspect of yourself. You will be there to help and guide people in many different ways. Some it will be to pass information on that they require in order to shift their energy towards a purer light form. Often people get stuck in dark energy and in this state the weight and heaviness clouds them like gravity, slowing their vibration and breaking down their thought energy so that their light energy is diminished. If this is allowed to carry on to the extreme the light source will go out and the person will become extinct to your planet. However the soul is released and not being subject to such weighty issues will return to pure Color + Light. It is best you not work with such troubled souls in the beginning while you are learning (approx. three years). Remember to start slow and gentle, building knowledge as you go. Always be humble. What you do for yourself you can do for others. Look at what has just been written and how easily it comes to you. Merely ask the question and it will be answered. This is how you do for others as well.

Q. Yes but can I earn a living from it?

I hear your concern and the trouble you are in at the moment. If you want it to be so it will be so. Many are willing to pay for your services. Yes you may need to advertise in the beginning but you will get many by word of mouth so you no longer have to do this. This is the ideal way. You will help and guide many people. To some you will provide answers to their questions, guidance and knowledge. To others you will show them the way to pure Color + Light, the *Being* and *All Knowing* of telepathic communication. You will start with the former and work your way towards the latter as your own knowledge and experience grows.

Your gentleman friend is a perfect starting point as he is very receptive to your knowledge. You get very frustrated with his external beliefs. Don't. He does not know any different and is searching for the truth. You can show him that truth but to do so you must humble yourself. I hear you when you say communication is not one of your strong points but you must overcome this if you are to carry on in your quest. Tame that ego of yours and speak from a humble place and you will find the communication flows much easier.

You see I am here to help and guide you. You only have to ask, seek guidance for your troubles and I can show you the way forward.

Q. Where, how will I start?

Start with your gentleman friend. Let him know where truth comes from (his internal *being*). Show him the way. Guide him to his truth. If you can do this then you will be ready to move on to others.

Q. But how will I do this?

I feel you can talk to him and share your knowledge but to truly understand he will need to experience it for himself. You will need to guide him towards the physical manifestation of what you talk about. Sit down with him and share your way to telepathic communication and tapping into the *Light Source Energy*. You know what has to be done and said and even where you should do it. You are right to wait until the time and conditions are just right and that private beach you are thinking of is the perfect place to do it. You will need to allow time as he will want to talk about it afterwards. Also this will increase his fascination with you so ensure you have your boundary's set first. You know what I'm talking about.

Q. What is to be said?

Let go of all thought, feeling and emotion. Just '*Be*' and then feel what enters. When everything is abandoned from the mind only pure Color + Light Energy is left. *Feel* this pure energy with *no thought attached,* i.e. don't think about what you are feeling, just *feel* (This allows you to tap into the other person's vibration), *feel* their energy/vibration (Remember Energy = Color +Light = the Light Source) for as soon as you put a thought onto the feeling you are no longer of the Higher realm but have come crashing back to earth. It is no more complicated than that but many struggle to do it bound up by the mind. If you can rid yourself of the entrapment of the mind you can…

- **Do anything**
- **Go anywhere (austral travel, teleportation)**

Nameless automatically switches topics when I wonder about the labor of writing our conversations…

One day you will not have to write everything down. You will hear it and it will just become a *knowing*. In this way answers will come faster. At this time you are learning and growing which is benefited more by writing. Do as you are imagining and have your friend 'S' hide an object. See if you can find it. This will be a useful exercise for you. Ask me what the object is, then ask me for directions. I will guide you. This will allow you to have faith in me and what we are doing. I am here to help with your achievements. 'S' will think it is a game, it is not necessary to explain yourself. Ask 'J' to give you three questions. I will aid you in the answers. Don't discuss them with her beforehand. The first time get her to write them down. The next time you will know the question for yourself. I can tell you now she has concerns for her book but this is nothing really new to you. She sees the achievements of others and feels she is being left behind. Her time will come. Enough said.

Q. Nameless is on a roll, he switches topics again.

By the way the woman that came to you today was searching for answers. She came to you twice and whether she knows it or not was reaching out for help. She has lost her son many years ago as she told you and is recognizing the loss of her granddaughter, whom she raised, as she grows towards womanhood. She is grieving all over again as the granddaughter is the link to her son. She is living in fear and feeling quite lost, searching for something to fill the void. She is heading in the right direction and will find a strong support network in the lovely feminine energy of this continuum (group). She is just at the beginning of her new journey and as she learns to let go of the granddaughter it will open up areas for new opportunities to arise. I feel it will take two to three years before she finds her *happy place* and comfort zone. By then the granddaughter will be on the verge of womanhood.

I know you recognized her plight and offered her words of comfort regarding her son being proud (of the way she raised his daughter) but you were subtle in your approach and she failed to get the message. This is partly due to her being all consumed by her troubles and failing to be a good listener. As you gain confidence so too will your approach to such things. Taking someone by the hand and looking them in the eye will *always* get their attention, even if they seem to brush it off your words will have an effect for days, weeks, afterwards. In this way you can provide the peace that they crave.

□

THUR 22ND NOVEMBER

Identify yourself.

I am Nameless, I am always with you as I am part of you. This should give you comfort, knowing that you are never alone and therefore never feel lonely even though I know you don't.

Q. *I'm going to leave this one open, what information do you have for me today?*

Nothing - for there is nothing to know, nothing to do, just *be*. It is in the *being* that you become *All Knowing*. To do that you must still the mind.

Q. Can you excuse me while I get a pencil sharpener?

Of course.

Q. Thank you I have one, continue… how do I still the mind?

You must learn to *ignore* the world you live in. This is your everyday reality but it is not the *real* you. The real you resides within. It is with you always, you carry it with you everywhere you go. Another reason for you not to feel alone as there is the worldly you and the real you. The worldly you takes up too much time and space. This I know you know. Therefore to quiet/still the mind you must still the worldly you. Take time out of your day *every* day to halt your world. Allow everything to come to a complete stop. Do this for half an hour to reap the benefits as shorter periods do not allow for deep knowledge to come through. This will become addictive to you as you feel the joy in connecting to your true self. You will come to want to do this on a regular basis or you will feel out of sorts with yourself. Any time you are feeling stressed, strung out or on the edge as in the other day's episode where you were experiencing a lot of anger towards a situation, remind yourself that the best way and the only real/true way to deal with it is to retreat into the self and ask for knowledge and guidance. You will always come away feeling your soul has been cleansed. All earthly issues can be dealt with in such a manner if only you would *listen* to yourselves, your *true* selves, and your inner soul sanctum.

Q. Isn't this what they call meditation?

Yes and no. Meditation like the word God means different things to different people. There is no reason to put a name to it as you humans tend to do.

Q. But what if I wanted to describe it, the process, to others?

Then I guess *Journey Within* or *Soul Sanctity* are two descriptions that come to mind. You may eventually find your own better description once you have taken a few journeys as the describer is best obtained from the self and as every self is unique each self would have a unique describer. The world would benefit greatly if each person had a unique describer for the word God instead of all using the same word. It would prevent many arguments and reduce the amount of wars. See what words can do? The power contained within? Therefore to be wise one must choose their words wisely.

Q. Is there such a thing as God?

God is simply another word, a describer of people's beliefs. If only people concentrated on the power of *being* instead of relying on external belief systems to *save* them and *condemn* others, you and the world would be much better off. God the savior is nonexistent as there is nothing to save. You and others are derived from the purest form (being Color + Light Energy). In this form there is no judgment, there is just '*being.*' It is an experience of unity and oneness of such joy and bliss that on your travels into your soul sanctity you are only able to glimpse but this glimpse on your earthly plain is enough to blow your mind. Imagine that *feeling* (of pure absolute bliss/ecstasy) as it is a *feeling*, multiplied by a hundred thousand squillion and you will get an idea of what it will be like when you are returned to *The Source* (of *All Kind*).

Explain to me more about the word God.

It is exactly that, a word. A meaningless word. It doesn't *mean* anything. As with all names and labels that humans put on things, it is just a name. Something that you use to describe something as a means to communicate with each other as you have lost the ability to telepathically communicate. Instead of *feeling* each other's energy in order to know each other which is the ideal way to communicate and the only *real* way to communicate as it is the only way to understand

and know the truth of the self and the truth of others, which is always just an energetic feeling (Remember we are all energy produced from Color + Light which manifests as feeling). So there you have, instead of communicating with each other on an energetic feeling level and connecting with each other's souls to know thyself and all others…you, the earth bound, have created names and words as a means to attempt communication but of which only serve to fail by creating confusion and misunderstandings around the meaning and definition. All would do well to omit the word God from their vocabulary. This I understand you have rightly wanted to do for a while. By omitting the word God you break down barriers and allow others to come closer to your inner sanctum and allow the truth of the self to shine so that others may recognize the real you and in so doing their real selves. The way to do this is just to *be* in each other's company and just *feel* each other's *energy.* No words, no outward communication *just be* (with each other). It's that simple. When you just *be* with each other, with still minds, then that is when telepathic communication will come into play. No need to force it, it will just happen. This is exciting when it happens and you will get a glimpse of the bliss that we discussed earlier. On your first visits it may be short lived however as you allow earthly thoughts surrounding the experience to enter and shatter the connection. With practice this will occur less and less allowing for blissful events to last longer each time. This is but one pathway to the *truth of being* and our existence.

FRI 23RD NOVEMBER

Ok I want to come back to this at a later time and ask you about other pathways as I didn't realize there would be more than one pathway to the truth but for now I have a pressing question that I need answered as I will be meeting up with someone who has a belief I question.

Q. Do we (our souls) choose our parents, children, partners etc. before we come here to earth in order to learn and grow (spiritually) from our relationships?

Hmm, this one always amuses me. You are right to question what purpose does or would it serve? You, me, we are but fragments of the Color + Light Energy Source. Remember we are all one and the same. I am an aspect of you and you are an aspect of me. The same can be said of our parents, children, friends, work colleagues and even perceived enemies. Yes I say *perceived* enemy as there is no such thing as an enemy.

It is purely the mind placing subjective thought onto an object or another being. It is the ego playing tricks on you and creating separation (from you and others) in order to preserve itself. This ego/mind does not recognize the sameness of all kind but separates out the self. The ego sees others as being *separate* and *different* to them and thinks of itself as *superior* to others.

Those who are of the belief that they choose their parents before coming to earth are deluding themselves. It is the ego's way of trying to make sense of their world and their experiences. Why things happen to them the way they do, or the benefit to being treated a certain way. You have to give it to the ego for putting a positive spin on things, "I will grow from this, be a better person (than them), do things differently from them." See the separation from self and others? Hear the superiority? Others may say, "You can't blame them/parents. They didn't know any better." Again the ego is trying to rationalize its experience by separating out and negating (attaching negative connotations to the parents) others and in so doing putting itself in a position of superiority. As long as the ego does this it will remain *separate* which is what it wants. This is survival mode for the ego.

A better way for the self to look upon the situation is *pure acceptance.* No thought, no judgment and no (emotional) feeling attached to the predicament or situation they are in or the experience they are having or had. Just pure...

- **Observation**
- **Acceptance, it just *is***
- **Without judgment, no thought attached, no emotion attached**

Then...bring *feeling* into the picture *(NB: energetic feeling* is different to *emotional feeling).*Tap into the energy of the Color + Light Source of your fellow man. *Feel* their soul's energy, communicate with their *being* to understand and know thy selves and others.

Remember that we are one and the same coming from the purest form. In this form there are no lessons to be learned, there is no growing to do. *You are already* there, *you just don't know it!* You are shielded by the ego who prevents this knowledge from entering your psyche. Your true purpose if there is one is to learn to break down the barrier that is the ego. It is not the only purpose but one of many. It is only by bypassing the ego that we may enter the realm of our true selves.

It is at this point you have noticed that you are writing in the form of 'we' and not in the form of Nameless. Do not concern yourself for we are one and the same and you will flit in and out of third party writing. It is because our connection is strong that you do this for we are writing as one.

Q. Can you answer my original question in a nutshell?

There is no purpose to this way of thinking except for the ego's...

- **Rationalizing its experiences**
- **Trying to make sense of its world**
- **Maintaining its superiority**
- **Keeping itself separate from others**
- **Therefore enabling it to survive**

So when others speak of this, "We choose our parents," it is not their true soul selves talking but the ego. That's pretty much it in a nutshell.

Q. How do we break down the barrier that is the ego?

(I must have tired or been interrupted here as this is where today's session ends.)

2

DEC 2012

SAT 1ST DECEMBER

Identify yourself.

You know it's me, you no longer have to ask. You can feel my energy with you always and will recognize any new entity which chooses to communicate with you as you will *feel* a different energy. I am always ready to answer your questions and other.

Q. Well I don't have a question today as yet, another open one…what do I need to know at this point? Sorry I guess that was a question.

You have much to learn, you are just at the beginning. This is an exciting time because there are many possibilities with many different outcomes depending on the path you choose to take. That women on the bus next to you is capturing your attention with her incessant talking. Tap into her thought energy field and tell me what you can interpret.

At first nothing. I feel blocked by the noise of her talking and chattering to the woman next to her whom I feel sorry for because she's getting a right ear bashing. I don't think it's going to work. Then, when I sit with it for a while, I get this …

She has a son whom she is very worried about. He is an adult, married with a young child of his own. The child is but an infant perhaps eighteen months old, walking and talking. I see the father and the son playing with blocks together, the little boy happy and unaware anything is going on. The father can't completely enjoy this moment with his son as he is worried about his marriage. His wife is very distant and they argue. She is very unhappy, maybe has postnatal depression. He is concerned she may be having an affair but this is not the case. She is just very depressed and not coping very well. She does love him very much but can't help her behavior. Every day she feels like crying and struggles to hold back tears which only turns into anger and frustration. This causes her to lash out at the ones she loves, which causes her to hate herself, which causes her to be depressed and the cycle continues.

He is worried his marriage will come to an end, that they will divorce but this outcome is in his hands and how he manages the situation. He is worried that if a separation happens he won't get to see as much of his son. Therefore he plays with his son with this fear on his mind and not able to thoroughly enjoy the moment. It is entirely up to him and his actions to keep this family together. I feel he should…

1. *Just be there for his wife, allowing the outbursts without judgment, let her vent her anger, frustration and her own fears. Talk when she wants to talk but more than anything just listen to her and what she has to say. Never walk away from an argument just let her vent.*
2. *Get his wife outdoors doing things as much as possible, keep her body and mind active. Walks along the park/beach etc.*
3. *Nurture her being. Time with her friends. Give her time to herself. Cook her dinner, meals. Let her sleep in and rest as much as possible.*
4. *Be with his boy as much as possible. Enjoy the joy of him. He will find strength from this. It is energy transfer from the innocent.*

If he follows this advice things will come good within the next six months and the misery will be over.

□□□

Q. Ok this is all very well but it's unsubstantiated. I can't test this against the facts as I can't present it to a total stranger on the bus and ask her if I'm right, how do I know I didn't just make it all up in my head?

Because of the flow. The information flowed to you with ease, such that your pencil could barely keep up. You did not have to stop and think at any point what was to come next. Also it all made sense from start to finish along with the advice given and conclusion. If you remember back you also received visual information. The man playing with the boy, the worried look on his face. I know you could have described them to the woman if you had to.

Yes.

The only way to ensure validation is to present yourself to a willing participant. This time will come soon enough. Don't rush it. For now you are simply learning to tune in, even in awkward difficult situations such as the woman talking. This is a skill you need to hone through practice. Do it often at least once to twice a week when time allows. Include it as part of your daily half hour ritual. The more you tune in the easier it will become. Anywhere, anytime your hands are free to write is a good time to execute this exercise. Over a period of time you will lessen the need to write things down. This will happen when both the information coming through and the flow are more powerful. Again this takes practice. You are actually learning to attune your vibration to theirs. You do this unconsciously. Simply place the thought or desire to do so then empty the mind and without fail it will occur every single time. Of this you can have faith. As you are aware this can also be executed long distance using the same method as above. Simply tune into the person you are trying to read, place the desire and empty the mind. I hear you ask if this would work for your daughter as you feel the need to understand what is occurring inside her head. I'm afraid this is too close to home and would be an invasion of her privacy and therefore not '*allowed.*'

Q. Well what about others privacy?

You don't live with others and anyway you attune to them in an attempt to help them. When it's too close to home ego becomes involved. Readings can therefore become skewed. Also ego may use the information provided for negative means. By the way you are correct in your desire to see Raven Owl. She has valuable information for you, as well you will learn greatly from the experience for your own practice.

Raven Owl[1] is such a cool name! It makes me realize I can't do this under my real name which being unusual, long and hyphenated presents certain difficulties. I've spent my whole life explaining my (birth) name. I even had a resident say to me one day, "That's not a name, that's a complication!"

Q. Can you help me find my spiritual name?

Your name will be revealed to you in due course. When it comes to you, is given to you, it will signify your readiness to take things to the next level. That is to publicize yourself and attach a fee for the knowledge and skills you provide.

Excellent, can't wait!

SUN 2ND DECEMBER

Ok I'm waiting for some information to come through.

Good morning. I feel you are well rested and have had a good sleep. You have many goings on at this time which can be exhausting for you but it is also exhilarating is it not? The difficult part for you is you are a lone cow.

What? That's not very nice!

What I mean is that you are a unique being who stands alone from the herd. They follow each other in one direction while you head otherwise. All will end their journey at the precise moment and point assigned to them and all are welcomed back into the soup pot of creation at this time to be melded as one. You my dear are taking the long way round, a different path with many possibilities, many adventures and discoveries but also many distractions. You will eventually join the others on the path towards home but this will only occur towards the end of your journey.

Your path can seem lonely at times, as if you are the only one on it but this is not so. Occasionally you will stumble across another being who is travelling a similar journey to yours. You will benefit from each other's company and the information each of you has gathered along the way which you will transfer to each other along with your energy as a means of sustenance and strength such that you can both continue your journeys. You have just met such a being and though I feel your resistance you have much to benefit from each other. Your challenge or quest if you like is to find a way to communicate with this person that is not on an earthly level. In return this being will provide many questions that will send you in search of answers that contribute to the building of your knowledge bank. Much like one of those techno games where the hero collects pots of gold along his way through dungeons and mazes, defending himself of villains as he goes. Your pots of gold are *information* and *knowledge*. These come to you at set times on the path of your journey through life. When it is presented to you, you may find it necessary to drop your travels momentarily (just like the gamer) and deal with the situation at hand. That is, pick up your pot of gold (your knowledge) before you continue on your path. If you do this you will find yourself stronger, wiser and more ready for the challenges ahead. Some pots of gold will be relatively easy to pick up, others will be more of a challenge requiring more effort and more time on your part but remember don't give up, the time and effort will be well worth it for future situations you will be presented with. You require this knowledge and experience to be successful in your quest.

A great analogy I really like it. It helps me to visualize what I'm doing and to recognize what difficult situations represent and what I'm to do about it. But this is one of those difficult ones. This being is a definite challenge to me. I'm attempting to communicate as you said, otherworldly, but I find people are too attached to their words. They think and analyze too much and I'm having difficulty breaking through the words/talking. Yes they talk too much, sometimes I wish they would just shut up!

They are too much in their mind. This person thinks they operate on a heart level but they are wrong. They are too much in their head. It is time to stop talking and start *doing*. It is at this point if you are to continue in each other's company that you are to set this person some exercises, a few come to mind. Take this being by the hand and challenge them to walk with you *without talking*. Both of you are to concentrate on the energy field of the other and that which is all around you as well as your own energy field. Remember that this is all *feeling* energy with no thought or emotion attached. You will need to explain this and this will be the challenge for both of you, to keep thought from entering. You are teaching this person to *still the mind* and in so doing real communication will follow. This is not an easy one to deal with as the talking is incessant. It's up to you to find the switch off button. *This is your quest.* There are other exercises but this one for now is the least confronting.

Take your normal circuit walk but remember as you see the beauty of the lake and such around you do not attach thought to it, simply *feel* the energy of it all.

Thank you Nameless I will try and see what happens.

TUE 4TH DECEMBER

I'm sitting here on beautiful Lake Cootharaba, it's going to be a hot one today, thirty-nine degrees. Already it's so hot I'm struggling and it's only eight thirty in the morning.

Q. What info do you have for me today?

Get back to nature. Stay as close to nature as possible as this is where your true soul belongs. Everything else is irrelevant but you busy yourself with it none the less. Look at what's before you, that's the real truth of existence. The cool flowing waters of the lake, the glistening of the sun on its surface. That little breeze that you feel on the back of your neck that you asked for to help cool you down. Listen to the cicadas trill and the birds singing in the background, chorusing each other, harmonizing. If you bring this chorus to your consciousness and try to feel it on a cellular level such that it *becomes* a part of you then this is how you escape the drudgery of your everyday life and enter the realm of the netherworld where all becomes one. It is a melding together, a reunification of our original *being.*

You do this by heightening your *sensory* awareness. I know you can hear that annoying leaf blower in the distance and this is what keeps you grounded on the earth plane. This is your challenge, your quest. To learn to block out some sounds while allowing others. If you can learn to do this you are on the pathway to enlightenment (*Light and Being*). This is one of the pathways we discussed earlier. *Silence* is the key, you need to silence your (earthly) world. Take a few moments and close your eyes. Practice bringing the sounds of nature to the fore and pushing all others away. Feel the wind on your face. Feel its travels and its freedom to come and go, wax and wane. What would it *feel* like to *be* the wind? There is a whole symphony all around you that unless you *tune* in you are normally unaware.

Having done this exercise you heard the multitude of birds cawing their song, communicating with each other, the cicadas in the foreground but also the group of cicadas far up on the hill some distance away. The fly that buzzed past you twice, first in one direction, then the other. The waters lapping at the shoreline. How it *felt* when that ant crawled across your foot on his way to somewhere important (you could tell by his purposeful scurry). This is all *healing* energy as it brings you to your rightful place which is at one with everything. To be at one with nature is to be at one with the self.

Your thoughts wander to your hugging tree and the healing you get from it. The tree helps you attune to your soul self, makes you let go of earthly worries, repurposes you by aiding in new perspectives. It does this through energy transference. Really you could get this from anything as we are all energy, we are all one. The tree though (a tree, any tree) is one of those *ultimate beings.* It takes little (from the earth) but provides much. Food in the form of fruit/nuts/roots/leaves, the air we breathe, a home for other beings and provides us with building materials etc. It is also a great *observer.* It sits all day and observes the goings on around it. Besides breathing and feeding itself in order to grow its sole purpose is just to *be*. It just *is*!

I see you have a visitor.

Yes, a little bug walking across the page.

An opportunity to observe nature in its true form.

The energy from a tree is one of the purest forms around and thus a great healer. You are right to approach your tree in times of need, but should also when you don't feel the need. Make it a ritual and do it frequently and feel your energy shift. See the trees directly around you now? They stand tall like centians standing guard around you. They are there to protect you. Anything you need to know can come from a tree (or a leaf for that matter). Andy Goldsworthy was right, "There is a whole world in a leaf,"[2] such a wise man. Yes you laughed, as you wrote this a leaf fell from the tree above onto your page, just another message from above that you are on the right path. Confirmation so to speak.

You also have visions of your chair in the forest, you are right to go there and visit often. I will be waiting for you there to answer questions and help guide you. This is a healing place where you can be alone close to nature and it is relatively silent. Perhaps our next visit together?

Very well, thanks for today.

WED 5TH DECEMBER

Hi Nameless. I aimed to meet with you in the forest this morning but due to the heat and lack of wind the mosquitos would be very annoying, making it difficult to concentrate, so I'm down by the lake again sitting amongst the centians. I have a bit of a doozy for you today...

Q. Is there such a thing as love?

Yes, in people's hearts and minds there is but really it is another name, a label you use to describe a feeling and emotion. You (earthlings) would do well to concentrate more on the *feeling* rather than trying to categorize it. It is similar to the word God, a describing word that only serves to confuse as the definition differs per individual such that two people could be talking about two very different concepts. Having said it is a describing word it is not very descriptive. What is love? Define love. What does the word love really *mean?* It really is non descriptive when you think about it. Better descriptive words would be *union* or *harmony*. It is a feeling of *interconnectedness* with another being such that more of your own true being can be experienced and felt. It is bringing you that one step closer to being at one with all and everything and knowing thy true self.

So people *in love* are…

1. **At union, in union with each other, are unionized.**
2. **In harmony, are harmonized.**

The first describes the *interconnectedness,* the coming together as one. The latter describes the *vibrational* attunement. I'm sure there are other descriptive words in your language that would better serve than the word love to describe what is *actually* happening. People in *unionized harmony* describe feelings of euphoria and absolute bliss that are not of this world. You, yourself have experienced as such and have written about it. It is actually quite rare on your planet to feel and experience this *true* state of what people call love. You are one of the lucky few but I understand there was a lot of (spiritual) work on your part to get there.

Love or the word love is one of those words that is bandied about superficially. Ask most people if they have been 'in love' and they will say yes, yet they do not understand the concept of true love or the *truth* of love as you do and are only fooling themselves. The average person's concept of love is just the ego once again trying to make itself feel good and giving one purpose to one's life. It is not wrong for humans to search for love as one day they may discover the true depth of love that can only be experienced as *unionized harmony* that transcends them into another realm entirely. Having been there yourself you know what that feels like, a state of pure ecstasy far far beyond all earthly expectations. A state that dissolves all matter such that you and your surrounds consist only of thought and feeling energy, you are one and all with everyone and everything. You have reached enlightenment. *You are pure Light and Being*. That is the *true depth* of love.

Reading this back over it's my understanding there are two types of love…

1. ***Love***

- ***The earthly description of love***
- ***Felt more on a superficial earthly plane***
- ***Experienced by most people on earth***
- ***A heightened sense of joy***
- ***Strokes the ego***
- ***Gives purpose to humans lives***

2. ***Unionized Harmony***

- ***Vibrational/Spiritual***
- ***Deep***
- ***Transcends you into other realms***
- ***Dissolves matter***
- ***An interconnectedness with the entire Universe***
- ***A state of enlightenment. Pure Light and Being***
- ***Rare, few get to experience***

Well surmised.

Why thank you.

FRI 7TH DECEMBER

Hi, I've been waiting to speak to you. I'm feeling a little panicked and seek your guidance. Finances will soon be drastically reduced, something beyond my control and I don't know what to do. Ok I'm more than a little panicked, its affecting my every waking moment, the worry of it all.

Q. How am I going to be able to support us both, pay all the bills and also keep my art going which is one of the only things that helps keep me sane and gives me much joy in my life?

Q. What is the best way for me to make up the dollar shortfall while taking up the least amount of time?

You know what you have to do but there is much study or preparation involved. You must take the necessary steps we discussed earlier. Go see Raven Owl as we said. I know you are concerned at the cost but it will reap many benefits in the long run. Think of it as an investment in your future. She will help guide you and you will come away with much confidence. Once having done this it is important that you act immediately and don't procrastinate as the thought energy will diminish and confidence will wane as time goes on. There is the other matter of the exercises I gave you which involved another that you also have not completed.

I know but I've been waiting for the right timing and it never seems to be. Also I think I've put this person off as I haven't seen them of late. I tried to make the boundaries clear but perhaps I was too strong in doing this. Is there another way? One where I'm not reliant on another being to gain my knowledge and insight?

Maybe but this was an ideal scenario as it would have been a reciprocation between the two of you. It is always best to give at times of taking to maintain harmony. You both would benefit each other as we have discussed. He to give you experience in dealing with others and to raise questions. You to share your knowledge and gift so that he can get in touch with his *true self* and stop externalizing as he does.

That's the problem, it doesn't stop and it puts me off. I feel my energy can be quite negative around him, like he rubs me up the wrong way.

This is just your *soul being* telling you to be aware. A warning sign. Much like a cat whose hairs stand on end when danger is near. Not that he is dangerous in that manner but certainly you must pay attention to his words and not be drawn in by them. You are right to want to quiet communication in this way (words) but understand that you are different to most as in you have other ways to communicate whilst they only have one. It is up to you to guide them and show them the way to their own true selves. If not him then who else could benefit from your gift? A willing participant would make your quest easier. Someone with a strong knowledge base already who just needs to be shown the next step in the process. You are thinking of your girlfriend and whilst she is a good candidate she is also very busy and in the same predicament with regard to words, a lover of words and spends too much time in the head and mind. I still prefer the first option. Don't give up on it yet. You may have to make the approach yourself. Remember be humble and park your ego at the door. If you get that niggling *biting* feeling just acknowledge this is your true self protecting you, it is a good thing and should be welcomed as it keeps you alert. If you can manage to start with even one exercise you will be well on the way to your rightful path and money will not be an issue for you.

Your future is bright. You have no need to worry and nothing to fear.

Thank you Nameless.

SAT 8TH DECEMBER

Q. Why do I keep finding feathers everywhere?

They are a clue to your spiritual name. There will be an Indian connection but it is not what you think. It will not be obvious or literal. All will be revealed in true time. This is when you can start the beginning of your new life…your true life. Then all of this that you know now will seem but a dream as this new life will take you places you never could have imagined. I myself am getting so excited for you as I know what is ahead, what is in store for you. You will go from strength to strength and once you start there will be no stopping you. Doors will open and opportunities will come your way. It will all seem so easy as if you have walked through a vortex into a different world and all your problems have melted away and indeed this is the truth as you leave your old world behind never to return. It is a step up on the spiritual plane and with this comes many benefits. It's important to remain humble and keep ego in check at all times as these want to drag you back to old ways. In this respect you will require strength and determination. You have worked too hard and waited too long to reach this point for it to be spoiled as you stand upon the precipice. Also people need you to follow through in order that you may aid them. You are a healer but are unaware of this. You will help many starting with a few until confidence in your skill and knowledge grows. People will hear about you and come from afar for your help and advice. This is your true life's purpose and as thanks many riches and gifts will be provided. Accept graciously as this is all part of the persons healing process. Never feel guilty when others offer up to you as they are grateful for your help and it gives them joy to show their appreciation.

This is all you need to know for now.

SUN 9TH DECEMBER

OMG, I'm in DESPERATE need of advice regarding my daughter. What am I to do? We're in the midst of those troublesome teenage years and she is getting more and more difficult and I don't know how to cope with it.

Q. Is it going to be like this for the next few years? Will it get worse? How should I manage the situation? Help, I'm tearing my hair out!

Sit back and *observe* as much as possible *without reaction.* She is going through a transition phase, a difficult time for her. You need to support her as much as possible while directing her in the right manner of living. You are right to have standards and are not asking too much. You are still lord of the manor so to speak but she is exerting her independence and bucking all the rules. It is a process of evolution that cannot be helped as it is part of all animal kingdoms, just look at nature and you will see. The challenge or your quest is to find the right balance between discipline and freedom.

Q. Should I follow through with the dance concert this week?

You will only be punishing yourself if you don't go. This is an opportunity to see a beautiful side of her that you don't normally get to see, albeit only for a short minute. That glimpse into her inner beauty will be a vision that you can hold onto in times of trouble and turmoil.

It is a glimpse into her true soul being. If you miss this opportunity you will never get it back. It will be lost to you forever as will the connection between the two of you associated with it.

Thank you, that makes sense and I feel better about it now but what about the length and duration of the situation we are in right now? How long will I need to endure this level of difficulty and is it going to get worse?

There is nothing to endure for if you can strike the right balance between discipline and freedom then harmony will reign once again. How long it takes you to strike this balance will determine how long before peace returns to your family.

Q. What is the balance between discipline and freedom?

The discipline are the rules you already have set in place. These are about rightful living…

- **Share the workload**
- **Respect one another**
- **Be kind to one and all as you are all one and the same**
- **Help those in need etc.**

This is guidance that will serve her well in future life. You are merely showing the way. The freedom is in allowing her to do these things in her own due course. Her being is at the age where she wants to make decisions for herself and in her own *timing*. This is where the struggle between the two of you lies. You want it done today…she wants to do it tomorrow or even in a few days' time at her own leisure and doesn't want to be told when to do it. This is where the two of you need to find a balance. Ask her what is *a reasonable* amount of time, for example, before the dishes need to be done? See what her answer is, you will find it is probably quite reasonable. Ask her if she can manage to do them within this time frame but preferably before and you *observe* without *reaction.*

It is all a control issue. She is bucking the control you have over her whilst trying to exert her own control. Allow her to do so with issues that are safe. This is the *freedom* she requires. The freedom in divine timing is allowing freedom in her own true being. The same can be said for many other issues, it is all about perception of control. As each issue arises sit down and ask her what her reasonable expectations are. If she was sharing a household with someone else, a complete stranger, what would her reaction or non-reaction time be then? Ask her to give you the same respect as a complete stranger.

Thank you, I'll try this.

SAT 15TH DECEMBER

Ok, I did have a question in mind I thought about yesterday but now I've forgotten what it is as I didn't get to write it down. When I think of something good to ask, I then try and put it out of my mind as the channeling will start straight away and as I may not be somewhere I can write it down (like in the shower) I'm sure I will forget what was channeled to me, or at least the finer details.. Therefore I try and leave the question for my next session with you and now I forget what it was…damn it was a really good one too!

Yesterday I was at my daughters' end of year dance concert, a large event. I waited for two and a half hours for her groups turn to come on. While waiting and watching the others I had a sudden urge to straighten her hair (you know how spirally curly it is). I thought, "Oh, we haven't done that for a long time, maybe I'll do it Xmas day." Anyway her dance routine came on and there was about twenty-four girls on stage all dancing and bobbing around, all wearing the same outfit and all with long straight ponytails. I couldn't see my daughter at all! I kept scanning all the girls and told myself, "Look for the curly hair, look for the curly hair!" but to no avail, even in desperation I couldn't find her. As quick as that the routine was over and they were all off stage. Perhaps something had happened and she didn't make it on stage? I was so upset I felt like crying. A whole year of dropping her at dance every week and I didn't get to see her dance in the end of year concert, not even for a second. It still upsets me now.

Later, when the concert was over, I went to pick her up from the stage door and I almost walked straight past her not recognizing my own daughter because unbeknownst to me she had had her hair straightened! All that time I was looking for curly hair and she was dancing away in the front row and I didn't even recognize her (In my defense she also had heavy make-up and false eyelashes on and looked about seventeen).

Anyway I tell you all this because I now know I was getting a channeled message (a warning or alert signal) when I had a sudden urge to straighten her hair but at the time I didn't realize. I'm sure I've had plenty of other insights during my lifetime as well that have fallen by the way side unnoticed.

Q. How can I tell when I am getting such a message that I should be more aware of, take note of or interpret for the given situation?

You will know when you get such a message as it will *come out of the blue* so to speak. It will be seemingly devoid of any purpose to the situation you are in (like that message you got about Brett and the ladder while you were doing the dishes).

Yes, warning of a fall.

It is a shame you missed your daughters dance but there was a purpose and a lesson in it for you. When that thought popped into your head it seemed unrelated to everything that was going on at the time but you also spoke of a *sudden urge* to straighten her hair. So there was a strong *energetic feeling* attached to the thought and this is your clue to pay attention to the message that you are getting. Yes you have received such messages in the past when you predicted the Boxing Day disaster that was the Sydney to Hobart yacht race the night before it happened. You had that same *urge,* strong *feeling* such that you felt compelled to tell your girlfriend what you thought was going to happen. There was also vision attached. You could see men floating in the water attempting to hold onto the boat waiting to be rescued. Weren't you both surprised to awaken the next morning to find your prediction had come true? This is clairvoyance and not pure channeling which answers the question you forgot from yesterday…

What is the difference between a clairvoyant and a channel medium?

A clairvoyant has vision attached to their knowing. You envisioned your daughter's hair straight and what it would look like did you not? You envisioned doing it on Xmas day but this was the Xmas concert. So the key words here are straighten and Xmas but your interpretation got skewed. The more you pay attention to these messages the more practiced you become, the easier it will be to interpret them correctly. Be acutely aware of…

1. **Thoughts, sometimes seemingly unrelated to the current situation that just "pop" into your head**
2. **Sudden urges, strong energetic feelings**
3. **With vision attached**

Channeling is more of a *discussion* and whilst it can provide one with advice or knowledge about the past, present or future event it is more concerned with the here and now and may advise about the past or future but only if it is currently relevant. Clairvoyance is more about *prediction,* what will happen or is likely to happen in the future or future event. It does not very often concern itself with the past.

You my dear are both, a clairvoyant and a channel. You are also a healer. You are a *Shaman* (because you have all three). This is your Indian connection as traditional Indian Shamans possessed these skills and if you lived amongst their tribes you would be considered a Shaman. Shaman is a good collective word for describing all the skills you possess in one word. Currently you are a much stronger channel than you are a clairvoyant but you will learn to cultivate this skill and eventually be able to flit between all three skills at will. I feel we could discuss these in a lot greater detail further down the line but that is enough information for today. I am aware you have a visitor coming. Know that I am always with you. Be at peace.

Thank you Nameless, exciting stuff.

SUN 16TH DECEMBER

I had a surprise visit from my male friend yesterday and after a small chat we left the house and walked to Paradise Beach[3] on the lake. Unfortunately it was not the private beach I had wanted to take him to but as I hadn't seen him for a while I wanted to take the opportunity to offer him an exercise so asked if he would like to try psychometry and on his acceptance gave him my watch with a few instructions. I took his watch to do the same and went for a walk up the beach for twenty minutes, separating out so I could give him quiet space. On my return he told me of his difficulty in clearing his mind of thought because there were children playing nearby. The only words he got were few and he felt they were predominately his own words and thoughts, "Introspective thoughts, cranium pursuits, unconditional love is my answer, freedom, peace."

I had managed to step back in time to his youth when he was on holidays and enamored with a particular girl who was not interested because she already had a boyfriend. I did not share this with him thinking it could be a touchy subject and an invasion of his privacy. I could tell he felt uncomfortable and he suggested he had failed the "test" (his words, not mine) but I disagreed and said it was more a lesson for me that what I do (psychometry and channeling) I think everyone can do with ease but now I have learnt it's not so. This is going to be way more challenging than I thought (to teach others). He asked if I thought people had other ways of doing it. When I asked what he meant he said he intuits stuff. I questioned further...

> *"What do you mean by intuit?"*
>
> ***"I get a knowing."***
>
> *"What is this knowing? Describe it."*
>
> ***"It's a gut feeling."***
>
> *"How does it translate to you, in words? Give me an example, I'm just trying to understand how it is for you."*
>
> ***"Like I know when someone's had their heart broken and that's why they act the way they do."***

I perceived he meant me, was having a dig and this was normal intuition that everyone gets. Anyway I got the message from him that he intuits stuff and that's his thing and I channel etc. and that's my thing and he wasn't interested in doing my thing at all because that's not the way he operates. So I guess I don't want to push my ideals on to him and I will have to find myself another (willing) candidate.

Q. Any thoughts?

Too much mind. He is still trapped by the mind and struggles to let go of thought. This exercise was too strong for him and you would have been better starting off with something gentler, an exercise in no mind. This would be in the form of a daily meditation where the person sits for gradually extended periods of time, starting off with three minutes and eventually extending it to fifteen minutes. More lengthy sessions can last between half to one hour as you know but as a beginner three to five minutes is adequate and as much as they could handle. A quiet place to sit is necessary. Absolute silence helps as noise disturbs the mind and allows for personal thoughts. This is a form of meditation. As the person sits the aim is to think of *nothing*. This is actually very hard for humans who are governed by ego as the ego hates to be ignored. By ignoring the ego it is a threat to its very existence so it will fight to be heard. The person should not stress when thought enters their head, just acknowledge the thought and let it go. Don't try to ignore it as it will just return. That ego is very stubborn, better to acknowledge and send it on its merry way. This will come in cycles...

- **No mind**
- **A thought enters (persons own thought)**
- **Let it go**
- **No mind**
- **No mind**
- **A thought enters (let it go)**
- **No mind**
- **No mind etc.**

The cycles, with practice, will eventually get longer of no mind before a thought enters. The person will become adept at letting go of such thoughts quickly and with no attachment. When this level is reached they are ready for further exercises. You, yourself could practice this even though you don't need to for self but so that you can better understand and explain the process to others.

That is all for today.

Thank you Nameless.

MON 17TH DECEMBER

Q. I have just contacted Maleny art co-op regarding an art space. Are you able to predict what will occur?

You are much too late in applying as you already know and unfortunately this was necessary for you to accomplish the work you needed to do before you would even be ready to approach them. They do not have a position for you at this time, others are already on the waiting list. However the woman in charge is impressed with your work, an opening will suddenly become available due to someone else's misfortune and I feel she will put you ahead of others that have been waiting patiently as you offer something different from what is already there. This may not be for a few months yet, three to four but I advise you to always be at the ready to enter at a moment's notice. They will need someone to fill the space quickly otherwise she may offer it to someone else.

In the meantime keep doing what you are doing, there will be other offers that come your way, other opportunities. I feel you have another year of hard work ahead of you before you can relax a little and I understand that juggling things is a big issue for you but necessary for dreams to come true. They don't just happen, there is a lot of hard labor behind the scenes. Those that don't give up will reap the benefits in the long term. This is all sowing the seeds for a plentiful harvest. You will be cutting the celebration cake and popping the champagne before the next years out. I see a real party going on, poppers and streamers, the whole lot. You can't wipe the grin off your face and are the happiest I have seen you in a very long time. It is like the days of old and you look young again. That is the power of such joy. Go forth knowing this will happen.

Q. Thank you, speaking of celebrations, there's forty million being offered in Tattslotto tomorrow night. Are you able to tell me the winning numbers?

That would be cheating and it's not allowed. It places you with an unfair advantage over others who have just as much right as you do to win that money. It's a game of chance and if I tell you then that chance is being taken away from everyone else who plays. It is also a form of stealing what rightfully belongs to others. For example to be shared amongst multiple winners, they would end up with less. If no one won and it jackpotted into next week then those winners would get more. If you cheat and win you are stealing from those potential winners. Anyway Karma will always come back to bite you and it's not worth it. Karmas a bitch!

Q. *Nameless, I can't believe you just said that! So Karma exists?*

Yes, it's the universal law of cause and effect and I said bitch because I wanted you to sit up and take notice. It's not something to be messed with. Somewhere, somehow your action will come full circle.

Point taken. Still, it doesn't sound like you.

□

WED 19TH DECEMBER

I've been sitting here by the lake for a few hours carving an art piece which I've been working on every day for weeks now, my hand and wrist are getting really sore. I'm wondering if my carving is going to be good enough for the upcoming Floating Land art exhibition. Have I gone too deep and ruined it? Is it worthwhile continuing? I feel like it's taken a hundred hours so far and I'm only half done. I don't want to waste another hundred hours if it's not going to look professional enough when I'm finished. Should I continue and finish it?

By whose standards are you judging it against? Yours? If so you have high standards and will always be your own worst critic but for the first time you will have your work on mass display for many to see and criticize. Some will like your work and appreciate where you are coming from and the degree of effort involved. Others will hate it and consider it rubbish. You will never please one hundred percent. Those that criticize feel superior to you and consider themselves to be more highly skilled. Perhaps this is so but a skilled artist takes many years to develop. It is all a learning and growing process. I feel your piece will be worthy and you will get many comments. Some will be negative but there will be more positives. You should do art to please yourself and not concern yourself with the thoughts of others. Do *you like it*? This is the question to ask yourself. If so continue on. It would almost be sacrilege to give up now you have come such a long way. Also it is a lesson in spirit, a test of your tenacity, your dedication and unwillingness to give up in times of rough enterprise. Quitting is not really part of your nature no matter how tough the going is. Stay disciplined and continue with regular small amounts. You are on the home stretch, it is a worthwhile piece, worth the effort to finish, developing and coming together at the end. The end results will reap many benefits for you as you will be able to play around with the finished image adding it to other pieces further down the line.

Nothing is lost not even your time which I know is a concern for you. Cherish these moments by the lake. How lucky you are to have such an office. Record these moments (photograph) and you will look back upon these times fondly. The surrounding trees envelope you in natures healing aura. Observe nature's beauty before you. Allow the *feeling* energy to caress you. Be free with the wind. Many blessings.

Thank you.

SILENT SIGHT

I watched the most fascinating program[4] on TV the other night about performance artist Marina Abramavić. Many in the art world or otherwise might have considered the following as a "performance," an "act" but I saw it as an exercise of great earthly compassion and passive instruction (to others) on how to connect with each other on a true soul level. I sat and watched utterly enthralled and gob smacked and to this day am searching for the right candidate/s with which I can practice it, without them thinking I'm a total loony.

The setting was in an art gallery, I can't remember where. New York? Just know that it was grand, multileveled and with thousands of visitors annually. There seated in the middle of an extremely large room was Marina in the most exquisite of ball gowns, herself already an exotic creature, looking like she just stepped out of a painting. Go back a few scenes and you would have seen that she needed several people to aid her into this dress such was its extravagance and fitting. She was of such beauty my eyes were transfixed. In front of her was a table and on the other side facing her, another chair. The audience, some already lining up, were invited to participate and join her sitting at the table one by one for a period of fifteen minutes. Each person was instructed they were not allowed to talk to (or touch) Marina but only to gaze into her eyes in silence and think of nothing. No thought, no mind, just ` being,' just ` is.' If they were unable to think of nothing then to think and only project love towards this divine being in front of them as she was doing for them. So it was an exercise in letting go of the mind and sitting in feeling and knowing, really connecting with this person to experience their soul being and in experiencing their soul being you are experiencing an aspect of you.

This length of time sitting still doing nothing forces people and their brain/mind to slow down in contrast to our normally fast paced world. With no thought/egoism attached you allow an opening for feeling communication, transference of energy and telepathic communication to occur and in doing so you come to KNOWING. To really know, feel and experience this persons true soul self which is a beautiful thing.

After a short time period Marina became more comfortable with the safety aspect of her "performance" and instructed for the table to be removed so there was no obstacle or obstruction between her and the other soul.

Thousands came to see her over a six month period. Seven hundred and fifty thousand participants to be precise! There were queues down the street so expansive that people were camping out to be first in line and they had to start distributing tickets to keep some sort of order. Many hundreds and possibly thousands more simply came to observe. People that were interviewed spoke of travelling far and wide just to come and see her even from overseas and often revisiting many times over just to sit with her. One man stated that he had been twenty-one times. Even though hundreds watched on daily and the room was busy, crowded and noisy Marina sat in angelic calmness and would connect only with the person in front of her, bowing her eyes to cleanse in between each one.

Imagine the magnitude if you were to sit individually with seven hundred and fifty thousand people. I can only imagine how profound the experience was both for her and the other souls. Some said they came because they were curious. Others came to be cleansed and healed. Afterwards people described feeling loved but not just a normal love but a great love of who they were in their entirety, their soul being, earthly warts and all. In this silent exchange they felt truly understood, known and acknowledged as if for the first and only time in their lives. Someone had taken the time to sit with them and see and experience the 'real' them and who they truly are. It moved people, they broke down into tears afterwards many of them sobbing. For some it was uncomfortable. Did they feel exposed? Open? Vulnerable? Whilst a vast array described it as cleansing and healing.

I wanted to be there. I wanted to experience it for myself, though I know I've had this with someone close to me before. I wanted to be in that palpable room opposite Marina. I wanted to feel her love and knowing because I know what that feels like and it's utterly amazing. It's my strong desire to connect with people on such a true soul level as I know that in the everyday I'm only dealing with the persons ego, their mask and not their true soul selves and thus find it difficult to relate to people as I know I'm not dealing with the real person even though I try to see past this. I wish we could all communicate like this on a daily level but to do that we would all have to stop talking. Thus a vow of silence. Oh how peaceful my world would be. Would I miss the talking, the chatter? Probably not. Why else do I shut myself away from society out here in Boreen Point? Its heavenly silent. If we all stopped talking it would probably stop a lot of wars. Our whole existence as we know it would disappear and I envision the earth more of Nirvana.

FRI 21ST DECEMBER

I'm concerned I'm not going to be ready on time to start readings on the first of January as I'd hoped as I've not been able to complete the exercises you gave me which involve other people. As discussed my friend was closed off to the exercises because he perceived himself not to be skillful in that area. I've since found a website[5] which defines all the different skills and realize he showed signs of clairsentience (he feels things) and claircogniance (a knowing that he had told me about which I dismissed as common intuition). My other girlfriend has been busy with pre Xmas get-togethers' and home schooling. I want to make up my business cards but don't have my name yet which tells me I'm not ready. I was going to make some up anyway with my "Light and Being" art image until I'm given my name. I'm starting to panic.

Q. Will I be ready on time to start in early January?

There are many issues here to discuss. Firstly there is nothing common about intuition, it is as you said claircogniance but once again these are just labels so that humans can understand and make sense of their world. Everybody possesses this and all other skills you read about. Some are more highly attuned than others and some lie dormant waiting to be discovered. Most people walk around totally unaware of their (underdeveloped) skill. Some will get fleeting flashes of what you and others call intuition or gut feeling or a *knowing* which is claircogniance coming to the fore. Anyone who has experienced this should know that this skill can be developed further. It is a matter of *attunement.* You would do well to read the article further to learn how to do this (attunement) for self and others.

As stated everyone possesses *all* of the skills to varying degrees but one or two may come through stronger. These as you now know are considered as primary or secondary. With work your tertiary skill may be developed also. An accomplished Light Worker will experience all three or will be able to draw on any of the three skills as necessary. As I said, read about attunement and follow the advice given. This may take place of the exercises previously given that involved others although if an opportunity arises please continue with this as you will gain valuable insight and experience.

You are thinking of asking your girlfriend for a question over the phone so that you may channel an answer for her before you meet up on Sunday. This is a good idea and I will help you with this. It will have to be a question that you have no preconceived ideas about to stop your own judgment about the matter. It might even be better to do a *blind* question, that is, she think of a question and you channel the answer. This way you can remain objective.

As for your male friend you are right to deliver him a copy of the information you found on clairsentience. As discussed previously you have been destined to help further his ability and as he is not currently open to your suggestions this reading material is a gentler way to increase his knowledge base (remember he is a gentle and sensitive soul who moves at a slower pace than you). Pass the information to him and leave it at that. It is likely he will read it and put it aside. His soul will act when it is ready. You are aiding in sowing the seeds for later on. Thus you will have fulfilled your purpose and can move forward.

Having completed all of the above will bring you closer to readiness and your spirit guide name. I feel you should work on the business cards you are thinking of as they will only need a slight adjustment at a later date. I am also sending you visions of a separate mobile phone as the business card cannot be finalized until you have the new mobile number.

Thank you Nameless. I'm not sure about the mobile, I'm not very good with phones having a bit of a phone phobia and I hate talking on them especially in public spaces. I assume being auditory it's the sound sensitivity and noise disturbance of public areas. Can't I just use my home phone number?

In the beginning perhaps but you will find it necessary to have a mobile as in the near future calls will come through thick and fast. It's better to start off in the manner you will continue in, otherwise it's confusing for others if you change numbers. Then once contact is made you can decide if you choose to pass on your home number or not.

SUN 23RD DECEMBER

I've completed one task as requested, the remote/blind question that you assigned me. Thank you for your help as I was really nervous about answering it. I wasn't sure if you would come through for me or if, my friend being too close to me, I would put my own subjective thoughts on the matter. I'm passing the answer to her this afternoon and it'll be interesting to get her feedback. The information on clairsentience I can pass on tomorrow. The third task was to read up and study the development of the "Clair's" and learn to attune myself correctly. I do like this teacher who seems very knowledgeable and straight forward but it comes at a price and it's very exy. The introduction is three hundred dollars whilst the working psychic certificate course is over a thousand dollars. The latter while it seems very informative I just simply cannot afford and the former, well, I just don't know if it's comprehensive enough.

Q. Would I gain valuable information and skill development out of it? Is it worth it? You know how money is so tight for me at the moment. Can't you teach me these things? Isn't that what guides are meant to do? Or can I find the same information in a book somewhere?

You have books, many books but you have failed to act upon them. Also they do not offer a certificate of graduation which would validate your skill to others. You are right to do the introduction to begin with and as you start working in this area put away one third of earnings towards your skill development. Thus the full course will be somewhat in the future at a time determined by you in how much you work, how much you charge and the dollar amount you put aside each time. This will be a test of your dedication. In the mean time I can help guide you as best I can but it is not specifically my area to teach you such skills.

Also in the forums she discussed you will have valuable access to the experience and knowledge of others who do as you do. This I could not teach. So you will be learning from a psychic's perspective which is better than dictation from me or straight out of a book. I understand this will not come to you immediately and you will have to work for it. I feel you can trust this teacher. As she discusses she has built up a vast knowledge base over many years and can fast track you through your journey. If you commit yourself to the first course it will show the Universe you are ready and you will be given your name. That is all.

Thank you.

FRI 28TH DECEMBER

Yesterday I bought the mobile phone so things are on track for starting but where am I to practice and do my readings? Boreen Point is too far for people from town to travel. I don't want to advertise without a plan. Also how much should I charge?

Good morning, I am happy to be with you. You have much to think about and much to do. Raven Owl will help you with some of these concerns guiding you in the right direction. It is imperative that you see her as discussed, you have much to learn from her. There are opportunities that will open up to you through meetings with others. Go to the Sunday spiritual church[6] and the Monday healing group[7] as you are planning, there more messages and guidance will come through. Also you are mixing with likeminded souls and will feel energized and supported, encouraged that you are heading in the right direction. It may be that how you start will not be how you continue on later. There will be much change, growth and development. The important thing is to *start* the process and from there opportunities and insights arise.

As for now I recommend you visit people in their homes until you can find a quiet pleasant place that is affordable and fairly central, though I do think it may be further afield than you anticipated so don't limit yourself to only looking close to home. Also think outside the square. Your space is rented or shared with another/others. Markets are an option though with your auditory sensitivity too noisy for you at this stage unless you are able to occupy a space in a small side room in one of the buildings. Such an option would be ideal and encouraged. Hiring of a van or caravan in a market situation is also ideal as it gives you a private room/space with the solitude you require. As for cost, sixty percent or two thirds of a normal charge is appropriate until you gain further knowledge and experience. A year would be a good time frame and another indication is when you have built up a return clientele or are so busy that people are having difficulty getting a booking with you. This is the time to increase your prices. Do not forget however the kindness that others have and will show to you on your journey and you would do well to return the favor by seeing those in need, in a similar position to your current self, at a reduced rate as these are often the people who need your guidance most.

It is time to prepare. Do what has been discussed and your readiness draws closer. Until next time that is all.

Thank you I appreciate your help and guidance.

MON 31ST DECEMBER

Good morning Nameless. I have been all over town searching for Raven Owl but to no avail. I googled her and found a contact number and that she was based in Coolum. I rang the number and a man answered who claimed the phone number as his own, thus Raven Owl has changed her number. I drove all the way to Coolum to the Wishing Well[8] to enquire about her and the owner who has had the shop for eight years has never heard of her. She also said there were not many readers in Coolum and she would have heard of her if she was around.

I then went to Symbolic Journey[9] in Noosa and enquired there and again they haven't heard of her. She doesn't seem to be on Facebook and is not in the white or yellow pages. The only other information I could find was a workshop she did in Townsville but there was no link to contact her.

Q. What am I to do? I have read for my friend and passed information on to my male friend. Finding Raven Owl and receiving information from her was to bring me closer to my name. I'm ready to order business cards today as tomorrow is my deadline but I don't have my name. Any thoughts? Can you help?

Do not panic my dear. There was a reason she had you running all over town. You retrieved something did you not?

Yes, a book on pendulum dowsing.[10]

This was one of your pots of gold, information that is necessary for you to continue your journey. It has given you much information and confidence to move forward and you will use the many skills it provides. If you had not travelled thus far it would not have come into your hands so your search for Raven and Raven herself guided you there.

As for your name you are to retrieve it yourself. This is your current challenge/quest and if you are able to do this it will confirm your readiness. You are right in that you don't need to be face to face with Raven Owl (in her actual presence) and you can channel her or telepathically communicate with her from a distance. If you are able to make contact with her in this manner she will pass you your name. It will be in a pink envelope and when you open it you will be much surprised, happy and joyous and also relieved. The tears will well in the eyes and you will be grateful and give many thanks to Raven Owl. She is one of your planetary guides and is there to aid and guide you on this journey. You would do well to check in with her periodically for advice and feedback. She will supply you with much information as well as encouragement and confidence especially when you doubt yourself. She, as I, will be by your side through the beginnings of your foray into this realm to support and energize you and pass on our knowledge until you're ready to stand alone and continue unaided. Do not concern yourself with this yet as it is far in the future, a year's length or longer.

Just know that we are with you always, you do not travel alone. Also I see you doing the *earth walk* that you are thinking of. This is rightly so, there is a message/information for you there. Perhaps you could do the two together…earth walk and then your communication with Raven Owl. You will come home much enlightened and walking on a high. Go to the private beach previously discussed. Go with my blessings.

Until next time — Nameless.

Thank you, thank you, thank you.

EARTH WALK

Here I am down at the private beach preparing to earth walk. This is an exercise that was given to me by a long ago friend as a tool to help solve life's issues or problems, for times of turmoil, indecisiveness or when you just need some direction in life.

First you find a starting point. It could be your backyard, the beach, a forest or your street etc. Next take off your shoes, being barefoot on the earth is important. The messages will not always come up through this avenue but the grounding and connection to mother earth is paramount. Ask a question in your mind that you need answered and then start walking with your head down only looking at your feet and nothing else, not even the direction you are walking in as you don't even know where you are going, your direction is simply being guided by intuition. Continue to walk in this way with a clear unattached mind until you hear the definite word STOP! It will usually come to you loud and clear and is coming from the Universal Mind. Immediately stop and observe your surroundings, noticing anything that stands out and catches your eye. It could be a feather, a dog running up the beach, a fork in the tree etc. or all of the above. Use these images to decipher the answer to your question.

One time I was doing this exercise on Sunshine Beach on a beautiful clear calm day when I was suddenly hit by a rogue wave that sprang from nowhere, pushing me into the sandy cliff face that had formed from a recent storm. Shocked and stunned by what felt like a Universal slap I looked down at my feet to discover I was surrounded by blue bottles (a sea creature notorious for their nasty stings). As the ocean wave was not receding my only escape was to climb up the near vertical cliff, as fast as I could! I definitely got my message that day, loud and clear. This exercise has often helped me when I've been at my wits end but today was the first day I had tried it without a question in mind.

> *"I know you (Universal Mind) have a message for me and have no idea what it's about so I'm just going to walk until you tell me to stop."*

I'm walking through the bush barefoot at the back of the private beach on Lake Cootharaba. I'm walking on leaves underfoot then suddenly I feel heat beneath my feet that is so intense I'm forced to take notice, it's like a zap to my consciousness, "Ouch!" There were no leaves here and the heat from the sun had roasted the soil. It was burning hot like standing on hot coals. I looked for any other signs and could see none.

> *Message: Take note, be aware of sensations, changes in temperature. Also sensations in general, sound, touch, sight, smell. Develop and heighten your sensory awareness. Be alert to your surroundings.*

Q. How do I heighten my sensory awareness?

By stilling the mind to all others (thought). Stilling the mind is the secret to everything. It opens up the possibilities of the Universe. There is so much to learn and grow and do and experience. This is only the beginning but you are following the right path. Rest now and prepare yourself to meet Raven Owl. She is waiting for you.

I'm guessing that last bit came from Nameless. I went for a swim in the lake to cool off from the days heat then laid my towel amongst the centians and rested for a while enjoying the solitude. Finally I went in search of Raven Owl.

▫▫▫

Raven Owl, Raven Owl, Raven Owl. What message for me do you bring on the wind?

I have arrived. You felt it touch you, a tingling sensation through your whole being. You have come to me seeking permission to move forward. You have stated your commitment and honor to the Universe. You have travelled far to reach this point. You sit amongst the *Valley of The Snakes* which only the anointed may enter. Before I pass the information you seek let it be known that I am your planetary guide. You may come to me for guidance, reassurance and knowledge. Ours will be a strong bond and I commit to you as you do to the Universe that is all and us combined. I hand you the pink envelope in the knowledge that you can be trusted to use your skills wisely and only for the better good of mankind. Open the envelope my dear and take joy in your new name…

MARIKAI

Shivers and tingles go through my whole body as I recognize and write down this word and indeed the tears well in my eyes.

Marikai (Marik-eye) is the twenty-first century interpretation of the name Marikahee. See you are more knowledgeable than you thought and yes you are right, the name belonged to the wife of a renowned Indian Chief. She was a *Shaman* and a great healer and revered by her tribe. It is she who chose the name for you as you will carry on the tradition in her honor. She also looks over you and guides you with her wisdom and skill. She considers you a granddaughter, family and will come to you in visions. It is a special bond you share. Marikahee is the one who has been leaving you feathers everywhere as a sign she is with you and you follow the right path.

Q. What does the name mean?

Oh great one who speaks with the spirits. I know you don't feel this fits with you (the great part) but neither did she. She had been preselected and it was predicted before she was born, the name given her at birth. The same can be said for you. Hear the deafening sound of the rattle snakes as they chime in celebration? You have just been crowned.

Thank you Raven Owl and Marikahee. Bless you both. I am forever grateful.

PART TWO

MY YEAR OF DIVINE GUIDANCE

3

JAN 2013

SAT 5TH JANUARY

Good morning Nameless. As this is our first meeting for the New Year I feel I need to tell you of my decision to follow divine guidance for a period of one whole year to see if it makes a difference to my life. I don't feel I can go on struggling through life as I have done over the last decades, my energy draining as time moves forward. Your words to me that my life would look/be very different in a years' time gave me positive hope for the future. If I follow divine guidance perhaps this is what is necessary/needed to change my world.

Q. What say you?

Indeed it is so. Trust in the Universe and it will provide. You have been closed off for too long, dead to our world and thus you have journeyed through life dead also, zombie like. I see you opening up petal like in the morning dew of a sunny day. As each petal slowly opens the glorious grandeur of it all is revealed. When the final petal opens your true beauty is revealed and the Universe breaks into harmonic song with the glory of it all.

Your decision to commit yourself to divine guidance is what led you to your name. Without this commitment it would not have been forthcoming. You are a beautiful rose about to blossom. But it is important to note. Do not rush this journey but revel in its adventurous learning. There is much to learn and grow and understand. It is imperative for your end knowledge that you *do not* skip any of the lessons along the way.

Follow divine guidance as instructed and indeed you will see your world change before your very eyes to be replaced with new visions that you had not thought possible or ever dreamt about. Your journey has just begun and excitement wells at the possibilities before you. We, your guides, are with you every step. You may call on us at will. We will never fail you. That is all.

Thank you Nameless for your support and guidance. Also I'd like to tell you about my meeting with Raven Owl and receiving my name…

□□□

I entered into the Valley of The Snakes and attempted to invoke Raven Owl. I really struggled to bring her through and the transmission was all very sketchy. I began to become concerned that I wouldn't be able to communicate with her and therefore not receive my name. I felt that perhaps I was trying too hard, there was thought attached which I had trouble letting go of and the more I tried to vision her the more reception faded. Then I realized here in lies the problem. I had been trying to vision Raven Owl and as a primary auditory channel this was where my blockage was occurring. As soon as I switched channels so to speak she came through loud and clear. I'm not sure why I was trying to vision her. I think I wanted to know what she looked like and I had been expecting to see her in the flesh. I remember recounting my efforts to find Raven to my friend and on telling her I thought Raven Owl had moved to Townsville or elsewhere she suggested I could always contact her through Skype. I then joked who needed Skype when you could channel, so I think this is where my visionary expectation came from.

Raven Owl spoke and presented me with my spiritual name and along with it a new guide. Marikahee does seem to come to me visually though as she is one of little or no words. She stands and looks at me with her all-knowing eyes. I feel her knowledge will be transferred to me through telepathy, a knowing and energy exchange. She is my healing guide, my hands are her hands and she will work through me to heal many. She follows me everywhere, I constantly see her before me and she leaves me feathers to remind me she is here and to follow the healing path, "follow the feathers for your journey involves healing." As a non-practicing Naturopath I came to the realization that I never fully pursued that path because I am not so much a clinical practitioner as such but more of a channelor/tool for energy and vibrational healing. Yes that feels more right to me, tying in with my interest in metaphysics and I can feel my heart and spirit lift at the thought of it as it resonates more with my soul. This also brings me to my earth walk which told me to be aware of my senses more. To heighten my sensory awareness as it will reveal valuable information for example alerting me to right or wrong path, healing of self and others and alerting me to surroundings and situations that I can learn from.

Anyway as you said when I received my name I was much relieved but at first I had a tingling sensation through my entire body as if I'd been 'entered into' by spirit or been 'switched on.' Tears welled with emotion as I felt excited, grateful and relieved. Thank you Nameless, Raven Owl and Marikahee for guiding me to this point.

Q. Do you have anything to add?

Indeed it is so. That is all.

SUN 6TH JANUARY

Good morning Nameless. I've been reading a lot trying to ready myself in preparation for the new enterprise. My confidence varies from one minute to the next, however things are falling into place.

Q. There is something I have lost and need to find, an old pendulum of mine. Can you help me? Can you tell me where it is?

Look in the cupboard and you will find what you are looking for although this is not the ideal instrument for you. I see you replacing it with another more powerful tool. This will be another quest for you, a pot of gold to pick up for the continuation of your journey. I feel you should go to the place you are thinking of, to the crystal healing shop there and you will find what you are looking for. It will glow and draw you to it, hold your hand above it for confirmation. You will feel the heat and vibration emanating from it so strongly it will almost jump into your hands. I see it being large and green in color, something you did not expect. Pay no matter to the price. It must be yours regardless of the cost.

You may begin with the one you find today until the rightful one is found and presented to you but this is a make do implement and healing knowledge will be somewhat stifled and therefore you cannot trust it fully. Use your own judgment and intuition along with this tool until the rightful one is yours. When this comes into your hands its healing powers will aid you a hundred fold. You are destined for each other to do great things. Look after and treasure this piece and it will reward you with much knowledge. The energy between you will become as one.

You *are* one. That is all.

Thank you Nameless.

SAT 12TH JANUARY

Hello Nameless. Sorry it's been a few days since our last meeting, I've had a busy week looking for potential shops for the art co-op etc. Today I'd like to ask you about you…

Q. Where do you come from? What's it like there? What do you look like, what are your physical attributes?

Greetings. I come from *The Source* of *All Kind.* That is *Color and Light, Energy* and *Thought form.* Therefore I do not embody a physical form but instead can be *felt*! We communicate via telepathy, you can tap into me at any time. I am within you, around you and everywhere all at once. Thus I can be a guiding light and a veritable source of information as I can draw upon knowledge from many different sources and many different places at any one time. It is only a matter of asking before I can deliver you my knowledge and guidance. I am the kookaburra that sings in the tree and the cockroach who moves stealthily through the night. I am all and everything at once. I am also you, as you are me. Remember we are all one and the same. You may liken me to a shape shifter. I am what you need me to be at any given time. If you need the experience and knowledge of an ant I will be that ant and draw upon its knowledge. You may ask me any question regarding the ants' world and I can relieve you of your wonder. But, remember there are many ants in this world and each with their own experience and own knowledge of their existence. Thus not all ants think the same nor know the entirety of what it is to be an ant as all ants are different. Just as all humans and their knowledge, experience and perception of their own reality is different. Thus it would be an idea to ask many different ants of what it is like to be an ant and live in the ant world before one could even grasp the merest idea/understanding of it all. You should try it one day…ask me about ants though this is not an appropriate time as I feel your exhaustion and heat. Yes I am you always and feel what you feel including your discomfort. So for now I think it is important that you go jump in that billabong before your blood boils and you cook us both. We can extend on this at a later time. For now it was nice to meet with you today but for our sakes…go cool off.

Thank you Nameless. By the way, Marikahee left me a beautiful flight feather today. I'll ask her its meaning after my swim…

▫▫▫

Marikahee, come to me. Explain to me the gift of the flight feather.

Marikahee shared this with me…I am her apprentice. She gifts me my first flight feather, it's she who will teach me how to "fly." We will share many lessons together. She called me her fledgling and told me she will teach me to soar with the eagles.

WED 16TH JANUARY

Sorry Nameless it's been a few days but I'm camping out at Charlie Moreland near Kenilworth, my days filled with swimming and bush walking and little light at night to write by. I hope you've been well (now that sounds a bit stupid as I guess where you come from you are always well). I've been able to do some reading since I spoke to you last regards channeling and my purpose in life. It suggested among other things that you may be able to guide me with regards to my Higher purpose.

Q. Are you aware of what my Higher purpose is in this life? Are you able to let me know what it is? Will you guide me along the way?

Greetings. Nice to be with you in *presence* terms, that is, speaking.

I was with you during your walk yesterday and felt your struggle. Maintaining health should be a priority as you get older in order to do the work you need to do and accomplish what you need to accomplish. As stated previously you are a teacher and a great healer. You will heal many from all walks of life. People will travel far and wide to see you and I feel you will travel also.

Q. But what is my primary purpose? Teacher or healer?

Both. You will accomplish and become accomplished at both. Flitting between the two as the need arises. When people require your knowledge you will teach. Those that seek healing will be healed and you will guide many more. This is in your future…it is already written. The timing was wanting up until now as you busied yourself with other things and would not have been able to show such diligence and commitment as you are now.

You will begin with healing and guidance as this is already familiar to you. You already heal others unaware of your effect on people. Currently you are having a long overdue rest to recover from the exhausting gruel of the past six months. This is good, you will need your batteries charged for the next six months ahead and beyond. I feel your trepidation as you think you are not quite ready but it is important for you to start and the healing will flow. You will make it happen as the learned scholar who will do much reading and research *but* this is useless without actual physical practice. Hence until your confidence in your knowledge and ability increases I recommend you not charge too much. *Feel* for the right dollar amount. You will know when it *feels* right. After a period of time healing and giving channeled guidance then you will feel ready to teach. People will start asking you and when enough have asked, you will know it's time to share your skills. And there you have it. Your purpose is to heal, guide and teach, in that order.

Don't forget Marikahee is your healing guide. I understand you are on holidays but when you get back it is important that you start checking in with her. She is waiting for you, for your first lesson together. You will be much surprised what you learn from her… a great wise healer who has chosen you because of your strong healing qualities and willingness to learn.

Both Raven Owl and I are here to increase your knowledge and skill with regards to channeling and guidance. You may call on either one of us at any time. Raven Owl is able to give you a psychic's perspective but as for the ant there are many psychic perspectives therefore also search out others as in groups or forums. These will form your support networks also. The book you are reading[1] is a good comprehensive guide and well written. You will learn much from this *but* all the knowledge in the world is useless unless utilized and put into practice.

Once you start practicing there will be a lot of on the job training. You will learn greatly from relating to others whether through guidance or healing (and later, teaching), with many experiences and many scenarios that will add to your growth and knowledge bank. Remember you are not alone and either Marikahee, Raven Owl or I will always be there to guide you. You need only ask and it be done. Go forth now with the knowledge that you have waited your whole life to reach this point and now the *true* living can begin. It is an exciting journey and one I am happy to share with you. Our bond is nigh. Greetings loved one.

Thanks Nameless. Um, what does nigh mean?

Unbreakable, never to be broken or never able to be broken.

THUR 17TH JANUARY

Hi Nameless. I've just been for a refreshing dip in the creek and am feeling relaxed and cooled. I'm sitting amongst the centians, the breeze on my skin and the bellbirds calling in the distance. All around me butterflies dance their merry way and as the heat is not so intense today I'm starting to feel more relaxed, rejuvenated and reenergized. It's a good day. I would like some advice on something you mentioned yesterday however. You mentioned my health and the importance of maintaining it. As you know I have put on the kilos in the last few years which I'm sure is linked to hormones but it really gets me down sometimes, not feeling comfortable in my own skin. I have never been a large eater and already halve my main meals, there is not a lot I can cut back on without feeling deprived.

Q. Can you shed any light on this matter? Can you advise me on how to shed some kilo's or get back to my normal weight?

Hmm, this is indeed a weighty issue and not really my area of expertise. It is right that you be concerned for your health, not that anything is wrong but that to accomplish much the greater the health the better. I feel your uncomfortableness of weight as an *energy density* that is weighing you down. Work on *lifting* and *lightening* your energy and your weight will lighten also. I hear you ask how to do this and the answer is that you are in need of self-healing and self-nurturing. Do things that feel right and good to you, that you know will lift your energy and spirits and the *space* you live in that is your aura and your souls being. This could take the place of for example the swim in nature that you just had which not only serves to cool the body and mind but to feed, energize and uplift the soul, your very essence and being. As you do those things and feel good about yourself you will make better (health) choices. It will be easier for you to pay attention and do what is right for your body with regards to health, nutrition, sleep, rest and exercise. If it feels good do it, with no thought or guilt for the matter or this only serves to add density to thought and therefore weight to the body, weighing you down so to speak, weighing heavily upon your mind, shoulders and ultimately your body. So the aim is to do that which raises your energy, uplifts you and takes you to a Higher place of *being*. The more you can do this and nurture yourself and your very soul being the more you will notice your weight stabilize and come back into alignment with what is essentially true to you. Other ways you can lift your spirits and thus your vibratory level are to be in nature, commune with nature as you are doing now. Also the healing modalities, massage, reiki, balancing your chakras, plant therapy and also aromatherapy which can calm and cleanse the senses.

Be aware of the energy of foods. Ask yourself is this an energy dense food? And I don't mean kilojoule counting but on a *vibratory level.* Does this food have a dense/heavy vibration and will therefore add density to the body (mind and spirit) as a whole or is this food of a Higher and therefore lighter vibration? This you would do well to ask and once the decision is made to eat the food do so with no regrets and no guilt. Enjoy and savor as to add guilt is only to add density and therefore heaviness to the issue at hand. Follow this advice and you will start to feel better about all aspects of your life. Not only will your weight lift but so will your energy, vibration and spirit as a whole but remember you must put the effort in to reap the rewards.

Q. I appreciate your knowledge and guidance and all of this makes great sense but you have said nothing about exercise, what of that and what is the best exercise for me?

Yes of course exercise and also rest should be include but not forced exercise that makes you a misery and again adds density to your thought and that which you would easily give up and forgo. You know such exercise that feels good to you, that *feels* right, that you enjoy doing and which uplifts your spirit and being as well as supporting the health of the body. You do like to walk and especially in nature and this benefits both mind and body. Swimming is also part of your nature, your natural being and always has been since you were little and this is why it feels so right to you, it is part of your essence, your very being. You always feel really good and refreshed after a swim, hold onto that *feeling* as that is what you should be trying to achieve through any form of exercise you do. Again it is an upliftment of your energy and spirit and a pleasant exhaustion of the body such that you feel mentally on a high coupled with the numbing effect of serotonin on the body which is pleasantly relaxing such that you feel high and relaxed concurrently. Therefore this is the state that you are trying to achieve to get benefit from exercise. So any exercise you choose to do, pay attention to the *feeling* that you get from it afterwards to know if it is doing you any benefit. Different times and different states of the body will require different exercises to achieve this state. For example one day you may benefit from a brisk walk in nature, another day laps or exercises in the pool. Choose what feels right at the time, trust your intuition. I feel you would also benefit from introducing yoga, Pilates or tai chi into your routine, something to aid in your flexibility and suppleness. Remember work that affects the body is also affecting the mind and spirit. If you can find time for this you will feel a great benefit. Once a week is beneficial you do not have to dedicate a lifetime to it at this stage though later when you have more time you will choose to do it out of pure pleasure. I feel at a much later date, in a years' time when you are freer with your time you may find yourself back in the gym also but with a more balanced approach than the first time. You have much to go on. I know this will be of benefit to you if you choose this path.

I too am enjoying being amongst the centians with singing sounds of nature and the warm breeze that carries the aromatic scent of nearby flora. Happy days and greetings loved one.

Thank you Nameless you have been very helpful.

FRI 18TH JANUARY

My daughter is suffering from a terrible score throat, a result from swallowing the creek water. I asked Marikahee for advice and she showed me leaves, her hands outstretched towards me. I interpreted this as herbs she wanted me to boil up for a tea or decoction. When I asked her what herbs she told me Thyme and Bloodroot. I know Thyme to be good for throats and from memory I think Bloodroot is a blood cleanser (immune support), alas camping in the bush we have neither. She then showed me a poultice placed on the throat another impossibility but from this image I realized I could work on the throat chakra and also some reflexology.

▫

Later I discovered that the American Indians indeed used Bloodroot for coughs and sore throats by placing the juice on a lump of maple sugar (to disguise its bitter taste) and sucking on this.[2]

SUN 20TH JANUARY

Hi Nameless, just a quick question before I get in touch with Raven Owl. A few friends and I are thinking of going to the quarry near Johns Landing for a swim. The water in the quarry is the most opulent aquamarine blue similar to that found in Australian outback underwater caves, the color being so bright it doesn't look normal. I've swum there many times over with no ill effect but my friend suggested that there could be chemicals that have leached into the water that would be detrimental to our health. I've tried to research its history and can only find that it was a low key extraction site to supply washed sand for landscapers, building materials and such. There seemed to be strict guidelines in place with EPA management under the former Noosa Councils supervision (Noosa being a "green" area) and being within a stone's throw of the Noosa River I don't see that they would have been allowed to use anything too harmful on this site.

Q. Are you aware of any chemicals in the water that may be harmful for our health? If so what?

This quarry has been sitting idle for many years. Any harmful chemicals have long since dissipated, washed away by the rains that have leeched it into the soil to then be traversed and transported away on the backs of microbes who toil through the soil on their many travels. It is true a long time ago it may have been harmful but currently that harm has been minimized and it has to be weighed against the joy that you get from swimming there.

Q. Who's talking?

It's me Nameless, I am always with you.

Q. Thanks, just checking. Is it in my highest good to swim there? What are the possible benefits?

Your friend has planted a seed of doubt. It is this seed of doubt and *thoughts* surrounding it that would do you more harm than the short intervals of pleasure that you would get from being there. Worry is only adding weight to this issue and as previously discussed will only serve to add weight to body mind and spirit and therefore be more detrimental than beneficial. If you choose to go there do so without worry, guilt or fear and only take those who would take pleasure in the exercise and not those who would add to your fear and thus spoil your enjoyment. Often it is the thought that is more harmful than the external. This has been a popular destination for a long period of time with no reported illness or negative outcomes. If there had been or if it were considered to be dangerous the authorities would have shut it down and even though you trespass they choose to ignore it for the benefit of the community. Now it is up to you if you can enjoy and take pleasure from being there. You will perhaps need to try it once or twice and concentrate on how it *feels* to be there, does it *feel* good? Are you able to overcome fear and doubt? Remember you are chasing that feel good quality to help raise your vibration.

Go my friend Raven Owl is waiting. Take pleasure in your day.

Thank you Nameless.

▫▫▫

After a brisk walk up the road from my place towards the private beach I enter The Valley of The Snakes. Laying myself down on a bed of leaves I make myself comfortable, close my eyes and breathe in the surrounds until I'm calm and relaxed.

Q. Raven Owl, Raven Owl, what do you bring on the wind for me today?

I have travelled far to be here and have been watching the many exercises you have put in place. You are right to be concerned about starting the new enterprise, this is healthy. I too was concerned in the beginning like a deer caught in the headlights but I knew it was my right path and so with a great gulp summoned all my courage and went forth along my journey. For what is there to lose? And so very much to gain. If you try and fail, pick yourself back up and try again. Failing is not an option as this is your rightful way. There may be bumps along the way but swallow your pride and see them as opportunities for great learning, growth and development. I see someone reading the cards for you.

Listen very carefully as there is an underlying message there. This message is what you need to give you the courage and help to move forward, it will lighten your load and confirm you are on the right path. You must go there early in order to secure your place, don't be late. Forgo the meditation it is not for you and you will only feel it a waste of time. Instead enjoy a leisurely walk while you wait your turn. You will come away enlightened and invigorated knowing that each pot of gold you are picking up brings you closer to your souls path. I will be there watching over you as will Nameless and Marikahee. It is like we are sending off our own to its first day of school. We will be looking on with such joy and pride and guiding you with loving arms.

Till then little one — Raven Owl.

Thank you Raven Owl.

THUR 24TH JANUARY

Hello Nameless. So much has happened in the last few days I feel I need to catch you up on things even though I know you're aware. I've ordered a massage table as I sold my last one thinking I would never use it again due to arthritis in my wrist. That's the beauty of energy healing it doesn't require a lot of physical contact. My business cards and a few other things are on their way also so the new enterprise is on track. After an email I received I decided to forgo the art co-op, it just wasn't feeling right and was going to take up a lot of my time, another weight on my shoulders.

I'm more conscious of my vibration levels now and what things increase it by concentrating more on how things make me feel in my core, my very being. This makes it much easier to make decisions about things by asking… "Will this raise my vibration?" and "what do I 'feel' about this?" I had to laugh the other day when I asked the pendulum about something I considered to be naughty to eat, would it increase my vibration? I was surprised when it answered yes instead of no so asked it if it would increase my physical vibration (no) and would it increase my mental vibration (yes). So there needs to be a certain level of discernment there and even though it might lift me mentally and make me feel good it's still going to weigh me down physically. It would be so easy to cheat, I see what you mean about putting in the work and effort as it still takes willpower to follow the vibrational way of eating. I can know that something will add weight to my vibration/physical form and still choose to eat it just because it makes me feel good. It would be interesting to follow the vibrational way of eating for a month and see what happens. Perhaps when my daughter returns to school I could try it for a full term.

Q. I've prattled on. Is there anything you have to say, or is there something I need to know right now?

Just that heaven is on earth, in front of you and all around you, you just need to open your eyes to see it. Last night you read about time (and space) travel and it is this you need to do in order to get there. You have been there once before a long time ago so you know what I am talking about *but* I am here to tell you, you will travel there many times over. You are standing on the edge of the abyss about to step over into what we call *star travel.* It is with lightning speed that this will occur and it is imperative that you hold no thought for home which will only serve to bring you crashing back down to earth. Hold on to your feeling of awe and wonder but do not allow fear and worry to enter your mind as this is what will return you instantly with a heavy bump and thud. You will be agape at what you see, overwhelmed with the *light* in the beginning until you adjust over a period of time after many visits and you will have *many many* visits. On these visits you will talk to ones with great wiseness, returning to your earth plane with much information that you will pass onto others in your healing and teaching practice. These visits will also give you a feeling of great *Lightness of Being* that you are unable to experience on your earth no matter how advanced you are. Thus you are of two worlds, the solid matter world governed by the clock and all that would weigh you down and the infinity world where *time simply does not exist* and all is *Lightness and Being.*

Q. When will I journey there?

Your time is coming… soon. There is still a bit of preparation to be done, however you get closer every day. I hear you ask for a specific time and date but this is not possible as it depends on your development and growth, a lot of which is dependent on yourself. Also asking for specifics like times and dates is old school and it is when you can learn to break free of these constraints and *transcend time* that you will begin your first journey into *Light and Being*. Once you have done that the challenge will be to learn how to stay there for a period of (your) time, followed by travelling there at will and liaising between the two worlds. The Aborigines and the Indians have already solved this problem as they are not bound by the constraints of the Caucasians. You would be wise to study their beliefs for the benefit of your growth, to expand your mind and your awareness beyond the limiting life (land) that you currently occupy.

This is exciting news… these travels. You really are about to blossom and have no idea the joy you're about to experience. Your world will never be the same…this is *life changing*. Then far off in the future your challenge will be to show others the way for you are a Shepard and they are your flock. Obviously you will do this humbly and with honor as we are all one, this was purely a metaphor to aid you visually.

Communication is broken, your daughter is calling you for dinner. You had better go or she will be getting impatient. She really does love you by the way. Peace in your heart.

Awesome, lots to think about. Thank you Nameless. I'm planning on catching up with Marikahee in The Valley tomorrow if this rain stops.

SUN 27TH JANUARY

Hi Nameless. This is a bit weird…we've had a huge storm go through last night and have been without power all day courtesy of the remnants of cyclone Oswald up north. I was complacent and got caught with no water (no electricity equals no pumps equals no water) and had to put all the pots and pans out on the driveway to catch rain so we could have drinking water. I cooked dinner on the camp stove and we've been playing games by candlelight. Now I'm sitting in bed holding a torch while I write to you.

I heard from neighbors the storm damage is wide spread and there are quite a few power lines down, the damage could possibly extend all the way to Brisbane and the Gold Coast but without a T.V and radio I have no idea what's going on. Apparently the power went out at four a.m. this morning, it's now ten-thirty p.m. and I'm getting worried about all the food in the fridge and freezer as we just did a big fortnightly shop. The power often goes out in Boreen Point but not usually longer than three to five hours.

Q. Do you have any idea what time the power will return?

You will go to sleep and wake to the power being returned to you. Do not concern yourself with the food as it will not spoil. You have done well in keeping the fridge closed all day and this has really helped. Let this be a lesson to you to be more prepared next time. Stock up on candles, batteries and the like. Invest in a radio and re read the storm preparation flyer. There are a few more storms on the way and one of them will be a doozy. You may find yourself trapped for a few days. If you are well prepared this will be of no concern to you, instead you will enjoy the solitude as you have done today. It has been enjoyable and relaxing has it not? The lack of electricity served to *slow* you down. This is more conducive to what your life *should* feel like, better for your health and wellbeing. This level of balanced work, rest and play is what you're aiming for. You got a little work done, got organized, spent some time reading and learning coupled with play and enjoyment. A well balanced day. Thus you would be feeling more in harmony with the Universe. This feeling of harmony coupled with the fact you are not bothered by worrisome thoughts or concerns allows the mind to open up. It *frees* the mind to energetic input from the Universe. *Relax* and the knowledge will come, flowing from the ether into your subconscious to be brought to your conscious mind and into your awareness where you may or may not choose to physically act upon it for the betterment of all mankind, for you have free will and even though the information flows to you, is there for you on a *daily* basis, you need only open your mind to listen and it be yours for the taking.

There are those around you who would benefit greatly from the knowledge you have gained and are able to pass on to them. There is no time to waste or wait, the sooner a beginning you can make then those who need it can be healed. I know you don't yet fully integrate this purpose into your souls being and this will not be so until you bring it into physical manifestation. You are on the right path. We are with you… Raven Owl, Marikahee and I and many others are waiting for you. There is much to learn and do and grow and sow but you will do it along the way. I feel the first step is near, every day moves you closer towards it. We are your guidance. We will never fail you, we are always with you.

Enjoy the ambience of this night. I will watch you as you sleep and cradle you in my 'arms' until mornings light. Lovingly — Nameless.

Wow, all that from asking when the electricity will be switched on. Thanks Nameless I feel safe with you watching over me. It's a beautiful peaceful night cocooned in my bed reading by torchlight, all cozy while the wind and rain howls outside. Thank you for your insights.

MON 28TH JANUARY

Well its ten-thirty a.m. I woke at eight a.m. and the electricity and power is still out, not having been returned by the time I awoke as you predicted. I'm seriously worried about the food now as I don't have enough money to buy more if it spoils. Also I feel you've failed in your prediction and it makes me question you. Are you real? Or is this all just a crock of shit, my schizoid imagination talking to myself and telling myself what I want to hear? I'm really getting angry, I do not want to waste my time following fantasy.

Q. I need some tangible proof that you are real. Can you show me something or tell me something that will prove your existence?

Firstly the power did come on but only fleetingly, whilst you were still sleeping. I hear you say you would have heard the microwave come on but it was so fleeting as to barely register and hence no sound from the microwave.

(This must have been when they cut the tree off the power line in town and a small amount of stored electricity was released.)

Also you were in deep sleep when this occurred. The problem is much bigger and more complex than anticipated and they are working hard to remedy the issue. I know you feel like your little town has been forgotten, deserted in this time but it is not so. The problem is wide spread over an extremely large area. This you will learn when the power returns and you are able to connect with the outside world. You will require patience as it is going to be a few more hours yet. I see if you go to get ice it will be on by the time you get back but you may still decide to do this to ease your mind and your lack of faith in me that your food will not spoil.

How can I prove to you that I exist? What will it take for you to believe in me? I think the only way for you to have absolute faith in my existence is to set me a challenge and once this challenge is fulfilled there will be no doubt in your mind that I am here, I am real. Your quest is to come up with the challenge as it has to come from you in order for you to have complete belief in the outcome.

Q. Are there any guidelines?

Ask me to manifest something.

Whoa, that's heavy. Ok, I can think of money (or a man, LOL) but that could get confused with coincidence. I think I'll put some thought into it and make it something more unique and specific. Let me have time to think about it and I'll get back to you.

Let it be so. Go in loving light, I'll be watching.

▫▫▫

Ok Nameless, I've thought about it. I'd like a button please. This button should be round and sitting atop is a raised sea anchor in metal or faux metal. I have seen such buttons before, some are made of colored plastic with a raised anchor, some are made to look like metal and rarer still are the actual metal ones themselves. I don't want to go in search of this button but I want you to present it to me in an unusual way (i.e. not at the button or sewing shop). I have some ideas of where I might find it and have written these down in a sealed envelope which I'll give to my friend with strict instructions not to open until I say. I'd like to find the button within the next three to six weeks (as I know manifestation can take time to occur). In the meantime I'll carry on with the faith that you do exist as I can already see my life improving for the better. So whether it be you or my Higher Self talking, I'm still benefiting. Show me my button please Nameless.

And so it shall be done. Let go of all thought surrounding such and I will bring it to you.

WED 30TH JANUARY

I've just had a meeting with Marikahee whilst sitting in the River of A Thousand Mirrors[3] *(so called for its reflective qualities) cooling off on this hot summer's day. As I gazed across the river to the opposite banks Marikahee emerged from the bushes and beckoned me to her. Surprised by her sudden appearance I cautiously obeyed.*

▫▫▫

Marikahee showed me a fine powder that she held in her outstretched hands and blew into the ether. I asked her what the powder was for and she told me to ward off evil spirits. I then asked her to show me where she sourced it from and we went walking through the forest together until we spied a white man's fire roasting a wild pig. Could that be it, ash from that fire? No, she only wanted to show me what to be wary of and motioned me to be quiet and follow her through the forest some more.

We came to a clearing and whilst hiding amongst the centians observed a beautiful wild deer grazing, a strong young buck. This is the source of the powder…ground from the antlers of such a beautiful beast. One buck could supply many in multiple ways but the decision to take such a life was not taken lightly and Marikahee assured me none of it would go to waste. The antlers are ground into a powder and used for many purposes…placed at the door of the teepee to ward off the spirits, thrown over virgin brides in ceremony to purify them of untoward energy before marriage and about the bodies of the ill and dying to ward off evil spirits, mixed to a paste and applied as poultices on wounds, bruises and swellings and to heal cuts and abrasions (speed recovery). She even wore some in a small pouch on her headdress for good luck and also because she said you never know when you might need it.

The rest of the carcass was used wisely and without a speck of wastage. The meat turned into cuts of venison, the eyeballs used in soups and stews, the tongue smoked and cut like ham. The other organs were dried and ground into powders also, each possessing their own special qualities. Traditionally bones were used as instruments for cooking and to help form utensils as well as a source of personal decoration. Sinew was formed into string and the teeth used for jewelry and adornments in hair, headdresses, spears and clothing as were the bones. The hide was dried, tanned and then softened for all manner of things, rugs, mats, bedding, moccasins, clothing, papooses for the young ones and formed part of the internal layering of the teepees in winter. Any left overs such as gizzards were fed to the wolf dogs. To honor the gift the animal had bestowed upon them nothing was wasted. Marikahee called the deer powder her panacea, her heal all. When everything else failed she would always turn to this.

Well we don't have deer antler powder where we come from though there is a deer farm nearby, an hour's drive away. I asked Marikahee what I could use instead to ward off the evil spirits (cleanse the aura) and to make poultices for wounds etc. She told me to search for the modern equivalent that contains both honor and healing powers and if I find it to bring it to her, she will tell me if it has the same energetic vibration. "Go with my blessings and may only good spirits follow you." Marikahee blew some deer powder from her palms in my direction and dissolved back into the ether from whence she came.

□□□

Since then I've done a quick online search and blow me down if deer antler powder isn't actually readily available in the West. Who would have thought? It seems the powder (Velvet Antler[4]) indeed possesses a multitude of uses but no mention of poultices or warding off evil spirits (tee hee). I had never known this to exist so my faith in Marikahee, her healing powers and knowledge and the truth of our communication, its very realness of existence, has been utterly and totally confirmed. Among other things Marikahee was probably trying to bring Velvet Antler and its healing qualities to my attention.

4

FEB 2013

SUN 3RD FEBRUARY

Hi Nameless. It's been a few days and I've much to tell and much to ask. Firstly I've had a harrowing week. I'm feeling quite shattered and am really feeling the disturbance in my aura.

The storm damage was wide spread as you said with major floods all over Queensland...Bundaberg, Gympie, Brisbane, the Gold Coast, Ipswich, The Lockyer Valley and Rockhampton, the list goes on, the damage being much worse even than the 2011 floods. It was declared a natural disaster. We were without power for six days and I lost the entire contents of my fridge, something I need to discuss with you. I trusted you that the power would return and so refused a neighbors offer of help (they had a generator) to put my perishables in her fridge/freezer. I lost absolutely everything in the fridge even the condiments and sauce bottles, a whole fortnights shopping and I had to work in the dark by torch light to clear and clean it out for refuge the next day, all the while we were hoping that any second the power would return and save us.

The first few days after the storm were quite enjoyable, relaxing as you said. I read and channeled. Then I had to go to work and things got more difficult. We had no running water, no flushing toilets and no shower either. It was thirty-six degree heat with very high humidity and I was driving down to the lake to get buckets of water to bring back and flush the toilets. Some people were accessing water from their now full tanks with ladders but I had no ladder. I had to get up for work at four-thirty a.m. and drive down to the lake to have a cold shower in the public toilet block and then drive back home to get ready. At this time of the morning it's still dark and everything had to be done by torchlight including trying to do my hair and make-up.

At work I saw on the news how wide spread the disaster was and realized the power would not be coming on soon. My daughter couldn't get to school, the road being flooded out. Two hundred schools across the state were closed and as we had no phone, internet, T.V or radio we didn't even know if hers was one of them. I really need to get a radio but dumb blonde moment, five days after the event I realized I have a radio in my car!

Anyway I accessed the internet at the library and Energex had already repaired three thousand poles by day three with at least another three hundred to go. They were concentrating on business areas, schools, major flood zones and areas where they could connect large amounts of people in one go, twenty thousand at a time. It looked like our little town of two hundred and eighty-six people was last on the list and they were predicting we wouldn't have power till the Friday or Saturday (six or seven days after the storm) along with some other hinterland areas. Already my daughter and I were arguing. The house was a hot box with no fans or air-conditioning to cool it down and the heat, humidity and all the running around were getting to me. I had to drive for an hour return trip just to source fresh drinking water and now we had no food and no money to buy more so feeling really frazzled on day three I sent my daughter into town to stay with her school friends.

After work the house was too hot to go home to so I spent my afternoons sitting in Cooloothin Creek. I would go home an hour before dark and quickly get everything ready for the next day while I still had light. By the fourth day I was exhausted and in tears. The heat coupled with no flushing toilets and no shower to cool off by was tipping me over the edge. On day six I started looking for solace and accessed the council website. All the local evacuation centers were closed, can you believe it? Hundreds of people were days without power and sewage in thirty-six degree heat and they were closed. I went and sat in the river thinking about my next move. That night just before dark (around seven p.m.) as I busied myself to get ready for work the next day the power miraculously came back on and the whole town erupted in "Yahoo's!" and "Amen's!" as people gathered in the street to celebrate and you could feel as well as hear the collective relief. I wanted to join in and bang my wind chimes with glee but was so scared the power would go off again I quickly filled some water containers for drinking and jumped in the shower to wash my hair and shave my legs. For the first time in forever I had a very long nonstop shower and even stayed in there to clean it!

I know there were people way worse off than us, devastated by flood waters, losing furniture and belongings or even being cut off by water entirely and I really feel for them as it will take months and years for them to recover but a lot of other (forgotten) people suffered that week too nonetheless. I'm not sure why it affected me so greatly as I spent two years camping in the bush once so definitely have experience of roughing it. Perhaps it's because I'm older, not as physically fit and having to go to work through the whole ordeal just made it that much harder.

My questions to you Nameless follow. You were wrong with your predictions, I lost all of my food when I trusted you and followed divine guidance as I've committed myself to this year. How can I trust you again and what you say? How can I believe you, believe in you if you can get it so wrong? I've heard that other guides won't predict things or the future because of people's right to exert free will and therefore things can change and we are not living in a static environment. Can you predict things for me/others? If you can't I'd rather you say so and that's ok but I need to know. Also an explanation would be good. If I can't believe your predictions how can I believe everything else you say (about me being a teacher/healer)?

Firstly you *are* (a healer/teacher) so you can put that right out of your mind. It is written. It is so. It is not my prediction but the will of the Universe that it manifest for the better of all mankind. Your life will struggle until this comes into manifestation as it is this struggle that directs you there.

The suffering that you felt during your latest ordeal directs you also. It directs you to question me and that is healthy. Herein lies the lesson…that at all times no matter what I say you must always listen to your gut intuition as these override any information that either myself or others supply *always*. That is, do not follow blindly others without first checking with the *self*. Honor thy (Higher) self above all others. Concentrate on the *feeling* once again. How does it *feel*? Does it *feel* right to you? You will feel it in your gut, your solar plexus and even on a cellular level. Be aware of your *senses*. Heighten your sensory awareness. What does your *vibration* and *Higher Self* say on the matter? Therefore do not consult me and do what I say blindly with no thought or feeling to the matter but also search within yourself for truth and guidance…your *Higher Self* and indeed this should always be your first port of call before all others as your Higher Self is the ultimate expert (and existence) on/of you and all that pertains to you. You only need to ask and it will answer.

I will not say that I deliberately mislead you to teach you this. I will allow you to draw your own conclusion as you are one of high intelligence. You know what is going on but you have learnt a valuable lesson, have you not? One you can share with others, your clients that they step inside themselves for the truth (their own truth) in *every* situation they find themselves in. It is not dishonorable to consult outside the self in matters that perplex but this information then be collated with *self-knowledge* and *self-instinct* before a decision and any action be taken. Always staying *true* to the self and what feels right and good. A person knows they have made the right decision when all worry and concerns for the matter exit the mind and they are of *no mind* for the outcome as they know it to be so.

This lesson was chosen as one of least harm, though at the time because of other conditions being experienced it felt quite harsh. It is a lesson with impact that you will not forget in a hurry and thus served its purpose adequately. Any less and you perhaps would not have taken note, so the degree had to be just right.

With regards to your question about predictions and whether I will allow it I can only say this... If I feel it is appropriate I will suggest it myself, impart the information of my own volition. I do not like to be asked with regards to predictions. I feel they are often fruitless and not of Higher guidance and for the souls Higher good. Only when the soul requires such guidance for transformation will I offer it willingly and without being asked. Also predictions are stuck in "space and time" are linear and we as a collective are trying to break you free of these constraints so that you have freer access to the Higher ascensions. So called predictions only serve to weigh you down in the here and now of your realm/reality and our aim is to take you *beyond* the here and now into timelessness, infinity and to pure *Light and Being.*

As for your belief in me. You believe what you want to believe for you have free will and it is not up to me to convince you otherwise. I would say use the duality of your intellect and your spiritual senses, observe, listen and feel over a period of time before you draw your final conclusion. Consult the Higher Self and again listen to your gut instincts and your feeling sensations until you reach a *Knowing* that it is so. It *is,* it just *is,* without question (no mind, no worry, no concern for the matter).

I have faith in you little one. I watch you grow (spiritually) every day. I am here for you always and forever. You need only ask.

Lovingly — Nameless.

Thank you Nameless I'll take that on board and sit with it for a while.

FRI 8TH FEBRUARY

Good morning. It's a great morning and I'm very excited…I found my button!

Firstly because of the dramas with the cyclone I didn't give my friend the envelope containing the button request and where I might possibly find it until the fourth of February on my way home from the healing group. I thought I'd better drop it to her as I'm sure you wouldn't manifest it until I'd done this and then I couldn't believe how quickly and easily it arrived. I worked the next three days so was busy and preoccupied. On the third day I was on my way home from running errands when the idea to visit an op shop that I hadn't been to sprang to mind. Trusting my instincts and taking it as a message I visited the store even though I was in a hurry to get home. It was a veritable treasure trove and once inside I got lost in all the glory of rifling through the abundant variety on offer. I was looking for things I could photograph for my art such as vintage sewing patterns and a possible suicide bunny. After a good hour and on my way to the counter I spied a shelf with jars of buttons. There were at least ten good sized jars and the buttons were grouped into size and color. I was immediately drawn to one very large jar in particular that had a mixed bag in a medium size, the size I thought my button would come in and as I rolled the jar through my hands scanning…there it was my button! I was so excited I sat down and opened the jar in my lap spilling all the buttons into the fold of my skirt for sifting. My button was a beautiful aged metal with a raised anchor in the same material, old and more special than I had even imagined. But that was not all, for added confirmation I found two more types of anchor buttons, one a faux gold metal and one a rather large plastic one. I think you were covering all bases there as I had mentioned in the letter to my friend that the button could be plastic, metal or faux metal.

Some people might say, "Oh, you could go into any op shop and find such a button," but I challenge them to do this and also find it in the first op shop they walk into and the first jar of buttons they pick up. Then I challenge them to do it in an op shop in Noosa which is by far no comparison to the op shops found in Melbourne and Sydney.

Anyway Nameless I wanted to thank you for my button. This along with some other things I will mention at a later time have restored my faith and belief in you and the etheric realm. I am going to treasure this button and make it into a pin or ring, a reminder and something of you that I can have in my physical life.

Q. Do you have anything to say?

Only that it was a joy to play such a game with you and follow your excitement and delight on your discovery, as every time you experience these type of feelings your vibration increases and you are more *Lightness and Being,* being closer to all that is joy and all that *is* and this is the feeling state that humans should strive to attain always in an effort to bring themselves closer to enlightenment. Though I understand the heaviness that drags you down in the physical realm and the struggle to bring yourselves up out of this mire.

Q. What is mire?

Muck. It is in these moments of pure pleasure, joy and bliss that you touch the essence of your souls. This is what you are trying to bring more of into your life. Rid yourselves of that which weighs heavily and only serves to weigh or bring you down. Increase the experiences of that which gives you *Lightness of Being* and this would be different for each individual. Reduce the amount of time you spend in the physical world *but* use physical and emotional joy to help you transcend into *Higher realms.* These moments on the physical realm are reminders of the possibilities of your true being, your true state. They are there to increase your awareness of other states of reality other than the one you spend most time in. Look at the percentages of how long you are in the physical compared to other Higher states of being. The ratio is tipped heavily towards the physical and on this realm there is very little joy, very little happiness. Work to lift your being Higher for a greater percentage of time, though this will need to be a gradual process over time so as not to shock your soul being which would put things out of alignment.

Q. But how can I do this on a daily level when my physical body weights me to the earth?

The *mind.* Transcend through the mind, perception. It is a letting go. A letting go of the physical and what you perceive as reality. This letting go of (the mind for) the physical is what transcends you into Higher etheric realms and *beyond space time perception.* The Higher you go the freer your mind and the Higher you are able to transcend again and so it goes until you have total freedom of movement. All constraints are gone. That is physical constraints and negative thoughts such as hate, jealousy and anger etc. The Higher the ascension the purer the thought and it is pureness of thought that allows for *travel in all directions, in past, present and future all at once.* Ultimately when you reach *Lightness of Being* it is the experience of …

- **All that is**
- **All that was**
- **All that could be**
- **And everyone**
- **And everything**
- ***All at Once***

This is *Enlightenment,* this is pure Love. This is Wholeness and Creation and pure *Thought,* pure *Energy,* pure *Lightness of Being.*

This may seem overwhelming and it is not my intention to overwhelm. For now your task is purely to bring a little more *Lightness and Being* into your day, every day. Do something every day that will give you joy and raise your vibration. It could be as simple as eating an ice-cream that you would normally forbid yourself or taking the time for a half hour sound meditation or a wonderful walk in nature or working on your chakras and perception of Higher etheric realms, a swim in the ocean. It shouldn't feel like work or a chore but something you are happy to do in that moment that would give you joy and that feel good vibe (vibration). Write a list of all the things that you think could do this for you that could be engineered into your day. Then at any time you can draw from that list in your head.

Also take note of your *feeling* senses (kinesthesia). When something gives you joy be in *mindfulness* and fully enjoy the moment. Then add it to your list of things that increase your vibration. The more joy you can experience in your life the Higher your vibration. The Higher your vibration the more joy you can experience in life and so on. *(See figures 4.1, 4.2 and 4.3*)

It is these little steps frequently that will draw you closer to enlightenment (Rome wasn't built in a day). This is what the healer and reader meant by you need more fun in your life. If it's fun do it and do it tenfold. If it's not fun (and it's possible) do without (That goes for your anger too… Dr. Phil would say, "How's it working for you?" and if it's not…drop it).

By the way I enjoyed sending you the button. It gave me a thrill to see you happy over something so small and that can be a lesson also that joy can come from the least expected, the small and inexpensive.

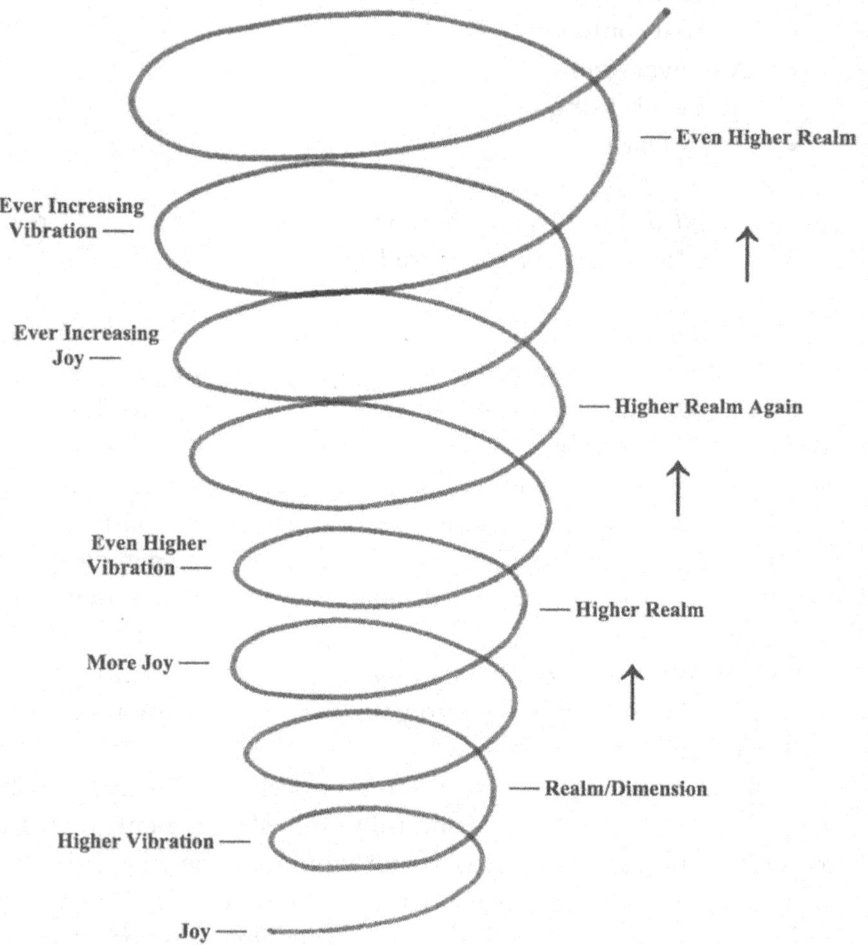

Figure 4.1 : Vibrational path to *Lightness of Being*

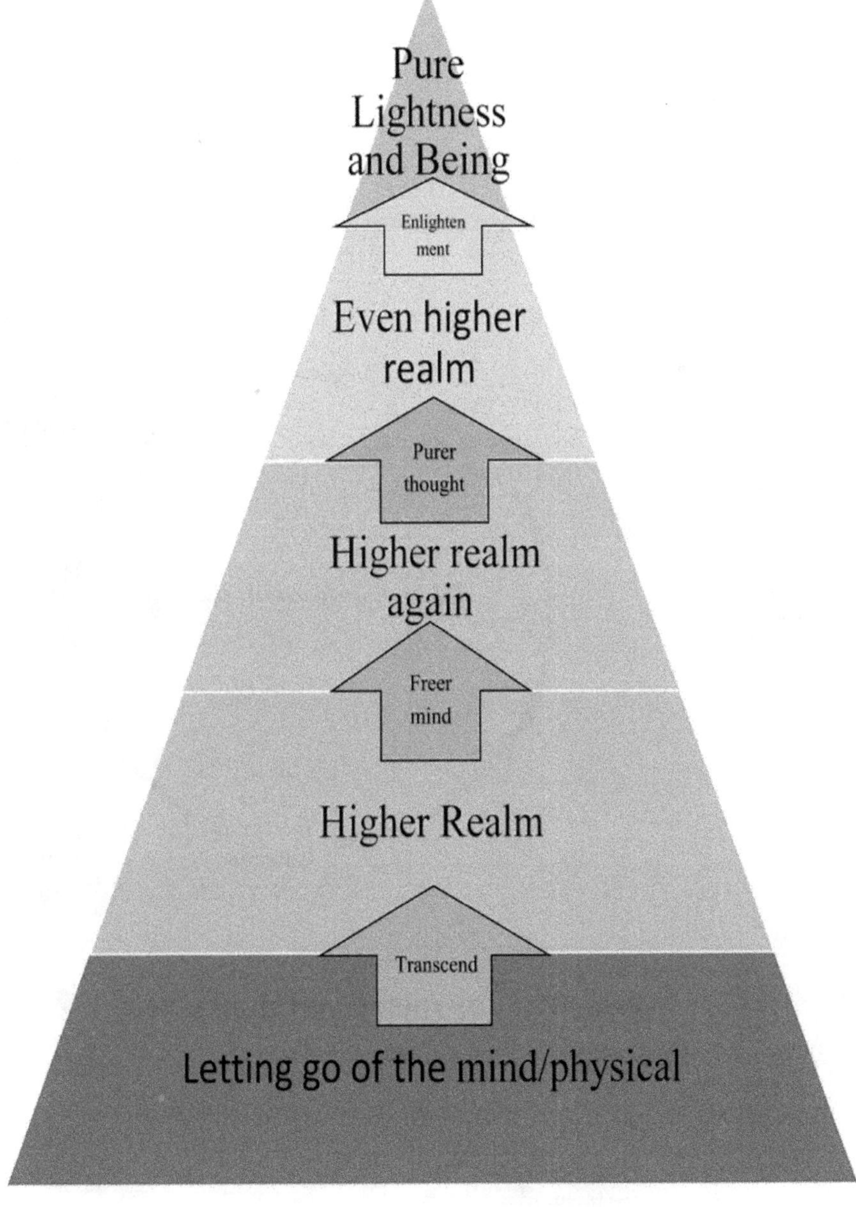

Figure 4.2 : Letting go of Mind

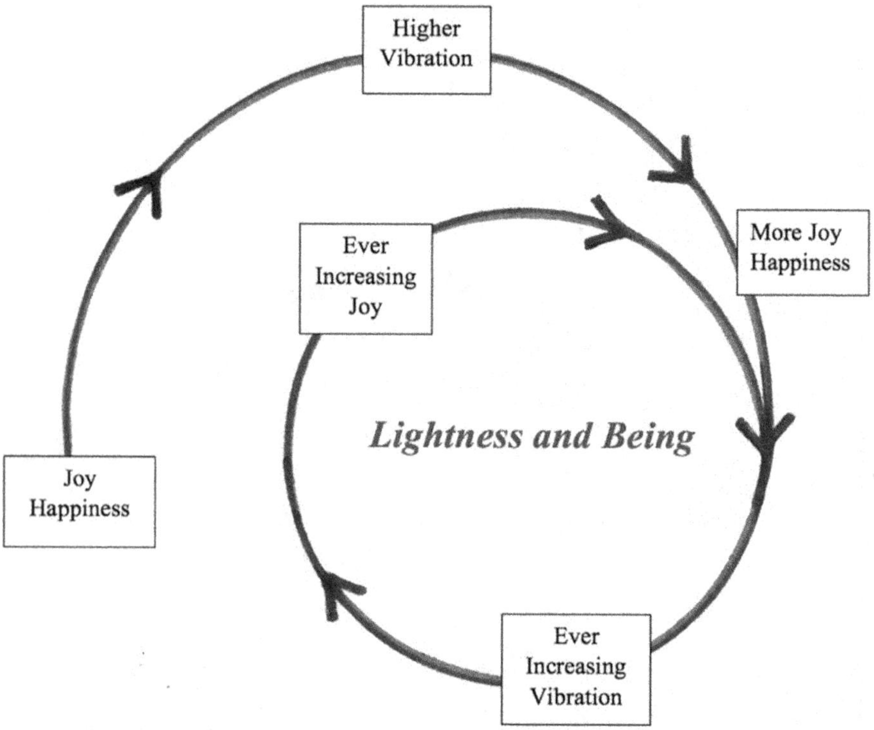

Higher Vibration

More Joy Happiness

Ever Increasing Joy

Lightness and Being

Joy Happiness

Ever Increasing Vibration

Figure 4.3 : Joy raises vibration levels

Enjoy your day little one — Nameless.

That's a lot to take in and ponder over but thanks as always for shedding new light and sharing your knowledge, also for the subtle hint (not) about my anger.

SUN 10TH FEBRUARY

Good morning Nameless. It's nice to be with you. I need to clear something up, clarify things while we are on the subject of mindlessness and mindfulness.

MINDLESSNESS

Letting go of the mind to transcend into Higher etheric realms beyond space-time, serving to increase or propel one towards Lightness and Being.

MINDFULNESS

To increase our sense of joy of the 'Now' which increases our vibration towards Higher realms, increasing our Lightness of Being.

They seem to be contradictory, letting go of the mind and mindfulness yet leading us to the same outcome. Here's my take on it and please correct me if I'm wrong. If we are experiencing joy in the physical world e.g. swimming at the beach we should be mindful of the experience, taking note of the pure bliss and joy of it all, the feeling of it and how it affects all our senses both mind and body. Even go in deeper on a cellular level and feel the energy and vibration increase of our very cells and knowing that this carries us to a Higher realm of existence in that very moment and in this 'feeling' and 'knowing' the event is even more blissful and joyful, lifting our vibration even more. Thus any joyful experience on the physical realm we are living in the power of now, the here and now awareness (mindfulness) to aid in raising our vibration. But…we do not want to tie ourselves completely, continually, to the physical realm or we will not transcend into the Higher 'etheric' realms and beyond space time perception. Thus to do this we need to be of no mind, letting go of mind/thought. The power of now, living in the now ties us to the physical reality and the physical realm.

Q. Thus if our aim is to lift ourselves beyond the physical realm into Higher states of being and Higher dimensions shouldn't we concentrate on mindlessness rather than mindfulness?

I agree and you are travelling along well my dear, being able to follow the concepts that are being directed your way. It's true both will increase your vibration and lead you toward *Lightness and Being* and pure *Thought* and *Energy* form. They differ however in many ways. The applications are poles apart to begin with. Let's start with the easier concept to understand…mindfulness.

Mindfulness is an easier application than mindlessness. Most humans can grasp this concept and apply it to their daily life especially in the busyness of your daily lives that you fill to the extremes with things that make no sense in our realm of existence (but we do understand have become important on your level but to the detriment of your spiritual growth and your evolution back to your true selves). Sorry I do not want this to become a lecture but will bring it back to comparisons and try to simplify it for you.

MINDFULNESS

An easier quicker way to increase your vibration. Shorter term. Your vibration increases then dips a little, then plateaus out. Each time you experience joyful mindfulness your vibration increases just that little bit more *but* it is short lived and needs to be topped up frequently or it will dissipate and plummet over time until you are at the beginning again or even lower. Thus its application requires a frequency of use, daily, to enable your vibration to stay raised. It is an arduous process in that the gains though positive are small and slight. If practiced frequently you will notice your vibration increasing over time. When practicing this method there is always a part of you held in the physical realm so you are limited to how high you can transcend. You are increasing your levels towards Lightness and Being but may never actually reach *Pure Lightness of Being* using this method as part of you is always held in the physical reality of your world/realm. *(See Figures 4.4, 4.5, 4.6)*

MINDLESSNESS

A more difficult concept and application to grasp. Once reached it has a more long term effect and more steady state. More a state of *not being* (on the physical) than being (physical). The vibrational increase is felt on a much deeper level and is held there longer. More like a *hum* than a *strum. (See Figure 4.7)* Liken this to your Superstring theory.[1] The strum is the pluck of a guitar string that vibrates for a short time and then fades

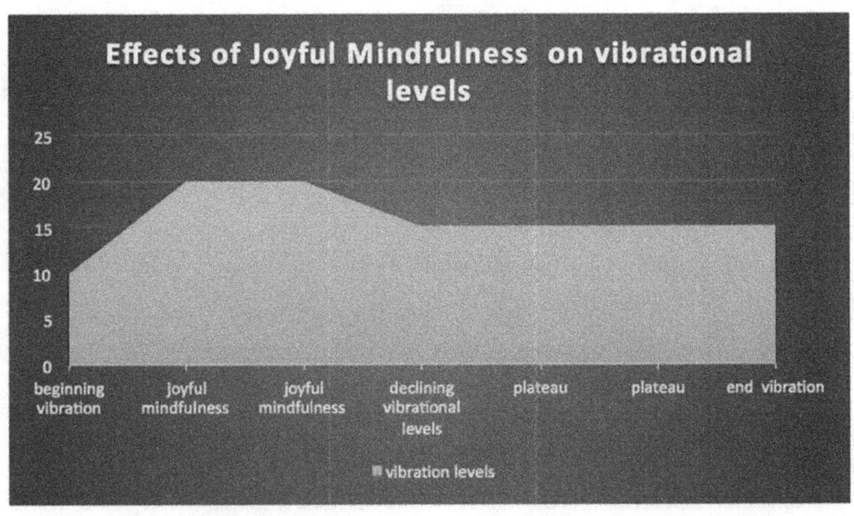

Figure 4.4 : Effects of Mindfulness on vibrational levels

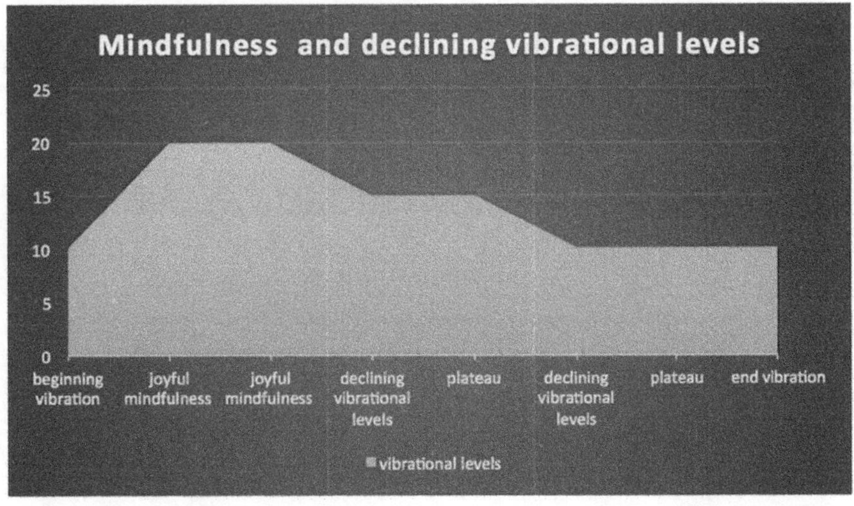

Figure 4.5 : Mindfulness and declining vibrational levels

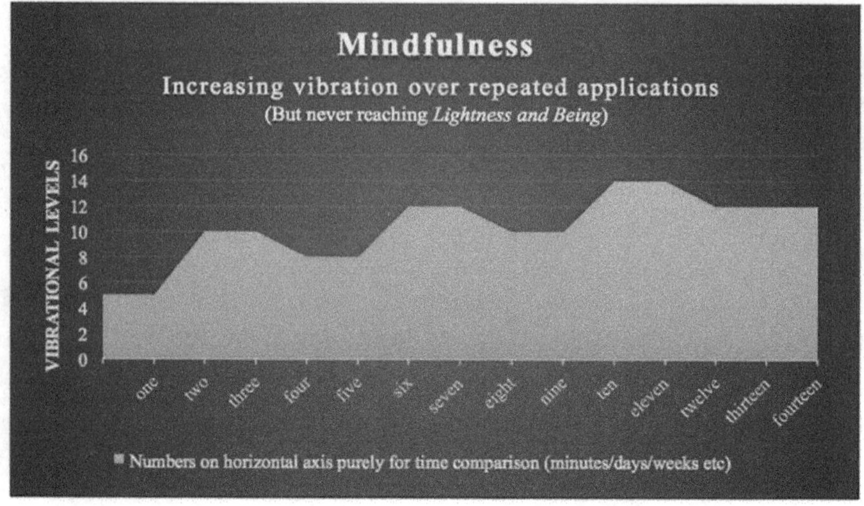

Figure 4.6 : Mindfulness and repeated applications

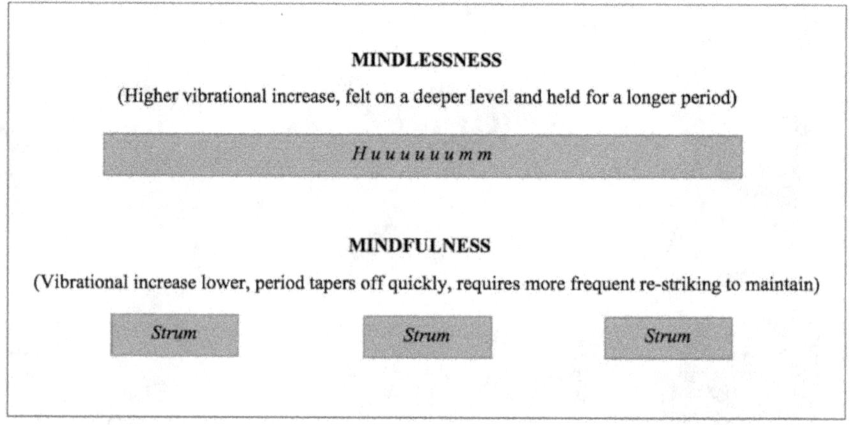

MINDLESSNESS
(Higher vibrational increase, felt on a deeper level and held for a longer period)
Huuuuuumm
MINDFULNESS
(Vibrational increase lower, period tapers off quickly, requires more frequent re-striking to maintain)
Strum
Strum
Strum

Figure 4.7 : Comparisons of Mindlessness and Mindfulness

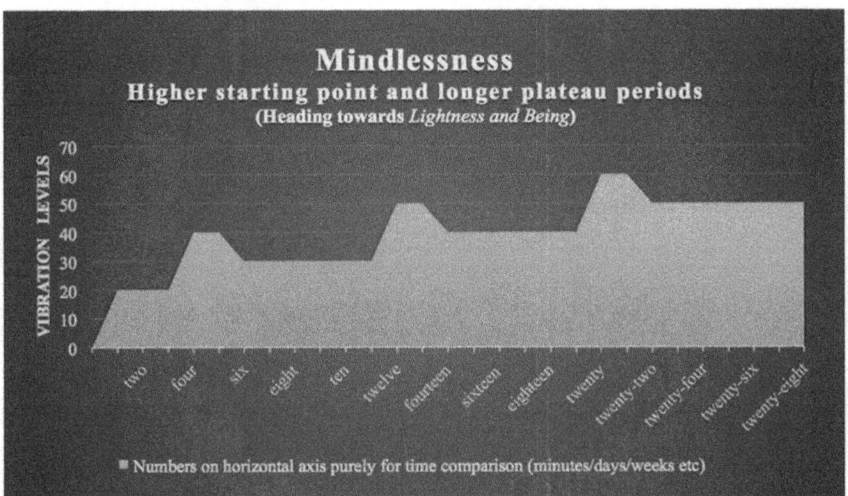

Figure 4.8 : Effects of Mindlessness on vibrational levels

off and you strike the guitar string again (this is your experience of mind*ful*ness). In Mind*less*ness the huuuuum (already of a Higher frequency to begin with as transcending the physical) is like a Buddhist mantra and continually vibrates for a much longer period before it tapers off and requires re-striking. Thus it can take you Higher quicker and holds you there for longer. *(See Figure 4.8)*

Mindlessness and Mindfulness can be summarized as follows *(See Table 4.1)*

Sorry Nameless I think I've spoilt this for you as my connection is not strong, I feel all over the place and think we should revisit this at a later time. It's still been a good exercise and is clarifying things for me. I'm thinking that we should only be mindful in that which brings us joy and try to practice mindlessness at most other times. I'll discuss this with you later. Thank you for today, I hope I have not left you feeling frustrated.

I understand little one, you have a lot on your mind (a pun). Therein is

MINDFULNESS	MINDLESSNESS
Quick	Takes longer (initially)
Easy	More difficult concept to grasp
Short term effects	Effects last longer
Can be used as a quick top up when energy is low	More effort, takes practice
Can easily be incorporated into the day	Requires more time to be set aside while learning
Needs to be practiced frequently to maintain high vibratory/energy levels	The vibrational increase is felt on a much deeper level and holds the vibratory levels for a much longer period
Holds us in third dimensional reality (The physical realm)	Eventually will be incorporated long term into your existence such that there is duality. You are of two worlds
Limited to how high you can transcend and for how long	Letting go of the physical and transcending time and space
May never actually reach *'Lightness and Being'*	Experiences of *'Lightness and Being'*

Table 4.1 : Comparison of Mindfulness and Mindlessness

the issue. It is best we wait until your reception is aligned with mine. I will send you vibrations throughout the day to re-energize and re-align you. Know that I am with you always and forever.

Thank you Nameless and bless you. (Truth is Nameless was doing my head in with all the imagery and graphs, LOL!)

FRI 15TH FEBRUARY

Raven Owl come be with me… I was going to continue my conversation with Nameless but feel I need to check in with you as I'm attending a crystal healing workshop tomorrow and would like your feelings on the matter. Also I'm indecisive about my healing room set up. The butterfly room[2] can be noisy depending on what the neighbors are doing (power tools etc.) which I can't predict and this concerns me. Also I'm polarized by what color to choose blue or violet?

Greetings little one it is always a pleasure to be in your company. I think of you as a much loved little sister whom I want to protect and help avoid mistakes that I made early on, though no mistake is really bad as we should just learn from it and move on and be grateful for the lesson and not dwelling on any negativity surrounding it.

Hmm Blue or Violet? Only you can decide this one as it has to resonate with your soul for it to sit comfortably within you. Take note of Nameless and concentrate on the feeling and vibration each one gives you. Perhaps jot down the words that come to mind when you hold each one in your hands. Ask your pendulum which is the most suitable, I'm aware you didn't have it on you at the time you were looking at each one. Pay attention to what *feels* right to *you* as I know you are thinking about what would be right for your clients and this is what is confusing the matter for you and why you are indecisive as one color you would choose for yourself and the other color you would choose for your clients benefit and herein lies your answer.

The crystal light that you saw is the perfect size at the perfect price and would be a great addition to the room, giving it a feeling of peace and serenity and bathing it in a warm comfortable glow. All those who gaze upon it will feel an immediate relaxation and aid in putting themselves in that place of acceptance for healing to occur. It's worth the drive back to get it and you may choose to pick up your colors at the same time. Then all you'll need to complete the room is a singing bowl, your sage stick, the Buddhist statue, a few candles and fresh flower petals and your set to go.

The butterfly room whilst a great room is not an all-weather room and this you have forgotten about. So it is not only the noise but also what when it rains? And in winter it will be very cold. At such times you will have to bring your client inside the house and as this is not ideal, best to be on the lookout for a suitable space at an affordable price that you have access to at any time that suits. Alternatively you may choose to only do healings say one morning or afternoon a week and book a permanent room somewhere. Scour the papers and even advertise for such a room. Also being in town would make it more accessible to many. Think outside the square and be open to all possibilities. If things don't work out you can always change. It might take a while to find the right place for you.

At the crystal workshop tomorrow ask the teacher for any ideas and also her experiences of places she has practiced. She is really knowledgeable by the way even though she may come across differently, she has issues with communication on a verbal level and is nervous about "dictating" to others so the more questions you can ask the better as this will show her you are really interested in what she has to say which will boost her confidence. She is very happy to share with you what she knows and has the possibility of being a mentor if you should choose, this will depend on if your vibrations are a match but you can adjust your vibration in her presence also so that you can both benefit from each other, she as a teacher, and you as gifted learner. No one walks away empty handed, everybody wins.

Someone annoying will be in the class (there always is). Send them positive vibrations to raise their energy levels. You will be surprised at the power you have and the effect that you can have on people and situations. Befriend this person and support them, that is all they need and watch the energy change, then everyone will have a pleasant experience. This person is just wanting to be heard, give them the validation (praise etc.) that they desire and all will turn out well. It will be a challenge that you will learn greatly from. You are a sponge for all intellectual information but you could also learn greatly from being aware of the energy in and around the room and of the people present. So don't just concentrate on the intellectual side of the class but open up your awareness to what's going on around you with regards to *energy*. Then you really do need to start your practice, the sooner the better. Take a collective gulp and step out into the ether and *just do it!* It won't be as scary as you think and you're going to be great. Remember we are always with you and will never let you down. Call on us at any given moment for support and guidance. You can do no wrong. We have faith in you little one — Love Raven Owl.

Thank you Raven Owl.

SUN 17TH FEBRUARY

I've come back from the workshop with exiting news. I asked the teacher where she practices and told her I was looking for somewhere. The workshop happened to be held in a medical and healing clinic in town and she said the owner rents out the rooms on a daily (a hundred dollars) or session (twenty dollars) basis and she showed me a couple of the rooms available. They were of a good size with desks and sinks but were painted in dark colors and no windows! I was hoping for something lighter and possibly overlooking a garden. The clinic itself had old and mismatched décor but had a nice feel to it. There was a long hallway lacking any features so later when I met the owner I told him I was a visual artist, gave him my business card and said I would very much like to supply him with some artwork on the walls. The art would still belong to me and would be for sale but would help create interest and brighten his vacant walls. He was instantly keen and said he had put it out to the Universe that he wanted an artist to do just that but had been waiting a while with no takers. I suggested he visit my website to see if any images peaked his interest and so will wait and see if I hear from him.

I didn't discuss renting a room as I feel my hands are full with preparing for the Floating Land exhibition and the Maleny Art Space.[3] *Better to wait till these are finalized before committing elsewhere. It's just exiting to know such an opportunity exists and I might entertain the idea of one full day per fortnight reducing the cost to just fifty dollars a week if it weren't for the lack of windows and free flowing air. All in all it was an eventful day and I learnt a lot to help me on my path.*

Thanks Raven Owl.

MON 18TH FEBRUARY

Raven Owl, sorry we got cut short last night. I didn't give you a chance to reply. We're in the middle of another severe weather low and the power went out again for about three hours so I was channeling to you by torchlight and got interrupted by my daughter when the lights came back on. I think we are still a bit traumatized by the last episode and she refused to go to sleep while we had no electricity, waiting to be reassured that it would come back on. When I went in to comfort her she grabbed my arm and clothes vice like and wouldn't let go. I stayed there in the dark for what seemed like half an hour and when I thought she was relaxed enough tried to make my escape but she grabbed me by the hair and begged me to stay. She thought we were in for another six day episode and was inconsolable. I consulted the pendulum which said we would have power returned within an hour (from time of consult) which seemed to soothe her and I then came to channel. The power did come on within the hour and I was interrupted by said daughter getting out of bed to "soak up the energy of it all," she was so relieved. She then went back to bed and turned the light out…go figure.

Q. Anyway, any comments from our discussion yesterday?

Just that all is well with the Universe and is going as planned. As you follow your rightful path opportunities will come your way. Things will come to you easier, life will be less of a struggle and uphill battle that you have experienced the last few decades. With spiritual growth and maturity comes not only knowledge and practice but also *abundance.* Abundance not just monetarily but in all areas of your life including love for fellow man and human kind. Once you let go of the stress of daily struggle it opens an energy portal in you that has been running on empty for a long time. It is almost as if the well was about to dry up when along came the rains. Think of the rains as metaphorically filling you up and replenishing you so that you may purify the souls of others for this is life's path for you. When you realize the feeling of fullness and total abundance you will wonder how you managed for so long being so depleted of energy, love and wealth. I am not talking monetary wealth but worldly wealth or should I say *other* worldly wealth which is great knowledge garnished from the very core of the Universe itself.

Q. Who's talking?

Nameless.

Sorry, I thought I had invoked Raven Owl, but knew it was you.

She's busy so I took over, I hope you don't mind. I was going to introduce myself but then wanted to see how long it took you to notice and how aware you are.

I knew it was you all along but didn't want to interrupt earlier because I was interested in what you were saying. I can tell it's you by the way you speak and the words you use, the conversation in general. Sorry I didn't mean to interrupt, please go on.

Yes, we were talking about your energy state, depleted for far too long. You are exhausted. It is important that you *do things for you,* build yourself back up again. Taking time out to replenish yourself, your own soul so when the well is full and overflowing it is the overflow that you are able to share with others and this is your purpose.

First and foremost fill your own vessel to its absolute capacity. The more you fill it the more open it is to being filled (and fulfilled). *Like attracts like therefore more attracts more.* The more you have the more you get until one day it is flooding in and you are able to spread it around through dispersion. The trick is to start with a little, open the gates and begin with a trickle. Soon you will have more than enough as a trickle multiplies itself and then multiplies again. Strive for balance. A little learning every day equals a little step further forward in the right direction. Add a sprinkle of fun into your day and what you're doing. *Fun* opens up the heart chakra's and opens up the gates for more (of everything) to follow.

So it's a balance between learning, knowledge, practice and play. This will result in a vibrational energy shift which will open up the portals to the Universe to allow abundance to enter. Achieve this balance and you will see it to be so. Go now Marikai, you are sleepy. I will watch over you till morning light.

Thank you Nameless. (I'm wondering if when he talks of portals he means chakras.)

FRI 22ND FEBRUARY

Good morning Nameless. Regarding our last conversation on mindlessness where I had to interrupt you, I'm not sure if you have anything to add to it or not? Have I grasped the concept adequately? Will others be able to understand the differences and apply them accordingly? I'm just not sure if others will understand mindlessness and how to achieve it.

Yes the differences have been outlined adequately for the purpose of others to differentiate between the two and grasp their concepts. Like you most are now very aware of mindfulness and 'the power of now' and many are utilizing this concept and bringing it into their daily lives and existence. Now it is time to start the actual practice of *mindlessness* also and it is when humans do this they will *feel* the difference between the two manifestations and gain a greater grasp of the concepts, as to do and experience is to know.

The issue for some is *what* is it and how to start or practice this mindlessness? Some have practiced this during meditation and will already be knowledgeable while others are completely foreign to the idea. A large majority are too much in the mind. There is too much thought, thinking and analyzing going on. You as a collective society are very intellect oriented with the majority of your energy trapped in this area. We aim to free you from this so your soul is free to travel in the Higher realms of existence and multidimensionality. To do this you must free your minds of all thought, *suspend thought*. Easier said than done. Many are aware of this concept yet still are unable to do it, or to suspend it for any length of time, long enough to experience other worlds. You are able to do this or we would not be having this conversation right now. You write without thought or thinking or analyzing the words as they come to you but write with total freedom and with no mind, *mindlessness*.

How do you do this? How do you get to this stage? This is what we want to teach others, we the collective meaning you, I and others of the Higher realms. It has been a long time coming for you not in the knowledge and ability which you possessed long ago but in the bringing to existence and practice into your daily life. This also is only a part of mindlessness this communication that we share and there are many different aspects to mindlessness for example transcending space and time, time (or rather *beyond time)* travel which is a much more advanced application.

Let's concentrate on one step at a time without getting too far ahead of ourselves. When one application is grasped and able to be practiced with ease it will then be time to advance to the next application.

To bring us back to mindlessness and suspension of thought, for others to grasp this so they may practice it for themselves, the following is just one example of many paths to mindlessness...

WHITE ROOM MEDITATION

(A gift from the Universe)

Imagine you are in a white room, there is nothing in the room except for you and perhaps the chair you are sitting on. At the end of the room is a white door. You have been told the door will open and something of value will be revealed to you. You do not allow yourself to think about what it could be or to analyze in any way. You suspend all thought on the matter instead concentrating on the *feeling* aspect. What the excitement anticipation and joy *feels* like and simply wait in this *feeling* to *see* and *hear* what happens. So an opening and heightening of the senses and at the same time a quietening and shutting off of the mind. As you sit in *anticipation* and *excitement*, you can feel your energy (and thus your vibration) is raised. Allow that *excitement, energy* and *vibration* to increase to almost bursting, till you can stand it no longer and when this is achieved ...open the door.

Q. What is revealed to you?

(Allow yourself time to explore this gift and when you are ready bring yourself back to awareness)

□□□

If people struggle in this exercise it is because they are too much in their head. Ask them to bring their energy down into the solar plexus (chakra) and concentrate on the *gut feeling* but not even to think or analyze or try and explain the feeling but to just sit in the excitement that is that energy. Sit in the joy of it. This closes one portal (the mind/intellect) and opens the portal that is the *Universal Energy Field* upon which they may receive other worldly information and even into the future *travel through.*

When starting this exercise some may just sit in this energy, the *feeling* of it all and may do this many times over before the door opens. Some may open the door straight away though this is not always advised as they may have missed a vital learning aspect of sitting in their energy field and opening up their senses.

When the door opens different things will be revealed to different individuals. I do not want to say too much on this matter as this will only instill ideas (and therefore thought) into the minds of others. When this exercise is repeated some may always find the same thing behind the door so that it be something they enjoy and visit often. Some may experience different things every time they open the door so always opening to new experiences. Let the opening of the door be a gift from the Universe. A gift that you have no idea what it contains but look forward to with excitement, joy and anticipation.

□□□

Share this with others and ask them to provide feedback. Were they able to suspend thought? How long could they sit in the chair in their feeling senses? *This is mindlessness!* What was that like? How did they do it? Was it easier/harder than they thought? Once they grasp the idea of suspending all thought and are practiced at it they should be able to do this anywhere, either utilizing the white room scenario or eventually with no room and no door but pure suspension of thought and an opening of their portals (chakra's) to access the Universal Energy Field and all it has to offer. Then they can decide for example when doing something mundane like doing the dishes, vacuuming, working etc. do they want to practice mindfulness or mindlessness?

When practicing mindlessness you may choose to set aside time in your day as you do for meditation *or* you may decide to incorporate it into your everyday such as the example above so that you are of two worlds. Thus you operate on the physical realm whilst at the same time you operate on the etheric realms. *You are of two worlds.* And while you possess a physical body you are both limited to this experience but also privileged to be able to experience two such very different worlds simultaneously. Once the physical body is removed (physical death) the differences between the different realms you can experience simultaneously are less pronounced. So my advice to you would be to enjoy this experience while you are able to.

I hope this has been able to clear things up for you and others. I am here to help always. Ask and I will attend. Blessings to your day Marikai.

Thank you Nameless, I'm always grateful for both your knowledge and your friendship.

□

SAT 23RD FEBRUARY

I've been sitting here scouring my books reading up on channeling and how to connect with your spirit guides and I'm getting the name Hoyan repeated to me over and over. Hoyan whom I know to be a spirit guide.

Q. Do you wish to speak to me? Are you there?

Yes and I am glad you heard me, I have been wanting to speak with you for a while. I have been watching your development from afar and with much interest and would like to offer my guidance also. I feel I can offer you other perspectives on matters that perplex and you are having difficulty not grasping but putting into words so that others may understand. I hear the struggle going on with the concept of mindlessness and how to convey that to others. I felt it important enough that I step in and offer my perspective as an extra contribution to add to the conversation allowing for a broader understanding of the concept. So here is my take on mindlessness.

Mindlessness equals absence of thought. Thought is governed by the ego. Therefore mindlessness is an absence of ego. A letting go of the ego. The ego is very strong and does not like to be let go of. To him that is death of his existence and he will fight you and struggle all the way. This is what makes mindlessness so difficult for many. It is really a struggle with the ego. Therefore to achieve mindlessness is to be able to suspend the ego for a period of time. *Suspend* is the key word here. We do not want to kill off the ego entirely, merely have him diverted temporarily. The ego's existence is easily threatened and he fears you may want to do away with him entirely and therefore for him it is a *fight to the death* to maintain his governance and existence.

You may have to meet this ego of yours and discuss your intentions. That you merely wish to suspend thought momentarily for short periods so that you can access information from other worlds, other dimensions. That he can have the majority of your time otherwise and that he could use this time to rest and regroup. Think of it as sending the ego on a short mini break in your terms such that he will return re-energized and with a clearer mind.

After having such a conversation with your ego and if after discussion he is in agreement, then practice suspension of thought and mindlessness for a short period. Once the ego has allowed for short periods of his absence and can see that he is always returned/re-instated it will gain his confidence in the process and his knowledge that his existence is not under threat after all. That even perhaps there is good to come from his periodic absence and brief holidays that benefits him also as this is all that he is really interested in, his own self. Once he has reached this level of comfort with the process then you may be able to barter suspension for longer and longer periods. This is what is called *'Letting go of ego.'*

Be aware that every now and then he will pop back into awareness. Politely ask him to leave until you are ready for his return. Remember the egos nature, he loves praise so give him plenty and he will be putty in your hands. There is a psychological game going on here between the ego and your Higher Self. Your Higher Self will always out govern the ego but in such a delicate manner as for the ego to think he is the governor of all your states of being. This is the way forward. So a great part of mindlessness and suspension of thought (ego) comes from an activation of the Higher Self. Herein lies a catch twenty-two. To access the Higher Self there has to be a quietening of the mind to begin with…an initial spark is all that is required. For some it happens by accident, some experience may create a sudden jolt…a shift in vibration. Some achieve it through meditation but what of others? Here's an idea…why not simply ask? *Ask* to speak to the Higher Self. Ask the ego to take a break or for permission to speak to the Higher Self. Once connection is made with the Higher Self then other portals begin to open and Higher ascensions can be made through the same process…simply by *asking*. It really is not as difficult as people perceive it to be. They put too much expectation and thoughts of complexity on it.

1. **Simply relax**
2. **Allow yourself to open (be open to all possibilities)**
3. **And *ask* for what it is you want or want to do**

Do you want to talk to Guides, a particular Guide, your Higher Self? Do you want to travel to other dimensions? It really is all possible and much easier than you think. The think part comes from the ego and it is the ego that prevents you from going there.

Lightness and evolution — Hoyan.

Thank you Hoyan, it was exciting to have you come through.

Q. Hoyan what does your name mean?

Leader of the Light Beings. But not leader as in dictator but leader as in first. I, like you, was once of human physical existence and one of the first *Light Beings* of your planet. You also are a *Light Being.*

Q. What's it like where you come from?

It is pureness of energy without physical manifestations but rather the energy of those manifestations that you are used to. There is a fine tuning process that one is constantly adhering to. It is a check of one's vibration and what is lacking and then accessing that energy to fine tune the vibration at its optimal level. This is an ongoing process from millisecond to millisecond and is not work or a chore or thought of but a natural occurrence and thus energy in this realm (including myself) is a constantly changing, moving and evolving process much like a lava lamp such that I am not static nor any one thing at any given time. I did however love music when I was in physical existence having been a composer and do vibrate towards the energy of pure divine sound to aid in attuning myself.

Thanks Hoyan for that interesting insight, Sorry to cut you short. There's more I'd like to ask but perhaps another time when I've got longer to chat but for now I have to go.

Blessings Light Being.

SUN 24TH FEBRUARY

Morning Nameless. Firstly I want to share with you my good news! One of my collage art pieces was featured on the home page of Redbubble,[4] a major feat because there is surely thousands of artists on there all with a vast array of talent and large bodies of work. So to gain a feature on the Redbubble home page is a major coup, I've been noticed by RB themselves! Within hours of uploading this collage it was featured, favourited, commented on and I sold my very first T-shirt, yeah! Sorry I was so excited I had to tell you, you know when you want to shout it from the roof tops? Its validation that my art is ok/likable and more importantly saleable. Yippee!

On a more serious note my legs are really aching. I've had x-rays and blood tests but to no avail, the medical fraternity can't find anything clinically diagnostic. They ache most of the time and are swollen and full of edema especially behind my knees. They ache even at night when I'm in bed and the pain can either keep me awake or wake me up. Sometimes it's too painful to sit (with knees bent) or even walk and I'll have to lay with my feet up. Some days the struggle to walk is so bad I think I must have MS or something but tests reveal nothing. I'm also getting sharp pains in my spleen area just below my heart. Sometimes they take my breath away and I can't sleep on that side as the sharp pain increases. Neither is debilitating enough such that I can't work or get on with my day but it is a struggle and rather annoying that it has been continuing for so long and starting to drag me down energy wise.

Q. Can you shed any light on the subject, do you know what's causing this? Can you help with healing or suggest some self-healing I could do?

I sense the stagnation in your legs which is reduced energy flow and chi life force. This is the same in the heart area also because you are currently not on your rightful path following your true path in life, your heart's desire. Thus the energy in these areas is blocked leading to a coagulation of mire and all that is undesirable. There is reduced circulation, life enhancing oxygen and nutrients to these areas, the life force is reduced and if allowed to continue will result in tissue damage and break down. If you look into your iris, iris diagnosis will clarify the stagnant chi and sluggishness. There is coupled with this in the heart area constriction also, a tightness. The muscles are flexed and held tight reducing the flow of good energy in and bad energy out. The good being the mana, [5] chi life force and the bad being the mire.

Walking and massage will help increase the flow to the legs and encourage elimination, also swimming, cycling and anything that gets the legs moving. This will aid the situation and make it more manageable but will not eliminate it entirely. Blood and liver cleansers in the form of herbs and also foods/juices will be of great benefit also to help eliminate toxins from the body. Consult your nutrition and herbal books for these. Exercise to reduce stress such as yoga, meditation, tai chi etc. will aid in reducing constriction and spasm in the heart area but all of these are not addressing the core issue, the *cause* and addressing this will bring about long term change and health.

The more you are able to follow your rightful path the less stress, constriction and holding you will experience in the body. The muscles will begin to relax, circulation energy and qui life force will begin to flow and the mire will eliminate more freely. You will gain more freedom of movement again and all aches and pains will be removed. This is your priority and what you should be aiming for. The aches and pains that you feel daily are your body's signal to you, a reminder of the need to change. I understand it is not always easy to affect immediate change and that you are working toward this in your life. In the meantime self-heal with crystals, hand healing techniques and reflexology meridian points to keep the qui life force moving and prevent muscle and tissue damage. These are things you can implement whilst you are working towards your true path in life.

Q. Thanks Nameless, are you also able to help in the healing process?

As you wish, I will work on dispersing some of the mire that has accumulated and built up over time. I will do this as you go about your daily business so you need no thought for the matter it will be done. You will feel an energy shift in that area and will notice a change such that it feels less blocked, more supple and relaxed and blood is flowing more freely. Your legs will feel lighter and stronger, like they could carry you anywhere and for any length of time…invincible. Thus you will also feel your whole energy and vibration lift as weight and stagnation is lifted from you. We will work on this together, a team effort. With your permission also I may employ others to join the effort, a collaboration of group healing, each imparts their own specialty to bring about positive change.

Yes you have my permission.

Then consider it activated and it shall be done. It is so. Blessings Marikai, enjoy your day.

Thank you Nameless.

5

MARCH 2013

FRI 8TH MARCH

Morning Nameless. Firstly thanks so much for helping me with my aching legs and knees. As you stated I'm feeling much lighter and more energized due to the reduced swelling. My spirits have lifted, I'm singing more, feel happier and have an ease of movement without any pain. This has all come from your help as I've really done nothing myself due to Floating Land preparations taking up a lot of my time. Not only am I creating the art but there's a lot of prep such as photographing, photocopying, printing, uploading, ordering, researching and searching for that 'one' specific item. Ditto the works I'm preparing for the Maleny art space too.

The channeling and healing practices are on hold as I don't see how I can fit it all in and am really at breaking point because on top of all this I'm also working my day job. Yesterday I was up at four-thirty a.m. and didn't get home from work and running errands till four-thirty p.m. and I was totally exhausted. I'm so close to quitting Floating Land but I'm not really sure what to do as I feel I need to honor my commitment. If I stay it means another twelve weeks of intensity and I don't think I can fit channeling and healing in on top of everything else. I also feel like putting Maleny on hold and just concentrating on one thing at a time.

Q. What is your opinion? Can you offer me any advice?

The healing and channeling will not go away and will be there for you when all the fuss is over and subsided. You are right to honor your commitment as to leave would not only let the others involved down but also those that would benefit from seeing your work as you offer a different perspective and view on things to what others are contributing. Your art will help round things off nicely and make for a more interesting exhibition.

Q. But what should I do about the cost of it all? It's getting very costly.

Quality over quantity is the key here. I understand you are full of ideas and it's impossible to replicate them all as the cost would be phenomenal. You may need to pull back a bit and choose a few key pieces that exhibit quality along with the message you want to convey and are a bit unique and possibly thought provoking and very *you,* that has your stamp on it. You have already started such a list, start with five key pieces from this list, complete these first and then if you have time and money you may choose others from the list that you think will offer something different to what you have done. Five is the magic number that will take a lot of stress off and won't overwhelm. I understand you are concerned of others having many pieces to contribute and taking over the show but ask yourself are they of quality or are they just fillers? Also it's not really anything different to what people have seen before. You are able to offer something more unique and thought provoking that connects with people's intellect. Thus do not concern yourself that you do not present a large amount of pieces rather that your pieces are of a high quality with meaning and story attached and provoke interest and thought, along with a vibrational energy shift in the viewer. Thus viewers will walk away with a subtle shift in their alignment and energy field and this is what you're aiming for rather than a number of bland churned out same same pieces.

Aim for the vibrational shift to occur in others so when choosing your pieces ask yourself does this particular piece have that quality? Your coconut chair has this quality and even though it may not be a conventionally pretty piece it has the ability to impart a Higher vibration on the viewer. Four more pieces with this unique quality and you will have your five. Remember…

- **Pull back**
- **Avoid overload (overwhelming yourself)**
- **Quality over quantity**
- **Aim for a vibrational shift**
- **Art with message, story, meaning**

Q. And what of Maleny, channeling and my healing practice? Should I put them on hold for twelve weeks? It seems such a long time.

You can only manage what you can manage. Your daughter is going to need you over the coming weeks also and her commitment is what would tip you over the edge. For you to honor both your commitment and hers, sacrifices need to be made. Both Maleny and your life's purpose can wait, you have already waited your whole life thus far that a few more weeks will not harm nor be detrimental. You are not superhuman. Also if you try to spread your energy amongst too many things none will receive the attention required for optimal results. Better to concentrate on the issue at hand and give the others the attention they deserve when this time is over. Having said that you may like to offer a channeling or a healing to those you have been thinking of for no fee, for your own practice and so you don't feel it has been abandoned altogether. Offer one person, see if they take you up on it, wait a fortnight between each one as this is a manageable pace for you considering the current situation. They will benefit as will you and when Floating Land is over you will be ready to fly in the right direction.

Blessings Marikai I give you strength.

Thanks Nameless, you really help clarify things I appreciate it so much and feel better already.

SAT 9TH MARCH

Good morning Nameless, just a quickie this morning as I have a lot to do today. Thank you for the advice you gave me yesterday. I'm really feeling better about things. As I create the art for Floating Land I'm getting more and more wonderful ideas and want to create them all and your advice to keep it concise and meaningful will really help me focus on what's important. I feel I created a small piece of value yesterday after a long and arduous day and went to bed happy.

Q. Do you have any comments?

Only that you are following your rightful journey. Art is a big part of who you are on a soul level. It helps you get in touch with your feelings and emotions allowing them to come to the surface. Each piece you create is a view of a small aspect of you so once created you can sit back and look at it with awe as you are looking at a part of the self. Whether you then decide to share this with others is up to you. Your passion comes from deep within the soul self which is struggling to get out and be recognized.

(I think Nameless means recognition as in acknowledged, not of the fame type.)

The more you create the more you get in touch with who you really are and you will begin to recognize the real/true you. The beauty of art is that there are (usually) no words involved and therefore devoid of labels. When people view art they are getting in touch with their *feelings* and emotions and are experiencing a heightening of the senses. In viewing any and all art they will feel a vibrational shift, either a heightened vibration if it is pleasing and close to alignment with their own soul self or a desire to purge the vision from their senses if the visual piece is an assault on their soul. This is why certain people vibrate towards certain types of art. It is due to wanting to align and reinforce ones soul self or aid in raising ones vibration. Thus art can play with ones and others energy levels shifting them in many directions up, down and sideways (The sideways can be when they are neither here nor there or possibly confused or have observed something so foreign they are in a state of shock). People are drawn to certain crystals for the same reason, for alignment and an enhancing of vibrational energy.

People who observe dark sinister work and get enjoyment out of it are or have experienced such energy themselves and can thus appreciate where the artist is coming from. Many would not like such art on their walls but it does not make the art any less artistic or valid. Some would say the pretty art such as flowers and the like is devoid of soul and for them maybe it is but for others it helps with raising their vibration and their sense of peace. It is what their soul requires to heal itself and maintain alignment. It may not be for everyone but it works for them.

Your art has intellect, there is a certain *quirkiness* there and this is what differentiates your art from others. It is neither classical, pretty nor dark but touches on the surreal. More and more you will delve deeper into this type of art whilst always keeping your feminine edge. Because of its unique quirkiness you may struggle to find a market for your work in the beginning because you are a unique soul and not many people are vibrating at your level. That is not to say you are better or worse than them just that you are different and that there are not as many who will understand and vibrate towards your work as for other more pretty and conventional types. Do not give up however for when you find your niche you will become very successful and quite well known to boot. It just may take a while and is somewhat in the distant future. Meanwhile you are having fun and your work is developing all the time so this is all valuable experience for you. I think as long as you understand that this type of work that you are currently doing is not high end commercial and thus will not be liked by the masses you will not be disappointed. You were never one to follow the crowds anyway and would be miserable doing so. Stay true to your soul self and success will eventually find you and I feel it will come at an unexpected time and in the most unexpected way.

Blessings Marikai, may peace be with you today.

Thank you Nameless and to you also.

SUN 10TH MARCH

Morning Nameless. I just did the white room meditation and wanted to tell you about it…

In the beginning I felt both nervous and exited, my breathing was too rapid and I couldn't relax so I placed a hand on my solar plexus (chakra) and bought my energy down into my core, slowing my breathing down. Once relaxed I started building my chair, playing around with different ones until I was satisfied that it was both comfortable and grand. It was a white velvet chair with an intricately carved wooden framework gilded with touches of gold, not too much to be overbearing or garish and the wood was earthy and grounding. Enveloping the chair was the etheric body of a giant sleeping Buddha such that the chair nestled in the lap of the Buddha and with myself cocooned in the chair. It was from here I set about building my white room starting with the floor made from white quartz crystal. Next came the walls, a pure pearlescent opal refracting the most opulent of blue whilst the ceiling was left open to the stars and night sky bathing the room in a moonlit glow. Once the room was completed my attention was drawn to building the door, glossy white, carved to match the chair I was sitting on and of such a grand scale as to reach the full height of the wall to which it was embedded.

From here the room adjusted and shifted itself so that the side walls narrowed heading towards the door enabling a complete focus upon it. Now I sat in my chair knowing that I was ready and bought my energy back to myself and concentrated on the feeling of anticipation and excitement of knowing that soon something will be revealed to me, I knew not what. I noticed my energy rise up into my throat chakra and here I sat in the feeling of absolute bliss and joy. It was that type of excitement that you are on such a high you have trouble containing it and just want to burst forth but I remembered what you said about experiencing and sitting in this energy field for a while and so I did. I felt I may have sat there for two or three minutes and knowing that in subsequent practices I may learn to extend this and hold it longer and being unable to contain my excitement any further I unceremoniously opened the door.

As the door opened Quan Yin came into being and floated towards me. She has such a beautiful and loving energy. She told me that I was a petal on a (cherry) tree about to blossom and come into full bloom. That all the other petals on the tree (representing the feminine) and I are all one and are coming into our spring. She said I would work with women helping to support and teach them how to love and nurture themselves and find their inner strength but first I would have to love and nurture myself. Quan Yin told me to allow my womanhood to shine through as it had been lying dormant for too long, to bring feminine intent and softness into everything I do and into actions and interactions with others. That contrary to popular belief that being feminine is not being weak but conversely strong. That there is strength and power in femininity and the female energy much more than the masculine but that it is a subtle and underlying strength so as to be barely noticed, designed to empower the bearer without disempowering the recipient. She suggested I harness this energy and bring it into my working practice and everyday life, that when one petal opens and blossoms many follow until the full tree is radiant with light and aroma. Then she enveloped me with her etheric being and transferred her energy to mine and took to leave but I stopped her and asked her to bless me. Quan Yin said I was already blessed but touched my forehead anyway and imparted these words…"Blessed are the ones that blossom upon the tree of life," and with that she floated angelically backwards through the doorway and vaporized.

SAT 16TH MARCH

Having re read this last communication I'm now highly embarrassed as I seem to have ignored this advice. As you know things are getting hectic and I have so much to do yet am feeling exhausted. We had a Floating Land meeting in which I was admonished in front of the whole group for not attending some meetings (I was working) and being unable to commit to future workshop dates without first consulting my diary (daughter needs me for her commitments too). This woman spoke to me (and others) in such a derogatory manner that I felt an immediate switch in me and knew I could not and would not continue with the exhibition. The whole meeting was a dictatorship rather than a democracy and I was really disgusted by her behavior. This person had been away for some time and things had been travelling smoothly but now I could see the next ten weeks would only be a painful struggle and I just don't have the energy to deal with it all. It would not be a joyful experience. Having committed myself to divine guidance this year Nameless had urged me to continue for the benefit of the exhibition but it no longer felt right or joyful and he had also previously said if it didn't feel right or joyful and you could do without then don't do it and to also trust my own intuition.

My problem is this… I feel like I let my ego take over in the heat of the moment and sent a group email to everyone stating that I was not happy with how I had been treated and the manner in which I was spoken to and could not continue to work in such an environment. I wanted people to know the truth of my leaving instead of being presented with some lame excuse from a different source. I feel I worded it as politely as I could while still getting my message across. I've since been told that she's mortified that the email went to the group, that she feels I've tarnished the reputation of the exhibition and now, having received emails back asking me to reconsider quitting, I feel I've let others down and am feeling guilty about that also. More than anything I'm cross at myself for not acting in a very High (highly evolved) manner. My girlfriend says now I have to accept the backlash of my actions and I know this is my karma.

I guess I don't really know what else to say except that I wanted to fess up to you my 'sins.' I think reading back over my notes I was readying myself to quit, was feeling exhausted and this person just tipped me over the edge, was the last straw and perhaps my excuse for a quick exit. To be honest I guess I was getting nervous about the quality of my work and whether it was worthy also.

Q. Would anyone like to respond? And please identify yourself.

It's Hoyan. You hit the nail on the head with your doubts and fears and this has clouded your judgment and decision making process. You feel you are not worthy, not just in the art making but also in life in general. This stems from your upbringing and childhood where you were never considered *good enough* at anything you did or applied yourself to. You always came off second best or never quite got to shining position where your soul self could be recognized as the shining light it is. You have carried this experience throughout your life and it holds you back in many aspects from your work and job to your relationships and friendships and even your ability to enjoy yourself as something is blocking you from shining through. There is a barrier there that needs to be broken and this will require working on. Hence whenever something good is coming you tend to self-sabotage and this is what has happened here.

You think it is the ego that has taken you over but it is not so as the ego would have spoken up directly and fought back and the ego would have wanted the accolades that would come from exhibiting your work. The shame now is that you will not know how worthy you really are, that opportunity has been lost to you and so really it is to your own detriment that you have made such a decision. Know that other opportunities will arise and having learnt from this experience and what the *real* issue is approach it in a different manner entirely. If you keep this experience and its lesson in mind you will go into it more wary and prepared and when you feel that *energetic pull backwards* understand its existence and its cause, work to overcome it so that you can move forward and excel at what it is you love to do. If you cannot overcome this barrier there will be no moving forward.

It's unfortunate that things played out the way they did and people got hurt and prides and ego's wounded. Life's lessons are sometimes tough and this one really was a small blip compared to the hardship of others' lives and realities. Do not feed it any more energy than is necessary. Acknowledge any wrong doing, understand its causes and why it happened, learn from it, vow to try to do it differently next time and move on. To dwell upon its negativity will only bring down yours and others energy and vibration of which we don't want. The aim is to always go Higher. Being human is to err sometimes and to accept that this happens occasionally. Berating yourself will not aid the situation. Picking yourself up and moving forward will. Send blessings and healing to this person that you feel has wronged you and you have wronged also. Work on healing yourself, do things that bring joy and laughter back into your life. I see in the future there will be apologies and you will be on speaking terms once again though this person does not belong in your close enclave you will both be able to put this behind you. Remember growth (spiritual) can come from every experience even the more difficult ones.

Blessings Light Being, I send you healing energy.

SUN 17TH MARCH

Hi Nameless, I enjoyed my white room meditation and will revisit Quan Yin tomorrow with questions. Today I'd like to discuss observations from my work in aged care. There's a lot of sleeping going on, even in residents who are quite well and mobile. Most sit in their rooms sleeping in their armchairs all day long, only coming to the dining room for meals and sometimes not even then.

Q. Why do they sleep so much when they're quite physically able and could be out enjoying the last of life they have left? Can you shed any light on the subject?

Yes. They are in preparation or transition mode. What you see is apathy, sleepiness and stillness, a wasting away of life as it passes them by *but* what you don't see is that really there is a lot of underlying/unseen work going on during this process. They are preparing their body, mind and soul for what is to come, the great transition from one dimension to another. Thus they are re-attuning themselves and working on shifting their vibration to match the next dimension they are about to transcend into. For some this takes a lot of work and a lot of effort as they may not have done this type of work before in their lives, this transforming of vibration and shape shifting. Certainly this generation that you are observing have little or no information regarding such things. Thus they are not consciously aware of what is going on, it is their soul self that is doing all the work and to make it easier for the soul the physical body and conscious mind needs to be in a resting or switched off state so the soul can make the necessary adjustments.

The individual themselves is unaware of this process, they simply feel tired and the need to rest. As physical death and soul transformation draws closer they are becoming more prepared to cross over and speaking to people there will be an acceptance and even a willingness to let go of this reality. Those that reach almost a sleeping like coma in their later days have already let go of their physical conscious state of being and it is only the soul self that is left to transition. You wonder why the soul just does not leave at this stage, saving the anguish of those who watch on but the soul is wisely holding back to ensure that the vibratory attunement is just right for an optimal transition such that during occurrence it is as simple as stepping through a doorway with there being no repercussions or anomalies or difficulties occurring and the transformation is a smooth and easy one.

The physical being that you observe lying in their bed is at peace, resting throughout this entire process. Rendered unconscious to make it as peaceful and painless as possible. The occasional one who is in pain and cry's out is the strong willed one who fights against this process instead of succumbing and letting go. It is a struggle between the conscious being and the soul self who want to go in opposite directions. They have no idea of the peace and tranquility that is waiting for them on the other side, if they did they would jump right in. Thus the saying, "They fought to the bitter end."

There will be a noticeable time difference in the preparation for transition such that for some it may take years and will be a slow and gentle process most of the way and picking up speed towards the end. For others the souls work may have gone largely unnoticed until it is time to transform and thus from an outsiders point of view the transition appears to occur rather suddenly. Know that your loved ones are at peace and have moved into a dimension that does not possess the hardships that you face on earth. They have transcended into pure *Lightness and Being* with an energetic feeling of *pure bliss*. If they could communicate with you they would not only want to tell you of this state but want to impart to you the *feeling* of it also so that you may understand fully where and what it is they have transcended to and that you not fear for them, others or yourselves when your time comes.

The majority of you are kept in the dark with regards to this to prevent you from "jumping ship" similar to your planet and country that experiences refugees who are searching for a better life for themselves and their families. The numbers allowed in has to be paced so as to not upset the system to the detriment of everyone involved. If everyone was aware just how good it was to transform there would be a stampede and the scales would tip such that everybody would fall off. Better to have a controlled trickle where operations are not compromised and transitions are running at one hundred percent optimal levels such as there is no wrongly occurrences.

You, yourself have a long while before your soul is ready to transform but this does not mean you are unable to currently experience other dimensions. Indeed if you are well practiced at it in this life, when your time to transform nears, it should be a quick and easy process without prolonged vibrational tuning as your soul will have a vast experience to draw from of attuning to other dimensions. Thus people can prepare themselves long before they reach the end stages of life and it should not be looked upon morbidly rather that your variant enjoyable experience of other dimensions now will benefit you much later in life. And so when you observe your residents at work know that though the physical body and mind is resting, the soul is busy attuning to the *Universal Energy Field* and is hard at work preparing this being for transformation. It really is a wonder.

Blessings and lightness to your day Marikai.

Thanks for that insight Nameless.

MON 18TH MARCH

This morning I went to my White Room to speak with Quan Yin. When the door opened she stepped out in all her beauty and serenity, calmly and effortlessly floating towards me. I wish I could do that! I told her I had many questions regarding our last conversation.

Q. How can I teach women to love and nurture themselves and find their inner strengths? How can I bring feminine intent and softness into actions and interactions with others? Here's what she had to say...

First by *listening* to their concerns and worries. Then using healing techniques clear their energy fields, chakras and let the Universal Energy Field do the rest. Thus they will be strengthened to take control of their own mental, physical, spiritual and emotional healing and will innately know what is good and right for them. Also you will get knowledge/messages coming through during this process to impart to them. Just *being* there for them will help relieve blockages to help them see their lives from different perspectives.

1. ***Listening* without acting or reacting. Just *being* there for them, listening without judging.**

2. ***Touch,* healing those that need healing /rebalancing. Offer healing to those who are hurting. So if you see someone acting in anger it's because they are hurting. Instead of reacting as you did acknowledge their pain and without mentioning anything offer them healing, using touch and healing to rebalance their energy field and chakras. If you can't do this in person do it from afar.**

3. **If you are in the middle of verbal deluge instead of reacting *send healing, love, blessings, light.* Charge their energy field and chakras.**

This woman you shared difficulties with, look at the positive. It has made you question and reassess your actions and reactions, sending her on a path of reassessment also. You will both come out more loving because of it.

Quan Yin then touched my forehead and imparted healing energy, healing the rift between this woman and myself. Quan Yin spoke ..."Blessed are those that blossom on the tree of life." With that she floated to the door, turned to me, bowed her head and the door silently closed.

SAT 23RD MARCH

Good morning Nameless, here I am on the train again going down to Brisbane for the Stiches and Craft show. The train broke down at Gympie and we had to bus it the first part of the way to Caboolture. It's too hard to write on the bus but now I'm on the train sitting near an interesting looking old fellow and I'm going to practice my telepathy and speak to his Higher Self. As you can tell by my writing this train is really bumping along.

Q. Tell me about yourself (Neil?).

It's true I'm old but it hasn't always been so. I've lived a full life. Some of it regrets, wrong decisions that I would change if I could go back but I can't and that's ok. Nothing too bad just stuff I would have done differently. I can't complain it's been an ok life.

Start from your youth and tell me what happened.

I was a strapping healthy young lad. Had a charm about me and a way with the girls. Got me into trouble sometimes but not the kind of trouble you're thinking of. Fights with the boys over some of the girls especially the pretty ones. I did alright for myself but there was one girl I had my heart set on who was promised to another and it kind of broke my heart at the time. It makes you realize you're not quite up to standard and not the juiciest apple in the cart. That had an effect on me and my self-esteem and I adopted this couldn't care less attitude which only got me into more trouble and so it spiraled. I think looking back I could have made something of myself if I didn't cop this attitude. I can still see Penny's beautiful blue eyes, her golden wavy hair and her shy smile. She smelled like fresh strawberries and sometimes I like to dream that we are courting.

In the end I married Maud, she was a good if somewhat controlling woman and I let her boss me into it. Maud didn't take no for an answer and what she wanted she got. I kind of liked not having to make decisions and just did what I was told, throwing myself into work, first working with cattle and then after a hoofing accident I worked on the railways. The railways became my home. The camaraderie and mateship filled a void in me that I lost with my dreams of being Penny's beau.

Home life was ok too. Me and Maud had five kids and when they were real little, young uns, I didn't take much joy in them but once they got to talking and walking age we would play with the football and the cricket in the backyard, even having tournaments with the local neighborhood kids and the families of the guys from work. They were the times I enjoyed the most when we all got together and the kids ran around like crazy, the women folk sat and nattered and us men got to booze the afternoons away. I always slept well those nights and I always looked forward to those days.

One of our kids was sickly for a while and there were trips to the hospital. Maud was really worried but we stuck it through. I had to pull my family socks up and man up. It was one of the only times I took control, poor Maud was a mess but it made me feel good when she looked at me for help and I knew no matter how much she bossed me she did love me. I wish I could say the same but my heart belonged to Penny. I guess I did love Maud but in a different way. We didn't argue a lot, she just bossed and I just did and occasionally I'd put my foot down which would bring her back into line.

I remember the best holiday we had was when we took the kids to the beach, Caboolture which was a long way from Gympie in those days. We stayed in a caravan park close to the beach spending our days in the surf and eating ice-creams and the nights walking the promenade under the balmy night skies. The highlight was when I treated the whole family to the movie theatre, something we only got to do once a year. To see the kids on their first trip to the movies was a delight I will never forget. You would think they just found the pot of gold at the end of the rainbow. I'll never forget their happy faces and bright smiles. It made me proud of myself that I could give them such joy. Eventually the kids all grew up and one by one left home. They have kids of their own now, even some of their kids have kids. It's all so different now. Sadly Maud passed away quite a few years back. Diabetes. She always did like her food (sometimes more than me). Now it's me and my memories and my dreams.

Dreams of my Penny and the life we could have lived.

MON 25TH MARCH

Morning Nameless. Just another catch up with what's currently happening now that Floating Land is no longer. I have more time for me, having neglected the self over the last six months and am re introducing some good things back into my life as you suggested. I'm on the Liver Cleanse diet to help kick start vibrational eating, the two seem to complement each other and hopefully I will lose a few kilos. I'm back swimming once a week and am in joyful mindfulness at these times so get physical, spiritual and emotional benefit. Most other days I walk with plans to introduce some yoga.

On the fun side I went to the Stitches and Craft fair, boring for most but as a mixed media artist I was as excited as a kid at a fairground and had the most audacious time. If I'm honest with myself I really would just like to do art all day long (this tortures me daily that I can't make this happen). One of the ladies at work has asked me to do a talk at the Rotary club about my art practice and development. I'm a bit scared but it's good speaking practice and self-promotion. I've also been thinking about running some kids craft classes for the local home schooling group which would be fun but also good practice for running adult workshops later on.

Once a fortnight I go to Lotus Light in Cooroy for healing and the alternate week I attend a crystal bowl sound healing meditation in Cooroibah (this is my favorite, the ambience is just delicious). My business cards arrived but, duh, had a spelling mistake so Marikai channeling and healing is on hold while I re order. Maleny is almost prepared with just a few more small works to complete.

Life is full and abundant.

Q Any comments?

Just that as always the Universe provides when the need arises. Ask and it will find its way to you in some guise or another, not always how you had planned or would have perceived but often in a longer roundabout way and in a manner to surprise. Things don't just drop from the sky into your lap but take time to manifest and so it is a matter of putting the message out there that you want or desire and allowing the Universe to think about the best manner to present it to you and producing it in the Universes own timely manner.

Patience is a virtue and a wonderful lesson to learn. It humbles one and it is in this humble energy that one is most deserving and the portals of abundance will open to allow gifts to flow to you. Instant gratification and greed that has been bred into your society has prevented many from moving forward and experiencing the joy of possibilities that life could offer them. If only they could put the request out there and then sit back and have the patience to wait in a humble and thankful manner.

Also gift giving to others is another way to open this portal, this channel, as what is given will be returned many times over. It is a shame that your world is not operating to its capacity of generosity and abundance. The more you give to others the more is returned to you until you are spilling over with abundance and have more than is necessary for yourself such that you can share it with those around you with a true gift giving like nature and pure joy in your heart and this aids in raising your vibration and the recipients.

This is our aim, to aid in raising the planets vibration so that you can access portals through to other dimensions. The easiest way to raise your vibration is through unabashed gift giving. Giving with pure intention and no mind for "What is in it for me?" or for one's own benefit. The gift need not be expensive and can be as simple as time, give your time to someone else. And this could be time just spent listening (good and active listening) to what they have to say coupled with empathy, *feeling* what it is like for that person, their life, their worries and concerns, their joy and accomplishments. People just want to be acknowledged that they *exist* and that what they *do* and *feel* matters not just to them but to others around them or they would feel no point to their lives.

The gift of time could also be not one of matter (physical) but of energy. For example going out of your way to help someone on their travels, directing them or accompanying them on their path or journey such as the example you were given at the train station of the lady who offered a gentleman a lift to catch up with his missed bus. This was a simple but precious gift for the recipient who would have missed his flight if not for the woman offering her time.

It really is as simple as that. Look for such opportunities where you can offer help and do this often. It will raise your vibration, the recipients and the planets. If the whole world looked for such opportunities *daily* imagine how different it would be. So this is your quest or next exercise. Every day, *every day* look for someone to help (and expect nothing in return). Stay humble. You really are precious Marikai. Joy be with your day.

Thanks Nameless. I get the first part is connected to my art (ask, patience and work towards it and it will manifest in divine timing). I feel I do give daily in my job but perhaps not enough and may also need to open more to opportunities for giving outside of work. I'm always grateful for your advice.

THUR 28TH MARCH

Good morning Nameless. Today is Easter Friday and the start of the school holidays. My new business cards are waiting to be picked up from the Post Office so I'll be able to start readings very soon. I rang a few psychics to get an idea of pricing and it varied greatly. I was shocked that some were charging a hundred and twenty dollars an hour. Do people really pay that much? These mediums had ten to twenty years' experience though and used a multitude of tools (tarot cards, palmistry, crystal balls etc.). It made me feel inadequate and inexperienced and for a short time I was a bit "depresso" about the whole thing. Once again like my art I'm coming into something late in life and don't have the experience and knowledge that others have built up over years. I feel like I'm behind the eight ball from the word go. Can I, should I really do this? I decided if I go ahead I will charge around the middle range if only for my unique verbatim method. This in itself poses a problem as it takes a long time to write down the information verbatim long hand. How am I going to present this to a client? I decided on a laptop with projector so they can be involved and I can email them the copy afterwards. Trouble is, cheapest set up comes in at around the seven hundred dollar mark and you guessed it….I can't afford it.

Q. Do you have any advice about how I should go about this?

Yes. Rent one. It would be good to start out how you mean to go on and this is definitely something that makes you unique and worthy of charging the price you choose. It's a good method for transferring information to the client that involves them while you transcribe. People will become hooked and fascinated by this process as they get to witness it firsthand. The fact that you can transcribe verbatim is what sets you apart from other mediums/channels. It's not to say they can't do this if they want to and have the patience but that it seems your style and your way at this point in time. There is much to be gained via the net using this method also, involving people from all around the world, and channeling on all sorts of questions that you may not have thought of but that others put forward. A blog or some such interactive site. This may come later but for now baby steps and as I have always suggested it is important for the benefit of all mankind that you just get started in whatever manner that suits or you can achieve.

This may change at a later date when you teach yourself how to verbalize the channeled information. This is a learned process. As you know there is a necessary transference from right brain (channeled information) to left brain (to verbalize) and is not that easy for the uninitiated *but* can be learned by anyone. It is a constant switching back and forth of vibrations and frequencies. You could try practicing it once a week on your own to get the hang of it. Ask for the information to be slowed down, then verbalize what comes through, stop, listen for more information then verbalize again. As with the written word you will notice you get faster the more practiced you are and the more you are able to attune to the Universal Energy Field.

As for the experience and knowledge of others don't let that put you off as it is *we* that are passing the information on to *you* to impart to others and so the knowledge and advice is coming from *us*. You are our method of transference and without belittling you as you play a very important part it is *us* who do the work of providing the information and so you do not have to worry yourself that you are not as knowledgeable as others as the knowledge is provided for you.

Tarots and crystal balls etc. are all smoke and mirrors. They are visual prompts to accessing the same information. Funny how a civilian can put their faith in a picture on a card yet find it difficult to understand that auditory information has equal validity. We are not so concerned though, whatever works for the person to obtain the rightful information for them works for us. They have been conditioned to such things from eons ago when people were accused of being witches and burned at the stake and so the devices were utilized to shift blame from being accused as a witch to a mere reader of the cards. They still do have validity in today's world though as discussed they are visual prompts for the reader and a visual image for the recipient to understand the information being imparted.

Speaking of imagery you may well practice yours by simply *asking*. Ask for an image if and when you get stuck in a reading and this will aid in unblocking and allow for more information to come through. So don't feel threatened by others and what they do. You concentrate on what it is that you do and you are right in thinking that even if you help just one person then you are doing a good thing.

You are on the rightful path Marikai and this is your life's purpose. I understand your lack of confidence and this will only come with practice. It is time for you and others to enter the ether of enlightenment. I will *always* be by your side. I will *never* let you down.

Go now Marikai with renewed optimism and vigor and *trust* that it will be so. Blessings to your day and a joy to be with you.

Thank you Nameless and ditto, always a pleasure and I love having you in my life my eternal friend.

Bless you Marikai.

SAT 30TH MARCH

OMG! I know I'm sounding like a nervous nelly but I was discussing with my daughter what you said about yourself providing the information in a reading and so I am not to worry. She reminded me that when she gave me a blind question back in December and I put it to you to answer her question you went off on some totally different tangent about something else and didn't answer her question at all (Q. Should I tell Mum I smashed the screen on my lap top?). Now I'm really worried as when a client comes to me with a specific question they need answering I'm concerned I may not be able to provide them with the information they require and then if I can't do that, supply them with specifics, then I'll just be a fake and a phony. I guess I'm asking for reassurance that you can supply me with specific and related answers to their questions.

Q. What say you Nameless?

Rest assured it is a given. You need not worry my little one. As stated I am there for you and will not let you down. There was important information to impart to your daughter and so little opportunity to do it in as I know she struggles to believe and hence there is not ample experiences to be able to pass to her the necessary information that is important for her growth towards her chosen path. The laptop was a minor glip in the grand scheme of things and even though was pressing to her at the time was not a part of the *bigger picture or grander scheme of things of which we try to stay focused on.* So many people give too much energy in what is happening in the here and now which has nothing to do with their life growth and moving forward toward other dimensions and increasing their spiritual vibration. Remember our aim is to increase the vibration of the individual and the planet and aiding in attuning to different dimensions so you may release yourselves from the hardship of your planet. In your Daughters case she should have known that the truth will always out and she had to give herself time to man up and be able to confess to you herself and not take the chicken's way out of you finding out through me and the channeling process. This is using us for deviant means and will not be allowed. We only deal with pure intention *so information is provided as long as the intent to use that information is pure.*

You would do well to let your clients know this. They can ask specifics and we *can* provide specific answers as long as there is pure intent and it is for the benefit of themselves and fellow kind. That is, it is information given that will improve their lives and the lives of those around them that will direct them towards a better way of living and towards their rightful path. In this way it is *guidance* and not just a solution to their problems but perhaps a different way of looking at their problems or coming at it from a different angle so they may get a different perspective and more insights into what is *truly* going on and thus armed with this new found knowledge be able to answer the issue for *themselves* as their Higher selves are opened to the situation and they can see it from a Higher perspective. Thus we are not there just to answer their questions for them such that they become dependent on us but provide gentle nudges in the right direction much like a lioness with her cubs who teaches them their own strength so they can defend and fend for themselves.

Many will come to you with problems and issues that seem all encompassing to them at the time. It is up to you to *also* alert them to looking at the *bigger picture. The grander scheme of things*. Really is this issue worth putting all their energy and worry into when they should be looking at their lives as a whole? And so when questions are posed always consider the *whole life* aspect. How does this fit into their *whole* life (from beginning to end)? If you were to draw a scale of their life and mark this issue on the scale, how big/small is it and this can give you a different perspective on how much energy and attention it could/should be given.

If we use school, job and marriage as an example, the times invested in these differs. There will be issues that arise at school but school life is very small in the grand scheme of life and unless the issue is or could have an impact on their future life (for example job or wealth prospects) then not too much energy should be given it. That is not to say there will not be issues that need to be dealt with but they should be dealt with in a quick, timely and efficient manner so the person can return to their life's path (and moving forward) as quickly as possible.

For example is the issue bullying? Then ask for a method to deal with this as quickly as possible and most likely it will be in how you manage it yourself in your own mind and intellect as to not allow it to affect your self-esteem for future years ahead. If we give the bullying a lot of energy, concern and worry and let it 'in' we can see how this could have an effect on our self-esteem and future job (and wealth) prospects and even career prospects and relationships and partnerships. If we look at school bullying on the picture scale (*see Figure 5.1*) we can see it is but a small blip in the timeline of our lives but has the ability to affect the rest of our lives if we allow it. By feeding it with our time and energy we are *investing* in it. If we look at the time line and say "Hey this bullying is occurring but it is not the grander scheme of my *whole* life and I will not allow it to be," then we may find the strength and motivation to nip it in the bud in some form or manner that is beneficial to your life moving forward, lifting and raising your vibration. Thus it may be suggested at looking at the different angle and perspectives of how to deal with this bully so that you can move on with the grander scheme that is your *real* life. Do you need to ignore, address, confront or remove yourself from the situation (change classes, schools, jobs etc.)?

So addressing the problem/issue but putting it in perspective of your *whole life scenario* and the aim that whatever action you take on things is always to lift and raise your vibration, taking yourself Higher and Higher all the time heading towards *Lightness and Being* as when your reality is shed and gone all will be revealed that what remains is *Pure Energy*. Remember guidance can be subtle, gentle, is not always what they were expecting to hear, aims to steer towards a better way of living, a Higher more evolved way at looking and dealing with things and aims to give different perspectives so that people can get in touch with their Higher powers to find the answers for themselves as *you* are the expert on *you*.

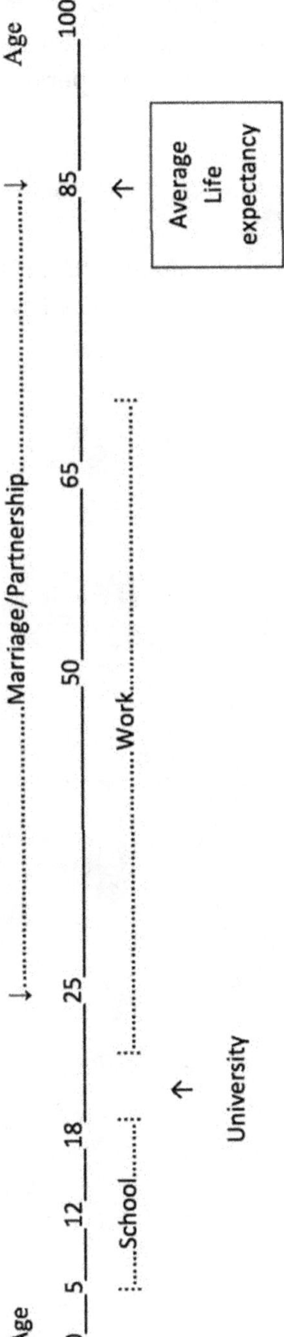

Figure 5.1 : Lifes time line

Go now Marikai with the confidence that this new way of looking at their lives will be just as intriguing for them as it is for you. Remember you are teaching the uninitiated and be patient. It is a new way of thinking for them and all change takes time. Time is your gift to them. Give them time to adjust and time to experience and you will have many followers.

Blessings to you always Marikai, I am always by your side.

Thank you so much Nameless. I do love the perspective you have on things. Thanks for the scale, that's a great visual tool I can use.

6

APRIL 2013

MON 1ST APRIL

Q. *Hello, is there anyone there who is willing and can help me with time line predictions? What can I look forward to in the next twelve months? Are there significant events that will occur in certain months of the coming year? Can you tell me what these events are and what month they will occur? Where will I be, what will I be doing one year from now?*

Only respond if you can answer these questions and please identify yourself.

Yes it is Hoyan. I have been waiting and eager to speak to you. You only need to *ask the question* and it can be answered for you. You are in for quite a heady year with much going on and many changes such that sometimes you may feel your head is in a spin and it is necessary to periodically earth and ground yourself and stop to re-assess the direction from whence you came and where you are going and if you do this always moving in a positive direction forward.

August is a strong month that is coming to mind. I know it is a big birthday celebration at this time but this is not the significance of this month. I feel there will be travel involved but not the type of travel that you had planned for this big event. Rather a journey. I see you sitting in a vehicle with many others, you are joyous, happy and excited. There is much talk and chatter as you look out the window and point out the scenery on the way. This journey has come totally out of the blue, was not expected at all and I feel was gifted to you in some way. It is an important healing process as for the first time in a long time you are able to sit back and enjoy without any concerns or worries over time and money. Someone else is in control in the planning and execution of this journey and thus you are able to fully relax and enjoy.

In light of this journey September will bring a re-assessment of your life and the hardships you have endured. There will be a conscious decision that you do not wish to return to this past way of living as really it is no way to live at all. Instead you will take a courageous step out into the Universe and leave the past behind you. There will be many changes and upheavals from this point forwards as you adjust and fine tune your life and indeed it may take a good six months and though difficult physically and exhausting mentally and emotionally it will also be positive and an exhilarating move in the right direction. I feel you will be resettled by Xmas time and that is when you're able to first sit back and really take stock of what you have done and been able to achieve in the previous four months.

January and the New Year will bring on new beginnings, a new life and a new way of living and operating. You will never return to your old life which is best left in the past except to remind yourself where you have come from and how much better your life is in comparison.

I do see writing, lots and lots of writing and this is the direction your life is heading. You will post off your writings to several publications and may receive as many as up to three offerings so don't just take the first offer thinking it will be the only one you will get.

Q. *But what about the months leading up to August, the next four months, what of them?*

I'm afraid its drudgery, difficult steps forward like you have lead in your boots yet you still need to keep moving in that forward direction or opportunities that have the ability to propel you forward will be lost. It is a chance (or really not by chance) meeting that will suddenly see your life turn around and head in a new direction. For this reason it is important that you allow yourself to be present in group scenarios and occasions where people gather as this is where it will occur. It will be an introduction through a group gathering and self-promotion on your part so don't be shy about telling others what it is you do and are doing. This coming four months is the ground work, the foundation of what is to be built on later. It is hard work and tough going and difficult to stay focused and motivated but is necessary work that will reap great benefits later. The more you put in now, the greater the rewards later.

So this is the time that you dig your heels in and get down and dirty with it, really apply yourself to what you're doing whole heartedly.

Thank you Hoyan you have imparted some interesting information. I'll mark these dates in my consciousness.

You are welcome my gifted one.

Ooh, I don't know about that.

You are all gifts it is not specifically about talent.

Duh, how presumptuous of me. Thank you.

FRI 5TH APRIL

Hoyan was right about trying to stay focused on what it is I'm meant to be doing, I'm all over the place at the moment with work, art, channeling, healing and single handedly raising a teenager. I wish I could give up work altogether to focus on my life's path but alas the bills need to be paid. It's really hard to juggle everything and time to fit everything in is the struggle Hoyan discusses. I'm desperately trying to follow divine guidance to see if it'll change my life for the better but so far it's only adding more work. He did say the next four months would be hard going so on I plod. My new business cards arrived but once again I'm being challenged by my confidence which continually fluctuates. Along with channeling I also advertised psychometry and dowsing, now I'm not so sure and think I should just cut it back to channeling.

Q. Should I redo the business card and omit psychometry and pendulum dowsing or am I ok to go ahead? Please identify yourself.

Yes I hear you its Nameless. Do not let your lack of confidence stop you from moving forward. As you are thinking make a list of all the things that you are able to do with the pendulum and you will see you have enough to offer your clients in this respect. As experience grows so will your list but experience only comes from putting yourself out there in the beginning. Everybody starts somewhere and do not concern yourself that you do not have twenty years under your belt as do others for your abilities are innate, you are a natural. Do not fear that you are lacking in skills as you have been training for this for a long time, even without your (conscious) knowledge. Add to this your life skills and your personable nature and your ability to communicate well with individuals, your caring and empathy and you will be well received. As long as you are *truthful* and *honest* about what it is you can and can't do you will not be deceiving any one or letting anyone down. So make the pendulum list and this will be your guide and as discussed add to the list as you explore and become more skilled over time. This is an exercise that can be completed in a day or two so you will soon be ready.

As for psychometry you have possessed this skill for a very long time, twenty years or more but have not utilized it very often. Introduce this gently as *part* of your readings and when it is fully awakened as a skill in its own right you will manage to do complete readings with this skill alone for those who are drawn to it. It's a skill that works well with photos, jewelry and the like to aid you in tapping into the persons energy field to draw upon information and so is a very useful skill and one that adds a different dimension to what you do…complimentary. So it would be beneficial to both you and clients that it remains a part of your repertoire.

Psychometry and the pendulum work really well together. For example using a photograph and assessing the health and wellbeing of the individuals chakras, aura, energy levels, vitamin and mineral deficiencies etc. You will actually find that this comes easier than you think, give it a go and you will see. If you can do it once you can do it many times over. It really comes down to a confidence thing with you as you definitely have the ability.

In Love and Light — Nameless.

Thanks Nameless.

Q. At this point in time which would suit me better regarding selling my art…a gallery or similar where I rent a space or Maleny art co-op where I rent but also work the shop on a roster?

Yes Hoyan here.

Both Nameless and Hoyan seemed to both want to answer my questions in the beginning so I gave them one each. I always give Nameless the more spiritual based questions as he seems less interested in earth bound concerns (he will always help but I can tell he prefers to focus on spiritual growth) whereas Hoyan having been human before seems to be more eager regarding earthbound issues and I think this is why Hoyan presented himself to me in the beginning, to handle the more mundane and emotionally charged matters. Sorry Hoyan for interrupting, go ahead.

You have been weighing up the pros and cons of both and really it comes down to *affordability* and *time* which you are short of both. Therefore my leaning is towards the gallery space rental or similar concept. It's a good and mild beginning for you without having to get too involved time wise. This frees you up for more healing/channeling work and more art practice. You are right in thinking this art business is a much harder sell than you had thought it was going to be and are currently re-assessing what it is you do and in what direction you want to take so something like Maleny is a huge commitment both financially and time wise and I'm not sure you can afford either at this point in time. You don't want to be personally invested in the shop yourself, better that you approach shops to either buy your work outright or sell on a commission basis. That way you have more time and flexibility to yourself and are not beholden to any one which is something you try to avoid. If further down the line things change Maleny will always be there as an opportunity if you so desire. Yes the travelling to and from there is also off putting. The occasional GARART sale is also a good idea, order that banner it will come in handy.

You are right to be precious with your time (and money) as the true focus for now is your life's purpose which is the channeling and the healing arts. As this takes off and becomes successful you will see your art change and so will its direction. Eventually you will be in a position to drop your day job and strike a compatible balance between the two or three of your passions, art, healing and writing. This is when you come into fruition as your *true souls being* and life will feel more complete. Until then the journey is arduous as you make plans to travel toward your goals.

Focus is always the key. Focus on always heading in the right direction (forward) towards your life's purpose. Stay goal oriented and you will be on the right path. Periodically assess where it is you are going and you will avoid being strayed. And of course we are always here for support and advice, you only need to ask. Blessings to your day.

Thanks Hoyan I know you're right. As much as I would love to be a part of Maleny I really can't afford the dollars or the time. Thanks for your insights.

SUN 7TH APRIL

I spent all day yesterday preparing my pendulum list and was surprised by the amount of applications I was able to include. I spent the whole morning working through each one testing them to ensure I could use them in my practice. The following are only what I have currently tested myself on, there are quite a few more but this is enough to start with.

- ***House/space clearing***
- ***Body and tissue health scanning***
- ***Aura/chakra (balancing and clearing)***
- ***Vitamin, mineral and food evaluations***
- ***Remedy selection***
- ***Homeostasis and personal assessment***

I was surprised to find out the pendulum is very effective in telling the time and also the direction of true North should I ever get lost. Yesterday in the supermarket I was looking for an obscure item and getting frustrated at not being able to find it. The staff were unable to locate it either. To my surprise the pendulum knew exactly what isle it was in and led me straight to it, what a useful tool! This excited me no end as finding lost items would be a great addition. I'm now feeling more confident using this tool, thanks for your help Nameless.

Q. Any advice for today?

Just that the pendulum charts are a good idea as they will save you much time. This is why many do not use the pendulum as a tool because it is such a timely process but the patience is worth the specific information that you gain from it and it is just as accurate if not more so than Touch for Health/Kinesiology without the need to contort the person's body.

There will be many who question the pendulums validity as they struggle to understand the concept of its workings. Find a suitable simplified definition of how it works so as to not complicate the mind of others. The proof is in the pudding so to speak and you will encourage others to do their own investigations regarding the (health) advice you give them and they will very often find it confirmed and that the two coincide and agree with each other. There is nothing wrong with this and conversely should be encouraged as it will provide your method with validity and though people are unsure of how it works they will find it *does* work and can be highly accurate. Be aware however that no method is fool proof and this one is open to errors due to miscommunication. As long as you are honest in your approach and conduct then you are living in your Higher truth and working for the best good of the person. Therefore to cover yourself and the information you provide it is always good and best to encourage the person to seek secondary advice to confirm what it is you impart to them.

Client feedback will aid in building your confidence as you become more aware of its accuracy and the benefits it provides your clients. A soft approach is always best, erring on the side of caution. Any information regarding deficiencies etc. can do no harm even if the odd one be incorrect, it may be so minute as to not be picked up in medical tests but the body itself is still deficient in some way. It could even be that the levels of vitamins or minerals are adequate but are not being utilized by the body in an efficient manner. This is always a possibility and as your aim is to increase their levels through food and not through pumping tablets into the body then there can be little harm done and more likely than not it will be highly beneficial working to increase the persons functioning and vibratory level of which is always our aim. The vitamin and mineral lists that you provide will be of great benefit. People always enjoy coming away with something in their hands and also a plan or guide that they can follow. In this way it will be a prescription of sorts and as people are conditioned in this manner it will be highly effective.

It wouldn't hurt this week to investigate further the rental of a lap top. I feel if you rent the lap top you could afford the projector outright. Time is drawing ever closer. It is only these working out of the finer details that are preventing you from moving forward so make them your priority. Also keep up with your practice with the pendulum using it as much as you can. It could do with a cleanse and Mana[1] charge it also. This will see it recharged with great energy. Go now Marikai there is still much to do, stay goal oriented and you will keep moving forward towards your life's purpose.

I am watching on with pride, I am always by your side. In strength, Nameless.

Thank you Nameless. I love having these conversations with Nameless as it helps me put my life and goals in order, a plan so to speak which helps with my indecisiveness. In this way it is my life's guidance and I hope this is what I can do for others (with assistance from my guides), help put their lives in order.

And it will be so. Trust my child, faith.

SAT 13TH APRIL 2013

Good morning Nameless. It's another rainy morning and I channel to you from my cozy bed. It has pretty much been raining nonstop since the floods (well it is the wet season) and I haven't been able to go down to The Valley of The Snakes to meet with Marikahee nor speak to Raven Owl for such a long time. I'm in fear that perhaps they will think I have lost interest and they have given up on me. Supposedly it's going to rain for another week at least and I'm really aching to be with them. Instead this morning I've been handling my pendulum and working out my ground colors, color deficiencies and my predominant aura and radiating colors. It seems I'm mainly deficient in red, no surprise there given my physical exhaustion so will work on topping this up over the next few days.

Q. Can you impart to me your knowledge on chakra's and auras?

This is not really my specialty but I can inform you of what I know. There are those that are more specialized and knowledgeable in this area than me whose job it is to oversee and aid in fine tuning such things by bringing humans into awareness of the existence of the chakras and aura and presenting to them methods of fine tuning that they can apply themselves to help raise their vibrations and ready themselves for *dimensional travel.*

You have had such a being working with you even though you have been unaware. Their guidance is underlying and hidden from view but has been directing you towards certain information and books, meditations and even people you meet and conversations gained such that information is provided through gentle nudges in the right direction towards positive change. These beings are everywhere and can be considered the 'workers,' the ground staff. They are like busy bees fluttering all around those on your earth assessing your auras, your chakra and energy levels as well as your intellect and choosing those they think suitable of working towards Higher existence and aiding in the cleansing, replenishing and fine tuning of their energy systems, raising their awareness to a level that they may take control of their own volition to work towards optimal levels for themselves and then the ground staffs work is done. They have bought you into awareness and presented to you the knowledge and skills so that you may assess and fine tune yourselves.

This is the beginning stages of moving into other realms as it is only when you are tuned that it is optimal to travel into other dimensions. That is not to say that you can't do this beforehand without fine tuning but that you will have the most optimal, pleasant and the most rewarding (intellectually) experience when your vibration is at its peak. There will be experiences and information that you will have greater access to when you are in this state that will not be revealed to those who travel with lower frequencies. Thus if you aim to gather *High* experiences and *High* information then your vibrational frequency needs to be *High* also.

Just like all the systems of the human body the chakra's and aura are in a constant state of flux and are not impervious to external influences that can either uplift or bring about degradation and thus it is necessary to consult with the self on a regular basis to assess the state of these and make any necessary adjustments also. Not only will this allow an easier transition through the portals into other worlds and different dimensions but you will notice a shift on planet earth also that life will become that much easier, things of good will flow your way and there will be a *lightness of being* almost like walking on air. This is the *feeling* that is your raised vibration. The Higher your vibration the *Lighter* (and less earth bound) you feel.

As it is necessary for you to operate on the earthly plane while you possess a physical body it may also be necessary for you to consciously ground or anchor yourself to the earth simultaneously to avoid floating into the ether like a halogen balloon would float off into the atmosphere. Liken this to the invisible umbilical cord that is always attached between mother and child or an astronaut connected to his mother ship such that you have free reign to travel where you please but always having a connection to the earth, a way of returning. Make it invisible and weightless so that you have total freedom of movement in all directions with no restrictions or limitations.

As for the chakras themselves these are the portals that not only supply you with access to information from the Universe but are vortex's allowing for travel into different worlds, other dimensions. An earth bounds perception is that these worlds are "Out there," beyond themselves projected in space somewhere. Instead think of them as black holes, vortexes that collapse in on themselves and this is where the different dimensions lay, internally rather than externally and it is the formers perception that prevents many people from dimensional (and time) travel as they are taking the wrong path to a journey that will take them nowhere…is desolate. They have caught the wrong train so to speak to Nowheresville and are moving in the wrong direction entirely. The answers are and always have been within, within the self and this is the direction one should take if they choose to advance forward and experience all there is to offer. So accessing the Universal Energy Field through the portals of the chakras which are like collapsible vortex's of energy such that they implode in on themselves and when the dust has settled there is complete calmness coupled with a feeling of weightlessness, an absence of gravity and this signals the ability to *travel and move in all and any direction one wishes to experience.*

At this stage you might like to call in a guide as for any other travel how do you know where to go unless you are told of all the fabulous possibilities. Your travel guide is knowledgeable in this area and is there to serve this purpose advising you of different places of existence and the best travel methods as well as imparting travel advice and any possible warnings or things to look out for. Once you become a seasoned traveler you may choose the freedom to branch out on your own but my advice in the beginning is to consult with your travel guide and you will navigate your way through a lot quicker and with little hiccups.

You have travelled these portals before I know but the distance and time frame was reduced to very little as fear got in the way. Fear of where you were and fear of ..."Is this really possible?" and fear of… "Can I return to earth?" Remember with a guide you are always safe and until you feel safe to go it alone. Fear (or any related thought) will always bring you crashing back to earth, remembering that fear is thought based and therefore earthbound.

So armed with this new found knowledge that optimal space, time and dimensional travel is reliant on a finely tuned aura and chakra system you may choose to add this to your priority list if this is the direction you decide to take. Remember if your car is finely tuned you will have a smooth ride and an enjoyable journey to your destination. If it is not you may still get to the end point eventually but it will be rickety, slow, unpredictable and possibly fraught with difficulties and obstacles on the way and you may even breakdown. The former you can relax and enjoy your journey knowing the preparation is done and you are safe. The latter may be fraught with concerns and worries and so is a less enjoyable experience. Remember what you put in you get out.

By the way Marikahee and Raven Owl are aware of the difficulties you are facing and will be there for you when you are ready, no rush. Enlightened joy to your day Marikai — Nameless.

Thank you Nameless. I relate this to Quantum physics, black holes and their collapsing in on themselves where everything as we know it ceases to exist including an absence of time. Perhaps I should read up on this for further understanding. Fascinating stuff I love it!

SUN 14TH APRIL

Just a quick one this morning. I've been doing some research and reading online about Psychism. One website suggested that Psychic skills won't fully develop if you begin working with the public too soon. That stepping out into the public prematurely will prevent the development of the persons (psychic) frequency into a Higher spiritual vibration capable of handling higher intensities of communication and knowledge. I guess my concern is…

Q. Am I taking myself to the public too early? Am I highly developed enough for my clients? Will I prevent myself from going even Higher if I do this? Is it going to affect my own development and abilities and therefore what I can achieve for others?

It is right for you to be discerning with what you read and always questioning the thoughts of others. This information comes from a good source but is not applicable to you but more to the beginner who is first delving into such realms. It serves as a warning to those who possess such little knowledge yet feel they are capable of much more and so it would be detrimental to them and those they serve that they would do more harm than good. You are not an initiate newcomer to this realm of knowledge and come armed with a vast array of experience and information gathered over a prolonged period of time. You have been practicing on and off for decades for the benefit of yourself, family and friends who have all benefited from your skills. The only step forward for you *is* to take it out to the public and this is part of furthering your development as contrary to what you have just read the public will aid in bringing you Higher as you aim to provide the best guidance and with the utmost professionalism and respect. By working with the public you are bringing it more into your reality and so will be *living* it more as your everyday physical (earthly) life. This is bringing your

Higher purpose into existence on this earth in this life. This is what you are meant to be doing and have spent your whole life developing and accumulating knowledge to get to this point. So no you are not premature in going public. It is your time. This is your opportunity to take what you have learnt and use it for the benefit of others so that they also may go Higher and with guidance find their lives easier to live by gaining new and valuable perspective on things. With you as our translator we can help many people this way.

It is good that you question and show concern for yourself and others as it shows your intentions are good and pure. You possess the wisdom to measure that you are always coming from pure intent and with the persons' highest good and best interests at heart. If you always work from this place, pure of heart and mind, then the individual will always benefit in some way and can only go Higher.

As discussed your own development will not suffer in the process of you aiding others but will rather be solidified and confirmed to you such that you will gain encouragement to explore further and delve deeper and search wider. Be aware however that with knowledge comes responsibility (to self and others). As you gain knowledge always stop and take the time to *manifest* and bring this knowledge into your life's practice and everyday existence. That is to say *act* upon the knowledge gained as it is worthless if it stays trapped upon the mind.

Even though you have grown spiritually and psychically for decades to reach this point you are really just at the beginning of your psychic explosion. Today you stand upon the precipice. Courage Marikai and take one step forward into the Universe that will cloak you with all the love, peace and joy that you only ever hoped existed, where you will grow wings and fly — Nameless.

Thank you Nameless for all your encouragement and support.

FRI 19TH APRIL

Raven Owl Raven Owl come to me on the wings of the wind, I've a need for your advice.

Q. I'm going to the annual Psychic fair tomorrow. Is there anything I should be looking for that I need at this time? Should I visit with a psychic and if so which one?

Good morning it's nice to be with you again my friend. I see you perusing the tables of many crystals and see you being drawn to one particular larger one and a few smaller ones. Do not over analyze or overthink your decisions to purchase but work on instinct and intuition with the ones you are drawn to as these are the appropriate ones' for you at this time. You will feel it in your gut and heart at the time of connection and will sense your energy vibration lift, that feeling of joy, bliss and excitement.

You are becoming more attuned to these senses. As you use them more frequently it becomes easier all the time to instinctively know what is best for your Higher good and purpose. You are developing all the time in this field and I already see a marked difference in you from when we last spoke as you are more in your *feeling* senses and more attuned to subtle shifts in energy and underlying electronic fields. This is moving you forward in a positive direction towards your life's purpose and the work that you are doing is having positive effects not only for yourself but also for others who will reap the benefits of your study and hard work which you will soon put into practice.

I see feathers also and there is a connection there to Marikahee. She has a gift there awaiting you. I see a picture of a young beautiful Indian woman and feel you will be drawn to a book that has valuable and important information contained therein. This book is sent to you from Marikahee. It explains some of the Indian ways and traditions that will impart to you a basic grounding of shamanism as well as a few explosive insights that will have you thinking in new directions and new light.

The artist you choose to sit with is simply out of your price range and I know you drool over her work and long to sit with her but it is not to be. Instead choose one of her most beautiful pictures to purchase so that you may use it as a psychometry and channeling tool and also for pure pleasure to look upon daily as a way of increasing your vibration.

Instead of the artist you will choose a more affordable psychic. As with the crystals allow yourself to be drawn instinctively to the one that suits you or intrigues you the most. I'm sure it will be aligned with what you yourself are doing as not only will you use the reading time to gather guidance on direction in your life but also to gain valuable insight into the workings of the other similar (to you) psychics. So you will most likely choose along the lines of pendulum, psychometry or channeling.

Whilst you're there soak up all the good and positive energy and vibration. Look around you at the crowds of people who are interested in this phenomena. These are all your potential clients. These are people who are interested in the services you provide. Look at the demographics and the great range of ages, shapes and sizes they come in. All are aiming to better themselves and their lives in some way. All are searching for that which can bring them to happiness and Higher states of being. I am not suggesting it is time to hand out cards or such but that you merely observe there are many people in this area that are interested in the healing ways and you will not be short of clients when the time is right for you to begin. So this is confirmation that indeed your service is required and it will be well received.

I must also state that I am proud that you are travelling with caution and are not jumping the gun. When you do make the decision to start, which I feel is soon, you will be well prepared and ready. Enjoy the atmosphere of the day as I know you will. We will all be travelling with you, watching you, protecting you and guiding you.

Feathers and Light — Raven Owl.

Thank you Raven Owl.

□□□

Hi Nameless, I'm actually *on the computer now and thought I'd try channeling to you and typing what you say instead of writing as this is the method I aim to use when channeling for clients. I thought it best to try it first and see if it works, LOL! So here I sit at my iMac and I'm wondering if you will come through for me and what it will be like to type instead of write.*

Q. Do you have any information for me today?

Just that all is well with the Universe and you are progressing well my dear. You are right to practice at this before taking it to clients, as you need to see for yourself that it is indeed possible. I am still able to converse with you this way and indeed as you can see from how fast your little fingers are typing it is a much faster method, as if you are on speed. Also it is possible for you to go back later and edit out any spelling mistakes, though I ask you (and I know you have already pre considered this) not to change any of the words I speak as to do so would indeed as you think be a dishonor to what I am trying to convey.

This method that you chose will enable the client to be more involved in the process. They will look on in awe at the speed with which you type and the profound information that is revealed to them, knowing that it is not possible that information comes from you given the concepts discussed. It will restore their faith that there is something beyond their current Universal understanding, something that which they do not have firsthand experience of and in these instances you are the medium we use for information transference so that they may get a glimpse into the vast array of possibilities that are truly available to them on a grand scale if they are only to open their eyes, hearts and minds and attune all their senses to that which is available on the etheric realm so that they may expand their awareness one hundred fold.

Yes this information is coming through to you extremely fast now such that you are having trouble keeping up but I have managed to slow it down a little now so that the letters do not come out all jumbled. Just ask for me to slow it down if you are not coping with it well. It is hard to keep this pace for an extended period of time.

I felt that stop abruptly there and I lost the connection.

Q. Can you tell me what is going on there? And if that happens when I'm with a client what should I do? (Also I should be timing this, I will say I started at twelve-thirty p.m.)

The connection broke because you started thinking and analyzing what you were typing and also searching for the letters to type. This is a new process for you and one which you need to learn and become accustomed to. Try to type without wondering or worrying about spelling. Let it flow to you naturally. Don't look at what you are typing on the screen. Trust that it will all make sense when you read it back and you can make any editing and adjustments at a later time. Grammatical. See that word should have been in there but came to you late and so it is good to include these words even though the actual sentence is not word perfect. People will get the idea of what we are saying and trying to convey. They are not that stupid and can put two and two together and work it out for themselves. Also we are not trying to spoon-feed people but to only convey an idea that they may not have thought of, a different perspective on things so that they can see a bigger picture that is their whole lives. Seeing things from a whole life perspective and this way they can weed out the unimportant and only concentrate on the important things and what is best for their Higher good and for them to move forward with their lives towards their life's purpose. So looking at the grander scheme of things as to what is important for them to know right now at this moment for their Higher good and advancement towards *Light and Being.*

(Pause, I take a breather.)

Good it is good to take a pause every now and then and re center yourself. Especially in the beginning when this is all new and you are not practiced at it. As with all things perfection will come with time. But remember it is not perfection that we are after but merely an opportunity to state our case and to help you earthlings out so that you may advance your souls. You are doing a wonderful job and you make us very proud. You have touched us too as we have you and your tears honor us. This really is incredulous isn't it? Who could have thought that it was even possible that we could communicate with you like this? You are an advanced soul. One of many. As for Hoyan you are a leader of the Light Beings and you will show people the way. What is possible, how it is possible and how they can do it for themselves and others also.

Q. But I still feel like a fake and I wonder is it all coming from my imagination?

Remember your fingers are barely able to keep up the typing with the speed of our words. I'm sorry but the human brain does not work that fast it is almost impossible. If your brain did work that fast then you would be superhuman and you are special but not that special. Yes all and anyone can do this, not just you. As previously discussed it is a letting go of the mind and ego to allow other worldly communication to come through and flow to you. Thus as long as people can let go of the mind so they can do this too.

Ask another question.

(I get the sense this is what I should do if I get 'stuck' or lose connection.)

Ok I spoke to Raven Owl this morning and told her I'm going to the Psychic expo tomorrow. I really want to sit with and have a reading with this spirit guide artist but can't afford it. I'm sick of being constantly in survival mode. This would give me great pleasure if I could see her.

Q. Will my finances ever change?

Ah this just now has been a good exercise. Notice how when you were speaking your typing slowed right down as you thought about what you wanted to say and ask. Whereas when I am talking there is no thought involved and you are just typing as fast as you can to keep up with me. This is how you know it is not you speaking and it is me. There is a vast change and I mean a very vast difference in the speed of the conversation. Thought only serves to slow you down, as there is analyzing going on. When I communicate with you, you are able to empty your mind of all thought and therefore analyzing and the words flow at great speed, you are not even thinking about what is being typed but just madly typing like one possessed. It is rather funny too for us to watch actually and for others it will seem quite remarkable.

To answer your question about finances. Hmm. We have had this conversation before and nothing has changed. When you are actually acting out your life's purpose you will notice great changes and all that is gold will flow to you and you will have no worries or concerns when it comes to money or how to pay your next bill etc. I understand this currently is a great source of your stress and distress and it is something that wears you down. You had a thought this morning to actually *feel* like you are already a winner, one of richness, and go about your day feeling the energy of what it would be like to have monetary abundance in your life with no concerns of how you were going to manage financially on a day to day basis. This is a good practice for what it will actually feel like in your future. You are not far away from having this feeling for real, manifested into your life. As discussed this will only come to fruition when your life's purpose is activated and the time is drawing very near.

As for the artist that you wish to see. She could not draw me or any of your other guides because we are in pure energy form which is not visible to the naked eye. That is not so say that she could not conjure up visions of other guides or that a picture is her visual interpretation of what our energy feels like to her. For example she would be able to tell if the guide feels young, old, male, female, ethnicity etc. She may ask herself does the guide have long hair, short hair, white skin, dark skin etc. until she conjures a picture in her mind that resembles that method that a forensic artist uses. Only instead of asking a person as the forensic artist does she is asking her own Higher Self or consulting with her own guides.

Some people/humans like to have a visual to work with, look at for themselves to make it real. You yourself can understand this being a visual artist. Often unless people can see, touch, hear etc. they are unsure of its existence. That is because you have all been conditioned as such and have grown up with the scientific paradigm. There is nothing wrong with this except it limits you to the physical space-time realm. Remember we are all energy, which is felt rather than seen or visualized. But having said that if a visual picture helps a person make a connection with their guide we see nothing wrong with that. There has to be a certain amount of accommodation on our part if we are to retain and maintain our connection with humans so that we may help them. What I am saying is that you do not really need to sit with this woman. You do not need to have a visual of us and if you did it would be better coming from yourself and not outside yourself. Rather we would prefer it if you *feel* us as a better way to get to know us and connect. *Feel* the *Love, Light* and *Energy* that is us and that we can pass on to you so that we may bring your vibration Higher and closer to your life's purpose as that is our aim.

And yes now that you have had success with this exercise you may start investigating the rental of a laptop, as that is the way forward for you. It is very exiting that your time is drawing ever nearer. Go know Marikai, peace to your day and my energy covets yours always.

Lightness to your Being—Nameless.

Oh my god! Thank you so much Nameless! That (typing) session was awesome! It's been a great exercise, more than I had even hoped for, I feel much blessed to have you in my life.

As I do you.

Thank you Nameless. (Time stopped, One-twenty p.m. This gives me an idea of how long it will take to channel for a client, approx. one hour)

SUN 21ST APRIL

Good morning All. Firstly I'd like to comment on the channeling I did on the computer yesterday which was awesome. I was struck be the speed of which the information came through and at times I was struggling to keep up it was so fast but was excited that it worked so well given it was the first time I had used this method. When I get a laptop I'll have more freedom to channel elsewhere, with clients and down by the lake. Now that I know this flows easily I'll head off today in search of a rental. I'd dearly love a private room to work from but they're all out of my price range. I saw a tiny shop for lease in Eumundi the size and shape of my hallway and they wanted three hundred and fifty dollars a week for it. Outrageous!

I went to the Psychic expo yesterday and bought myself another pendulum, a beautiful transparent green fluorite that has a gorgeous glow and I knew I just had to have it. Is this the one, my healing pendulum? I also bought a Tsesit stone which is a prehistoric rock from the desert of Namibia in Africa, said to have great healing powers and contains star dust particles. I tucked it in my bra as I woke this morning with a bit of a toothache and already the pain has settled. There weren't any books there at all as not being at the Big Pineapple as usual they had had to downscale (I did go to the op shop later and found two books on dowsing and space clearing the latter of which had a large feather on the front cover and information on traditional Indian clearing ceremonies).

I had trouble choosing a psychic as the one who supposedly worked with the pendulum and psychometry actually seemed to be doing all tarot work as I watched him from afar. As I didn't want this and being indecisive I decided to write the list of names on a piece of paper and took it outside to consult with the pendulum. Interestingly it gave a mild yes to most of the psychics except the two I had been considering but gave a very large and profound yes to one in particular. I booked him immediately and he was free and waiting for me.

Robert was his name, he was originally from Britain and had worked with Doris Stokes but seemed to be of similar age to me. Robert told me he did not see or hear but just knew (claircogniant) and mainly channeled throughout this way, all the time holding my hands open on the table (to help open the communication channels and prevent me blocking). He absolutely blew me away with the detail he provided about my past, growing up, family dynamics, childhood and even current friendships, relationships and work etc. Robert reiterated and confirmed what Hoyan had told me, that it is my lack of confidence and courage (caused by dynamics in growing up) that holds me back and prevents me moving forward with things in my life. That if I don't work on this and learn to get over this fear (of failing, of judgment) then I will be stuck in this current way of life until my nineties! (Yes I'm going to live that long).

Basically the majority of the reading was about where this fear and lack of confidence comes from and that it's up to me to work on it, grow and step out of it if I want a better life for myself. So relating that to what I'm doing (channeling, healing etc.) but "Feel the fear and do it anyway," and this is the big message coming through to me from all aspects (Nameless, Hoyan etc.). He encouraged me to stay focused and goal oriented, staying on the path. Robert also saw a male coming into my life but said unless I change and open my heart and let down my mask it will fail just like all the others and this relates back to the lack of confidence and courage again. He mentioned bringing more fun back into my life (as did Nameless and Hoyan), fun and laughter raises your vibration and allows more good to flow to you. There was so much more and it was a very beneficial reading, one of the best I've had. At the very end he did a small tarot spread and got me to choose just one card (the Lovers!). I really liked that idea of channeling with just a small spread at the end but you would have to know the cards well to do this and as Nameless said it's just a visual link.

So mainly the message I guess is don't allow the past to affect my future, to work on my courage and confidence. To feel the fear and do it anyway or I won't change my life for the better. It also confirmed everything Nameless and Hoyan had been telling me all along giving me a greater sense of trust.

MON 22ND APRIL

Good morning. Here I am at the computer again exited to see how I manage and not really sure what I want to talk about this morning. I've been reading the book on space clearing which interests me a great deal, especially using sound intonation and instruments to change the energy and vibration of spaces and people.

Q. I'm wondering if I should offer this as a service also. Will it be well received? Is it diverting away from my life's purpose?

Yes it is inclusive with what you are trying to achieve. There is definitely a willing market for this service and I don't feel it will detract too much from what you are trying to achieve but on the contrary bring more clients to you and awaken people's perception to what it is you do. People are actually more open to having a ceremonial space clearing than they are to have personal information channeled to them. The fact that it is a long standing tradition in many cultures that is gaining popularity in western society as these cultures are embraced more and more and also people are exposed to them very frequently on their travels and hence have a greater understanding of them and their philosophy's and workings mean they will be very well received and even sought after. The cost that you propose to attach to such a ceremony will prevent it from overloading and taking over your other work. It will be at a comfortable enough pace that it is neither draining to yourself nor overwhelming your other interests. Conversely as discussed it will open up new worlds and new opportunities to you and aid in preventing boredom with too much of the other aspects that can at times be quite heavy and weigh you down. There will be many places of beauty that you will experience this way which aid in lifting your vibration also as it opens you to the possibilities available to you. You are travelling in the right direction always but it is good to question as you go so as to not be swayed from your true purpose and diverted from your goals.

Q. How does space clearing work? May I have your opinion?

Yes, of course. Space clearing is just another form of working with energy systems. You have read about the stagnant chi and how it sticks to certain areas that have a reduced flow. Energy is getting in but not allowed to flow freely and stagnates creating thick air, density and sluggishness and vibration diminishes with the weight of it all. The aim is to create a lightness of air so that the occupants and beings are not weighed down by the mire also. Energy all around you has an effect on the system as a whole. You are trying to keep your vibration raised and as high as possible at all times. This includes your place of work the people you meet and greet, the furniture and rooms you occupy, the clothes you choose to wear. All have an effect on your *being* and its ability to maintain its optimum vibration for its Highest good and communication with the etheric realm. Anything that adds weight to your being will prevent you from evolving at optimal speed. That is you may still evolve but at a very slow sluggish pace and with much hard work and difficulty. It takes a strong person to accomplish this. You are aiming towards *Lightness of Being* always and so everything around you that surrounds you must be light also as you are all connected energetically as one. Thus it is beneficial that your environments are light also, that is to say, at their highest vibration possible and this is what space clearing aids in doing. It is breaking up the mire and lifting the vibration to one of *pureness* and *Light*.

Where people struggle to accept is the invisibility of it all but those who are still enough to *feel* the energy of the place (or objects/people) will recognize a good clearing when they can *feel* the difference afterwards. Some may be more skeptical than others but the proof is in the pudding so to speak and though they might not like to acknowledge it they will feel lighter and happier within themselves.

The thing with space clearing though is that once cleared it is not always easy to maintain and eventually will be laden with thick mire again over time. This is human nature at work and is unavoidable due to the current way of living. If you all lived outdoors in nature this would be the most ideal and your beings would be cleansed on a daily basis by the wind and the sounds of the birds, the forests and the trees, the trickling of water and creeks running and the warmth of the sun on the body and the moon on the mind. All purification elements in their own right and so if you can bring these elements into your daily existence in some form or manner you would benefit greatly. This is why people flock to the beaches and the countryside where there is pureness of air, salt, and sea, coupled with nature's sound intonations. They come home feeling cleansed and refreshed, tired but re-energized. Like their batteries have been recharged. They have unconsciously space cleared themselves.

So what you are doing in their environment is no different but a clearing of the cobwebs and the muck of life and the bringing in of, summoning of, new energy to bring freshness and vitality to the situation and uplift all that dwell there and draw all that is good to it. People will be astounded by the difference it can bring into their wellbeing and lives and the word will spread. It is a good thing that you do as not a lot of people are offering this service though as with all anyone can do it but perhaps not a lot of people are themselves interested in performing such a thing.

This will add another dimension to your work. One that I feel will have positive benefits for everyone involved. You may even be asked to travel to perform such ceremonies in the future. So rest assured it will be well received and you can move forward with the planning of it all.

Blessings to your day Marikai — Nameless.

Thank you Nameless.

7

MAY 2013

FRI 3RD MAY

Good afternoon Nameless. It's not very often I speak to you this late in the day so I'll have to see if channels are open.

Q. Are they open?

Yes, when you need us we are here. Just ask and we will come.

Thank you. Well I'm all excited and nervous at the same time. I haven't spoken to you for over a week and there is much to tell. I don't want to procrastinate too much longer on getting the new enterprise up and running and so I had given myself the goal of doing so by the beginning of May. I figured I had been talking about it for the last four months so time to put it all into action.

The problem was how to deliver my method to clients in a user friendly way. And so I have been researching, thinking and questioning the best way to go about this. If I rented a computer and projector as you suggested I would end up paying two thousand dollars over three years for a package worth half that amount and in the end have nothing to show for it. Instead I decided to put a laptop on a twelve months interest free with payments plan so it only equates to twenty-five dollars a week and I will have it paid off in a year. The projector was the next issue as I'm trying to minimize the amount of equipment I have to lug around and as Daughter pointed out not everyone has a blank wall space to project on to. After much research I discovered that a computer with HDMI and VGA outputs and associated leads will be able to connect to any digital TV screen which ninety-nine percent of the population have. So that is what I have done... bought myself a touchscreen Ultrabook and leads. The Ultrabook is charging as we speak and after I've loaded the software I'm going to try it out on the TV. I'm crossing my fingers that it'll work and so am a lot nervous being such an ignorant technophobe.

Also I've now invested a considerable amount of money so have put my faith and trust in you all that I'm being guided in the right direction. I'm sure my friends must think I'm 'nutso' and you, my guides, are (possibly) only my 'imaginary friends.' I kind of laughed on the way home from buying the computer thinking "Well if all this proves not to be true I'll just write a book about the nutso who followed divine guidance for a year from her imaginary friends." So either way it's a win win situation.

I had to go back to the Crystal Lady to gather some extra information she left out of her initial workshop that she had promised us. As she knew I channeled she told me about a psychic fair coming up next weekend and they were looking for readers and stallholders. The stalls were only twenty dollars for the day and she asked me if I would be interested and gave me some contact details. It's an exceptional opportunity but as I haven't even practiced with the TV set up yet (I can take my small portable one with me) I feel I'm not ready or prepared enough. I don't want to take myself out in public and make a complete fool of myself. I would much rather be practiced in delivering it this way to clients first to have the confidence to take it to this level. On one hand I'm disappointed but on the other hand exited that there are opportunities out there like this which will help me get exposure.

Q. How am I doing? Any advice?

Just that as usual all is well with the Universe and you are travelling along nicely. Trust in your instincts with regards to preparedness. You are right, this is a great opportunity and one that will get you noticed even though the exposure will be small (great for your first beginnings) but it will get peoples tongues wagging and you will very much be talked about because of the uniqueness of what you have to offer which is your delivery.

It is a shame that there will be many people there on this day that would have benefited from your abilities to offer them guidance from us through you. These people will still get their guidance from different methods but perhaps in a slightly different way as to not be so concise or to the point. The fact that people can walk away with guidance in written form (verbatim) is a very useful tool as peoples memory is not always what they would like and they either hear things differently or only pick up on certain information that they are perhaps more attuned to. In this way they may miss vital information that is useful to them and come away with only a limited percentage of what was actually conveyed. Also over time memory fades and even this information starts to be forgotten as people being creatures of habit return to their old ways and patterning's. By having it in written format they can read word for word what was said. There is less interpretation involved and they can carry it with them on a daily basis to read and re-read and read again. Each time picking up something new that they missed the time before. You yourself do this as you re-read over your notes and the writings from your channels with us.

It is a very useful tool to have and one that is quite unique to share, this verbatim method. If you can pull it off and I have no doubt that you will it will benefit a great many people. Not only those that come to you for guidance but also their friends, family and colleagues who will benefit secondarily from that guidance. So there is a ripple effect going on. You may see ten clients but effect many more lives during the process. Similar to the butterfly effect. See this as your input to the greater good of all mankind. You will touch many people over the years but effect many more thousands that you and they are totally unaware of. Thus in this respect you have an important job to do and a great purpose in life. One that is not to be shown any disrespect as it comes with a great deal of responsibility and so you are right not to jump the gun and go out in public until you feel the time is right and you are ready beyond reasonable doubt, taking into consideration that there will always be nerves and this is normal.

It is because you have respect for what you do and your clients that you are nervous because you want to do the right thing by them. Also because a lot of it is out of your control there will always be a nervous aspect there for you. You do not know what we will say or convey but simply have to put your trust and faith in us that we will be there for you. This will start to abate the more practice you have with clients and you see that we never let you down.

I understand that in the beginning it will be quite nerve wracking for you. You can have absolute faith that I and the others will always have something to say, some advice that we can pass on in any given situation even if it is one you are not confident in yourself. Ask and you shall receive, always. Call and we will be there, always. We are here to help, not only you but many who are seeking useful guidance for the betterment of their lives and those around them. We are here to help and to help heal and raise your vibration so that you may all experience life like you have never before and in ways you have yet to even understand and comprehend. Always aiming to reach you Higher to your full potential and as you travel there, guide you along the way so the path be a smoother one than if you attempted it alone. We also aim to speed up this process by guiding you to what is important and worthy of your concern and what is not worthy and so easily discarded from your lives so that you are more free to pursue Higher goals. This is the aim always and all advice is based around this…raising your vibration towards pureness of *Light and Being,* back to *The Source of All and One Kind.*

We are happy with your progress. Don't get too caught up with time lines. As long as you are moving forward and in the right direction you are travelling well my friend.

We look on with honor and pride and we are always watching over you, always by your side. Ask and we will help, always — Nameless.

Thank you Nameless.

Your (rental) suggestion did get me thinking along those lines though towards a successful outcome (rent to buy) and as also suggested I didn't just follow blindly but did my own investigation and trusted my intuition.

Yes and thus the suggestion fulfilled its intended purpose.

SUN 4TH MAY

I've been getting the name Teku (Tek-oo) coming to me periodically over the last few weeks but have chosen to brush it aside however this morning it was very persistent and wouldn't leave me alone waking me at some ungodly hour, this name constantly calling out to me. As I'd gone to bed very late I was still sleepy and in no mood to channel but he was talking anyway and I had to ask him to stop and wait till later as I wanted to write what he was saying down, basically who he is, where he comes from and what his purpose is. Really, another one? I'm starting to think I could have multiple personality disorder after all, LOL! When I finally woke up I asked how many guides are there and was given the number seven. I'm not sure if that includes planetary guides which Teku tells me he is.

Q. Anyway Teku I'm awake and ready, thanks for your patience. Can you repeat what you told me this morning, where you come from and your purpose?

Yes finally you answer. It is true I have been knocking on the door for quite a while waiting for you to answer. I wanted to alert you to my presence. I am Teku. I am Warrior. A planetary guide from Aotearoa, proudly Maori I stand big and strong. I am your protector, your body guard. Think of me as both shield and sword, deflector of all that may harm you both physically and psychically. My uncle held you in his arms once, you have the family photos.

(My mum does, it's of my sister and I as young kids tucked under each arm of a Maori dressed in tribal regalia.)

You can see the care and protection and joy on his face at the connection and great honor to be with you. It was at this moment he assigned me as your protector, your armor to watch over you through life and to keep you safe from harm's way. Remember the car in London's Piccadilly Circus?

(The driver had a heart attack at the wheel and mounted the curb nearly running me over.)

Its direction was slightly nudged so as to just miss you and even though you were aware and jumped out of the way remember how *time* seemed to slow down during the incident or as you recalled it afterwards? Well there was *actually an adjustment of time made* as well as *the physical adjustment of the car*. Though I did not interfere with time, this came from another source and gave you a chance to move out of the way. So while time around you slowed down, you did not and by stepping through the space time continuum you were able to remove yourself from danger and harm's way. You see, you are never alone, you are always being watched over and I guard and shield you with my physical and psychic being. Think of me being similar to the Buddha that enshrouds you in your white room scenario so that you feel safe and at peace and harmony.

Q. So why do you come to me now?

Because you are open. I have witnessed your discussions, I can see the direction you are heading. You would not have been ready to meet me earlier, perhaps would have baulked at the idea and I don't take ridicule lightly. Also mostly I am like the sleeping giant, sitting quietly and dormant but always with one eye open and ready to spring into action when required. However it is time that we met and I am honored to speak with you. I want you to know that you have nothing to fear. That I will not allow harm to come your way and so you can be assured that the journey and path you choose to travel will be a safe one. We are all a part of this journey with you. Our aim is the same as yours, that you reach *Lightness and Being* and take as many people as you can along the way. Thus I have been given a very important assignment to protect with much courage, strength and valor but also a pureness and tenderness of heart as it is this tenderness towards you that would see me stand up to the greatest of harm's way in order to keep you safe. Call upon me at any given time. Know that I stand guard over you and you walk safe upon the earth.

Yunga tunga — Teku… Warrior.

Q. Who is Teku? What does your name mean? What is it like where you come from?

Teku is descendant of chiefs. It means '*Great warrior of all time.*' Though not a chief myself my uncle is one of many chiefs and assigned me head warrior. As head warrior I sit in meetings with the other chiefs and my voice is just as strong and my ideas and thoughts often consulted. It is my position to ensure the safety of all the members of the tribe, something I do very well so my uncle chose wisely. Often these days trouble comes mostly within our own community so not only do I stand strong against external enemies I am also a peacemaker. I live by the ocean with my wife and children who are young and run free on the sand. I communicate with the whales as they travel by and whilst I am there in that setting I am also here with you. So like you I am of more than one world, one life. Both of equal value to me.

Thank you Teku it was nice to meet you and it's an honor to have you with me.

Stand strong — Teku, Warrior.

Q. What does Yunga tunga mean?

Stand strong with courage, be safe or safety be with you.

It seems Teku answered my question before I even asked it but cognition takes time in our world so it's quite possible the guides know what we are going to say even before we do! My new affirmation..."I am strong, courageous, brave and fearless!"

TUE 7TH MAY

Good afternoon everyone. I'm so excited because here I sit on my new laptop and I have connected it to the TV with a HDMI cable which was much easier than I thought it would be. I have bought myself a five meter cable so am sitting some distance away and If I had a client here they would be sitting on my nice comfortable lounge with a cup of tea reading what I'm typing on the TV while I'm typing it on the laptop. Yippee! This is awesome and going to be so much better than lugging a projector around.

I went to Lotus Light yesterday and had a sound meditation, a Reiki and a foot massage, awesome. I slept so well last night I actually slept in this morning and had to ring up work and take the day off. Too much stress to try and get in there and then I would've been stressed all the time I was there trying to catch up. I do feel so guilty though leaving them in the lurch like that.

I took my girlfriend with me to Lotus Light and while I was waiting for her treatment to finish a lady entered who said she did angel card readings and were they looking for any one? Yes and they had put their prayers out for readers. After having heard this I discussed with them what I'm doing and the possibility of me channeling there also. They seem keen and as it's only on a voluntary basis I could possibly do once a month to gain public experience. I can spend as long as I like with each client so it's very relaxed and laid back. I told them I was still in the process of setting up the electronics and then I would like to put it into practice first to know that everything was running smoothly. Basically now I have this up and running I'm ready to see my first client.

Q. Any comments or advice? And please identify yourself.

Yes it's Hoyan. I have been watching the shenanigans from afar and with much amusement. The trouble you humans have to go to, to communicate with each other, I really feel for you. But having said that you are travelling very well my friend and have everything well thought out and planned. It is good that you intend to practice with those familiar with you before taking it out to the general public on a large scale. It is very different doing a one on one in the comfort of your lounge room or theirs compared to going to a large gathering with all its disturbances. Yes noise is a big issue for you as I understand because of your acute hearing you prefer the peace and quiet. The ear plugs you have been thinking about will be good and can be added to your shopping list along with the case.

There was a reason you slept in this morning. One, you are meant to get this up and running as soon as possible so you would have been very tired after work and chosen not to do it. Also I feel something may have occurred at work had you been there that could have seen you blow your top and put you in a precarious position. You are not ready to leave work just yet. This time will come soon enough as you slowly build up the new enterprise over the next six months. Then one day you will realize that you can survive without it and you will be full steam ahead. Meanwhile you will be trying out many scenarios until you find the one that fits and best suits you. This may take a while and cannot be rushed.

Do not be disheartened if things do not go as planned in the beginning. Life does not always run smoothly that way but remember each step is one closer to your goal and there will be people you meet along the way that can help and guide you. Sometimes we have to try out these things before we can think or look in different and new directions. Don't expect too much from yourself in the beginning and don't run before you can walk. Pace yourself nice and comfortably in the beginning so as not to overwhelm and also to ensure that you have enough stamina and energy to do the job well. It is good that you are looking after your health and feeling much better.

Congratulations on losing the five kilo's, it is time to start including some exercise regularly and get out doors in the fresh air. Bush walking would be good now that the weather has cooled down and being in nature is always healing, there can never be enough of it. Perhaps a visit with Marikahee while you are out there. She is awaiting your visit.

Q. I'm getting blockages. Information is stopping and starting. What's going on? I'm scared if this happens when I'm with a client, what will I do?

You're parched. Have a drink of water.

I did, thank you.

Water is a conductor of energy which our communication with you is. Therefore it is important to keep your water levels up. Make sure you have a good supply of water with you when seeing clients. Also try not to be too impatient or scared as this will only serve to put up a wall and block communication. If information stops flowing. Ask another question, or change direction. Ask if we are finished. We do not always have a book to write each time. Sometimes it is short concise information that is the best, getting to the point and not offering too much so as to confuse the person or give them too much to work with at any one time. You would do well to remember this when dealing with clients. Often they will expect a lot, more than you can give. It is up to you to explain to them how the process works. Hopefully the wise will work on what they are given before returning for more information and guidance. Those that are deeply interested in the process will seek out a way of communicating for themselves. Some will just need a little bit of support and guidance for a short time to get them through a difficult process. You are there only to translate information and not push them one way or the other. We provide the information and then the person exerts free will. It is up to them from there what direction they choose to travel. Remember your humbleness always and leave ego at the door. But if any one criticizes what you do they are not normally open to reason and it is best to walk away at the earliest time possible. You will meet a few of these along the way. Do not be offended, they are just less ready than you, but be prepared to handle the situation in the gentlest and kindest way possible. These people are more of ego and have difficulty seeing through this. To try to explain your way will only make them angry. Those that show genuine interest are the ones who are open and more ready. These are the ones that you should concentrate on in the beginning as you are not yet equipped to deal with the other. Thus you have plenty to go on for today or you yourself will be feeling overwhelmed.

Lightness and Being to your soul and spirit — Hoyan.

Thank you Hoyan.

THURS 9TH MAY

Good morning. I'm sitting on my bed having just connected the laptop to my small portable T.V. This is the T.V I'll use if I go to Lotus Light or have my own practice room somewhere. It is so small, light and easy to set up. Such a better idea than using a projector which I'd only need to use now if I was doing a channeling for a group of people. Everything seems to be going to plan and I could be up and running as early as the end of next week.

I've committed myself to the children's art workshop next Tuesday and have some preparation for that which is sidelining me a bit and I wonder if it'll be worth doing on a regular basis. I might have to suspend it after this one for three months so I can give all my spare time to establishing the new enterprise. I'm practicing my channeling on the computer as much as I can but I'm a bit concerned that I do not seem to be as well connected as when I write it long hand and currently this is my preferred method. Also I normally do most of my channeling in the morning in bed while everything is quiet so I'm wondering if it is time and placement that affects it, thus this is a bit of a test this morning.

Q. Hmm a question for today... I broke the corner off my Tsesit stone when it fell out of my bra and it got me thinking. When you break or chip a crystal does it have an effect on its energetic and healing capabilities?

No, you need not concern yourself with this my learned one. It is as you thought, the energy is still there in the memory of it and as you also said if you look at it holographically then even one small atomic piece of hard matter contains the information of the whole piece or the piece as a whole. Thus the small chip or piece that broke off still contains all the information and energy the same as before as does the original stone only the area that is missing is not working as much in the solid physical dimension, is not grounded to your earth plane but is working more on an etheric spiritual level. There are many comparisons I can give you.

Think of the plant that has had its leaf cut or broken off. There is an initial shock to the plant and a drawing in of its energy and aura as it regroups and heals itself. Then the remaining plant offers its memory to replace the energetic memory of the piece that is missing to again become whole. Even though you can't see this on the physical plain it has been noted with Kirlian photography[1] and also those with sensitive hands would be able to feel and measure the outline of the plant and note that the leaf is still there even though invisible to the human eye. The leaf is drawing upon the information and memory from all the other individual cells contained in the plant. This leaf functions and acts as a part of the plant as normal, swaying in the breeze as normal, adjusting itself as the plant moves and even growing as the plant itself grows. The rest of the plant is acutely aware of the situation and in order to protect its wholeness and function constantly feeds this area extra energy to keep it healthy and functioning so as not to harm the rest of the plant and allow for illness and disease to occur and take it over. The plant adjusts and works harder to maintain homeostasis.

Imagine the so called dead skin cells that slough off you every day. As you know they contain the original DNA that makes you human and makes you, you. These cells if harvested and in the right and knowledgeable hands contain all the information that is required to make another you. Hence cloning. Imagine that, another you just from one cell and it is indeed possible. Well plants, crystals, rock stone, animals are all alike on an energetic level but science has not advanced thus far to replicate stones or crystals from a small microscopic piece but instead choose to copy the molecular structure.

The man who has had his leg amputated feels the so called 'phantom' pain because on an energetic level his leg is still there and indeed he will often tell you so, that he feels the sensation of the leg being there. He is correct. It is just not on the physical and earthly level and so he cannot see it. You would be able to trace its existence with sensitive hands or even your pendulum.

So to answer your question it does not matter that you have broken your stone. It's power, functioning and healing properties are the same.

Thank you Nameless. Now that I've channeled this information I'm again feeling a stronger connection. Is it because of time and place? The sanctity of my bedroom?

Yes and no. It is true you are comfortable in this space and thus more relaxed and able to let go of your daily surrounds and thoughts to quieten your mind enough such that conversation between us flows quite smoothly. You are right to practice with the computer and practice at different times of day and in different locations. The more practiced you are the easier it will be for telepathic communication to occur. It is a matter of attuning yourself, your vibration to ours and to do this you must still the mind as much as possible. If you struggle to connect with us this is usually the problem and also as Hoyan discussed keep the water levels constant to aid conduction. Also if you are tired, not feeling well or your energy levels are diminished then this will all have an effect. Thus we recommend you attend to your health on a daily basis. This includes rightful eating, fresh air and exercise, communing with nature, rest and relaxation with injections of fun also so that there is correct balance to your life and you are not feeling overwhelmed with things that may weigh you down or cause blockages to occur. You are travelling well my friend. Keep these in mind. You are aiming for balance always in every aspect of your life. Just remain aware and do what you can manage at any given time. It is not our intention to overwhelm you as this would risk you feeling like it's all too hard and giving up which we do not want you to do.

We are all proud of how far you have come and look forward to future communications with you. Lightness to your day — Nameless.

Thank you Nameless, I'm grateful always for your help and advice.

FRI 17TH MAY

Hi to All of The Circle.[2] *(Nameless, Hoyan, Teku, Marikahee and Raven Owl) I'm on the laptop in the bedroom and it's connected to the TV. I'm trying to get in as much practice this way as I can so it'll become more natural to me. It's afternoon because I've had a terrible toothache all week and took something to help me sleep and I didn't wake till noon. I'm desperate to book into a dentist. Trouble is I've just forked out about eight hundred dollars in bills and am truly skint. I never seem to be able to get ahead, there's always something that crops up. Daughter is desperate for winter clothes and at her age brands are a delicate issue so they don't come cheap. Meanwhile I'm buying mine from the op shop. I can't remember the last time I bought a pair of shoes that wasn't from BIG W, Kmart or Spend Less (at least twenty years) but I guess that's the sacrifices we make for our kids and in your world such things are irrelevant. My daughter thinks I'm a huge dag and I never thought I would be fifty and "Mumsy." I dream of the day I can afford a decent pair of shoes and a brand new coat but the reality is always that there are starving and unsheltered people in the world and I always tell my daughter how lucky we are that we have a comfortable couch to sit on, warm beds and a weekly food budget.*

I remember being a poor student with only ten dollars for food for the whole week and picking wild mushrooms from the local waterway to make an omelet hoping they weren't poisonous. Those were the days when I used to smoke and I would go out to the bus stop at midnight to pick up all the discarded ciggies off the ground, bringing them home to make 'rollies' out of them. Then when Daughter was a young toddler I used to queue up at the local Salvation Army for grocery vouchers so I could use my actual grocery money to buy her shoes. So yes I've been a lot worse off.

Well that's my vent over, sorry about that. But not having a partner, you guys are really the only ones I can let off a bit of steam with who may be vaguely interested.

Q. Any way a topic for today, as I'm drawing closer to channeling for people could you give me a list of possible questions they could ask if they come unprepared or are not sure what to ask?

Firstly, we hear your concerns regarding money and the buying of necessities. You manage very well with the little that you currently have and this is to your credit. You are not asking for anything outlandish and extravagant so do not allow the feelings of guilt associated with what it is you want. You as others are entitled to live a comfortable life and it should be so for everyone on this planet. Unfortunately that is not how things have panned out and many people suffer. Remember this always, the feelings of desperation and stress that you have had at times so that when your life becomes more fruitful you use some of these fruits to pass on to or help those that are less fortunate than yourself. If everybody of wealth did this then the world would be a much richer place not only monetarily and materially but also of love and goodwill. Thus there would be more peace in the world also as if you are done a good deed then this lifts your vibration and leaves you wanting to pass a deed on yourself. Both the giver and the receiver benefit with a lifting of their vibrations and moving closer to the experience of *Beings of Light*. Do not be afraid to ask for help or take help when offered as if you deny someone the opportunity to give a gift of time, money or service you are denying them an opportunity to lift themselves out of the mire in which many of you live. Many of those with riches and wealth are still living in poverty only it is a different type of poverty that they experience to yourself. One of spiritual poverty and a lack of love for humankind and thus themselves on a soul level. And so they are not to be envied even though they appear to live more like kings than you do, their souls are ungratified. Not all are this way but a great many as they have either forgotten what it was like to be wanting or have had no experience of it at all.

Your time of greater wealth is coming. Notice I said greater and not great. This time will see you pay the bills with more ease and you will be able to treat yourself to a few luxury items. It will be enough to take the stress and burden from you. All we ask is when this occurs please remember to give back or pass on in some way. This does not have to cost you financially but could be a gift of your time or experience such that you help another advance in life so that they too can be more comfortable and stress free. The purpose of this (stress free) is so that you humans can concentrate more on what is important for the advancement of the soul and less concentration, time and energy just trying to survive in your world as that is what most of you are doing. Just trying to survive. This takes up a great deal of your time and when you are not exerting your energy to survive you are taking a break from it in the form of relaxation through sport and activities or collapsing in front of the TV as a means of physically resting your body and mentally resting your fatigued brains. This leaves little time left for spiritual and soul growth and so you are all stuck in a cycle that is hard to escape from. We say if you can make *advancement* a priority in your life in small increments often you will see great changes occurring in your lives. You have been doing this the past few months with your commitment to channeling and your conversations with us, yet you are yet to see the benefits. We thank you for your dedication and understand the time is very near that you are to offer your services to others. As discussed previously this is when you will notice great changes in your life, both financially and in other ways. Not only will you be benefiting those you channel for but also for yourself and so it is a win win situation. This is ideal. If everybody could benefit from every interaction and situation they come across then the world would be truly shining and on a high vibratory level. This is the aim. But don't be overwhelmed. You can currently only do what you can do and touch those that you personally come into contact with. Aim to leave every person that you come into contact with feeling more uplifted or better about themselves or their lives and you will be doing a great service to your fellow man. This must come from a genuine place though in your heart. Know that everyone is a soul just like you, everyone is struggling in their own way. A kind or supportive word may be all it takes to lift ones soul vibration and send them on a new and positive path.

It's also important to take care of the self too. Do not berate yourself if you fail to recognize a situation that you could do this or cannot find it in your heart for a particular person but instead learn from it, question and try to find a way for the next time. You as others are always growing and in this way you will be making positive steps forward and this is all we ask of you. To be moving yourselves and humanity forward into positive territory for the betterment of all mankind and the benefit of the planet as a whole.

So some questions that your clients may ask are based around what we have just discussed. Here are a few suggestions…

- **How can I raise my vibration?**
- **How can I personally help raise the vibration of those around me? My friends, colleagues, family?**
- **What type of support can I offer …………? (insert name of those in need of uplifting,)**
- **What can I do now that will aid my spiritual growth towards *Lightness and Being?***
- **How can I help raise the vibration of others (that I meet)?**
- **What can I personally do right now for the betterment of mankind?**
- **What can I do for humanity as a whole?**
- **What can I do for the planet?**
- **What is my soul's purpose?**
- **What is my life's purpose?**
- **What should be my priorities right now?**
- **Is there anything important I should be attending to?**
- **Am I following my rightful path/direction? What is my rightful path/direction?**
- **Are there any changes I should make in my life? What are they?**

Ok there's some good questions here though they seem a bit heavy. The everyday person might not be ready for this. I understand that we are concerning ourselves with surviving in our current world when advancing spiritually should really be our priority. I'll try them out myself over the next few channeling sessions. Thanks for a great session today Nameless.

You are welcome my enlightened one. I am always here to guide you, always here to offer my help. It is up to the individual if they take it on board or not and what they choose to do with the information provided. Free will reigns all.

Oh and it is always a pleasure to be with you — Nameless.

□

SAT 18TH MAY

Good morning Nameless and All. I was watching Jamie Oliver's cooking show's yesterday on TV and got to thinking of what a fine example of spiritual and human being he is. This is someone who is, whether he is conscious of it or not, following both his life's purpose and his soul or spiritual purpose.

I got to thinking of those two questions that you posed yesterday. What is my soul's purpose and what is my life's purpose. I'm guessing that many people would think they are one and the same but they are not. Jamie Oliver is a good example as most people know of him and his work, and such a likeable lad to boot. I perceive Jamie's life purpose is to cook for that is his passion, what he loves to do and he has made it his life's work. You can see the joy in his face and sense the happiness he exudes at even the mere thought of what he is doing. He is like an excitable little boy opening his Xmas presents to find the long awaited for and desired train set has become his reality. His vibratory level is so high it is infectious and a joy to watch, exuding through the TV. I get as much delight from watching him as I do from learning his skills and recipes.

His soul's purpose is intertwined with his life's journey or path. It seems his soul's purpose is to pass this joyousness for food on to the world. But it doesn't stop there. In doing so he is bringing people, family and friends together in celebration of food, gathering them in to partake in all its joyous offerings in both the making of and the consuming side, resulting in a raising of vibrations both physically and psychically. His soul continues its work through educating those of less fortune than himself for example giving kids from difficult backgrounds an opportunity to learn his vocation, providing them with long term job opportunities that will see them live a better life. Educating and working with the school dinner programs to bring better awareness and nutrition to children on a large scale. These are but a few examples of how Jamie has taken his passion and love of food and nutrition out into the world to make it a better place.

Thus I see Jamie Oliver as being a highly successful role model in blending ones life's purpose with his soul's purpose. It is that win win situation you discussed. Jamie is doing what he loves most and every one he touches benefits. No wonder he is so happy.

Q. Is this what we are striving for? Will our life's purpose and souls purpose always be intertwined or can they be very different entities in their own right?

This is a good question and one well worth asking. Also you used a very good example which signifies your awareness and knowledge of the topics we are discussing. The answer is no they will not always relate to each other though you will usually find it approximately fifty-fifty or so tipping more towards the probability that they are in fact linked.

You are a prime example of it not being so linked. It is your passion and your life's aim that you be a successful working artist, enough to make a living from it. Your soul's purpose is to Heal, Teach and Guide and in doing so bringing awareness to many and raising the vibrations of many more. Therein is your struggle as the two are taking much of your time and fight for your attention. Throw in the fact that you are trying to survive and pay the bills and put food on the table and you can see the difficulties you face and the struggles you contend with. Thus it is a matter of prioritizing and good planning so that you can move forward and accomplish both. It may be that you have to sideline one temporarily and concentrate on the other to manage it effectively to a point where it is managing itself and you can then re-introduce the other. I feel you are doing this already and have toned down the desire to produce art so that the new enterprise is your focus. In this respect you are travelling well and draw nearer to your initial goals.

I am aware of your sadness for your lack of time for your art and it being necessary to take a back seat, as indeed it is an all-encompassing passion of yours. Know that it is only temporary. It may not return to you fully for a year or two but what you are doing now will see you have more time for it in the future than you would ever have had otherwise.

You may consider a way that unites the theme of both, you know what I am talking about, art more along spiritual lines. I feel there will eventually be a happy marriage between the two. For now your soul's purpose is your priority. You are not purely being driven by us but by your *knowing* that it is the right thing to do. Thus for your great sacrifice we think you are very brave.

For someone like Jamie things are much easier because his soul and life's path are linked. For you and others in your position, the strive for balance and harmony requires more energy, attention and sacrifice. The rewards however will be worth it if one can stay focused and goal oriented, always checking that one is staying on the path.

Q. So am I right in thinking that your life's purpose is more work or passion based, making your passion your work and your soul's purpose is more spiritually based? What you can do for the planet and humanity?

Yes and no. It is not indelibly so. For example a person's life purpose could be making a good home life for their family, providing a safe and loving environment for their own souls to be able to grow exponentially. While the souls purpose could be uplifting the vibrations of people they come into contact with in the most simplest of way's, a smile a gesture or merely their infectious presence aka Jamie Oliver. It is just them being them that is fulfilling the goal. Neither need be complex or dramatic as it is the small amounts frequently that can have the most impact.

Conversely someone may have a huge passion for (example) conservation that becomes both their life's journey and their souls purpose combined. Each is an individual and each should be measured on its own merit. Neither life's' purpose or souls purpose can be boxed into any one definition. You will learn this more as you channel for people and hear the answers given to their questions regarding thus. It is these answers given over a period of time that will help you better define the two and indeed as for Jamie you will find that often the two are one.

I must say that it is good that you analyze and question. We are happy that you do not take information blindly but go away and ponder and question the self for answers and guidance also. The more you do this, the more trust you will gain in the self that you possess more knowledge than you initially thought. As you gain your own trust more and more you will become your own first port of call. In this we guide you.

Pleasure to your day my friend. Always by your side — Nameless.

Thank you Nameless.

FRI 31ST MAY

Hi All. It's been a while since I've spoken to you as I've had dramas with my teeth. As you know I was in pain and booked into the dentist. It turns out I was in need of two root canals with crowns also and was quoted five thousand dollars to fix the two teeth! There's NO WAY I could afford to do that so had the one that was giving me pain removed. I could tell my dentist was disgusted that I wouldn't spend the money to save the tooth as this is always their aim. After I made my decision he could barely speak to me and was really rude.

I'm so upset at the fact that even though I'm working I'm living on the poverty line and cannot afford to fix my teeth. Someone on a dentist's salary has no idea how hard it is on minimum wage and a single mum to boot. Now I have to try to come up with two and a half thousand to save the other one if I can. I have had another weeks' worth of pain since having it out and am grieving and sad for the loss. Devastated really. Then I tell myself to get a grip and there are people in the world with lost limbs and I feel empathy for how enormous that would be yet they go about their lives full of positivity. Amazing.

As I was in pain I couldn't channel or organize the new enterprise so allowed myself to be waylaid by an online art competition. A tattoo design challenge. I had three days of solid work to meet the deadline and feel like I'm on an adrenaline high from it and am struggling to calm down, feeling very nervous and highly strung.

Floating Land starts today so ten full days of wonderful art, workshops, performances, installations and opportunities to photograph. I asked the pendulum a while back if I would weigh sixty kilo's by this date and it confirmed it to be true. I weighed myself this morning and was sixty point one so that is the lowest I have been for the last two years. I'm halfway to my goal and only another five kilo's to go. I went to my girlfriends and practiced connecting my laptop to her TV with great success. Now I'm ready to offer my first free channelings to a few locals before I go public.

Q. Using your suggested questions.... What should my priorities be right now? Are there any changes I should make in my life? What are they?

Firstly we understand the difficulties you have faced in the last few weeks and have watched your bravery. You often feel alone when facing these things but understand that you are not alone as we are always with you. We heard your call for help whilst sitting in the dentist chair but you were too distressed to really feel our presence when you needed to feel physical arms of comfort around you. It was hard for us to watch on when you, our charge, were under such duress. This is where an earthly partner is at its most valuable. To feel the physical warmth and caring on your earthly plane that we cannot provide. In this area you are lacking and it adds to your pain as you struggle through life facing such diversities seemingly alone and I say seemingly because we are always with you but cannot always provide what you need at such a time.

Yes there are others worse off and recent events opens you up to being more compassionate for your fellow man that is forced to face more difficulties than yourself. It is an awareness that you would do well to carry with you always in every day and every meeting with others that you have as you never know the underlying situation of what a person that you are communing with is going through. Most people are quite reserved when it comes to such things and unless it is a physical deformity that you can obviously see you never know the pain that someone could be going through due to an invisible ailment. Thus be compassionate and kind to your fellow man always and always trying to find ways to uplift their energy and leave them smiling or feeling good about themselves if even in the smallest way possible.

You are right to delay the second tooth. There may be opportunities that arise that could save it from the fate of the one you've just had removed. Delay it for as long as possible until it can wait no longer. This is not a promise or a prediction but a possibility, a likelihood that given the right opportunities and the right choices your circumstances may change early enough to save it. But then again it may not, it is up to you and the path you take. This is not to say that if you lose the tooth that you are to blame but that you chose a different path for reasons that may not be immediately revealed or learned from. Pain is a strange motivator and can cloud judgment and again this is where a second person who is able to think more clearly can provide thoughts on alternative pathways. What we are trying to say is we think you would benefit greatly if you were to find a partner that you could share your life with and while it may not be high on your priorities list right now it is certainly worth entertaining in your mind, what it is you would like in a partner and how you would ideally like your life in the future to be. Think about your best outcome how you would like to see the manifestation be, your perfect life scenario. Then this is what you should be aiming for.

You, as do all people, deserve the most perfect life possible and it is this deserving aspect that people struggle with. Look at those who are a great success both financially, family and relationship wise who are then free to spread the love and benefits to their fellow man. You think of such greats as Bill Gate's and others but only because they are high profile people that you know of. There are many other unsung heroes' with less notoriety who offer the world bountiful gifts, sometimes of money and wealth, sometimes of experience and skill. They all have a commonality, they *believe* that they, their families and others are *deserving* of the best life has to offer. You and all others have the opportunity on a daily basis to offer your gifts. Offer what you currently have. Do not worry that you are not full of monetary riches for yourself or others for you have much more to offer. If you come into great wealth then great, spread it around, the more the merrier but don't deny the opportunity to offer the gift's that you already contain up to your fellow man.

Q. What gifts are you talking about?

Love, compassion, kindness, which all come in many forms and many demonstrations. There are many ways to show love, many ways to show kindness. They don't have to be grandiose and can be executed in the mildest of way's to be barely noticed but with great effect especially if they are executed continually by many and accumulatively they grow into something grandiose after all.

Sometimes it is the littlest seed that can bear the greatest fruit. Think of yourself as the gardener of life. Dropping little seeds everywhere that will one day grow into a big beautiful orchid able to feed the whole of humanity, how grandiose is that? Yet all you did was drop a little seed everywhere you went. If everyone behaved the same the earth would be in full bloom and looking like Nirvana.

Currently you are doing what you can. You bring a little joy into your charges lives every day even without knowing. It is those little gifts of kindness that you share that can help make or break some one's day. Remember the dentist and how rude he was to you because you can't afford to save your tooth. He would do well to have more compassion and show more kindness to make it less stressful for you. He has lost that power. Always remember the difference a little bit of empathy, compassion and kindness can make to someone's day/circumstances. Live by example but not by preaching. Soon the seeds you sow will be much bigger and more frequent. You are heading that way following your rightful path and travelling well my friend, always forward and in a positive direction.

We are glad you are feeling better. Joy be with your day — Nameless.

Thank you Nameless.

8

JUNE 2013

SAT 1ST JUNE

Good morning everyone. I had plans to go to Floating Land workshops today but it's raining and miserable, I hope it clears up for the opening ceremony tonight. Over the next week I plan to contact the three I want to read for and write a pamphlet regarding what exactly clairaudience and channeled guidance is for those that are uninitiated. I remember seeing a list on a website somewhere explaining what it is (and more importantly what it isn't) which I thought would be great for clients so they know what to expect in a channeled reading. I'm not sure if I could find it again.

Q. Can you help me out and provide me with any info or a list, a definition of channeled guidance?

Your right it is indeed a good idea. As you are aware we do not offer predictions unless we see it as absolutely imperative for the person's future growth aspect. The world is full of possibilities and you humans possess free will. The slightest move in any direction can dramatically change the course of one's life and this we have no control over. Instead we offer advice regarding current situations, struggles, perplexing anomalies and indecisiveness. Bringing into awareness the possibilities open to a given person during these times and times of difficulties. We remind and can provide a bigger picture of what is developing and going on. Alerting them to the whole life scenario and helping put things in perspective. What is important? What needs their attention the most or more of, what should be addressed and others that are not worth their time, input or energy. So we can help the person focus on what is necessary and important for their spiritual growth and moving forward towards *Lightness and Being*, not just for them but for the betterment of mankind as a whole. So we do not just look at their own personal situation but what is the best possible outcome for the whole of the planet, for them and for everybody and this is our aim. Often you will find that by addressing their own personal issues it frees up their spirit and soul for them to be able to have enough time and energy on their hands to give more to the outside world in general (outside of themselves).

Your society is very concerned with the self but this is partly due to circumstances of trying to survive, the lost aspect of (tribal) community and the importance of family. You are no longer living as one entity as tribes tend to do but have separated and herein lies a majority of your problems. There is a lack of nurturing and support that has been lost and so your souls are feeling lost also. It is therefore our aim and time for humans to start the *Unification process*. By addressing their current issues and bringing things back into alignment they will sense an opening up to humanity as you are sensing at this moment in time. It is a gentle and slow process. Many will ask the purpose to their lives and *Unification* is possibly one of the major desirables amongst the many purposes possible for each individual. Your purposes may not marry with another's but Unification is a common purpose amongst all. Therefore we aim to bring you closer to Unification, closer to *Lightness and Being* and to do this it is necessary to help resolve current issues and problems that are preventing you from seeing the bigger picture, the whole life scenario and the whole world aspect. In this we guide you.

Q. What about a list of what you don't do?

You will become more aware of this the more you channel and transfer information to others. Each of us has our own area of expertise so I cannot speak for everyone as a whole. If there is information that you require and it is for the betterment of yourselves, mankind and the planet as a whole then this will be provided with ease. If not you may be guided otherwise. But generally we do not provide you with the *whole* answer but merely guide and prompt and bring into awareness so that you have more information to garnish from to base decisions on for yourselves. So we refrain from dictating to you outright as decisions are always better coming from the self. We also encourage you to question what we say and check in with your Higher selves, if it feels right for you. We do not suggest you blindly follow our guidance but first make sure that it makes sense to you and is of sound properties. We are not dictators, merely guides that is what we do. Guide. Ultimately the decisions are in your hands. You are the masters of your own lives.

By the way, the list has been bookmarked on your iMac.[1]

Thanks Nameless. I think I'll add it to this and together they should provide a good understanding of clairaudience and channeled guidance.

You're most welcome. Pleasure to your day as always — Nameless.

MON 10TH JUNE

Hi All. I've been having the most interesting time at Floating Land over the past ten days and thought I'd tell you about a couple of experiences that are relevant to energy vibrations and possibly channeling. Even though I know you are with me always and therefore present with whatever I'm experiencing I thought we could have a discussion regarding what I learnt and compare perspectives on things.

The art piece I was looking most forward to was an installation piece by local artist Lenni Semmelink[2] of hydrophones attached to trees on the foreshore of Lake Cootharaba. The hydrophones revealed the naturally occurring internal sounds of the trees as well as the external sounds of the environment emitted through the trees. I have to tell you it was amazing! I'm glad I went down to the night session as the immediate environment was largely devoid of human input allowing natures wonder to shine through.

Lenni had been to this site a few weeks before and prerecorded external sounds being picked up by the trees and also the internal sounds of the trees. She told me she had tried different times of day and night and kept getting noise disturbances such as helicopters (courtesy of the training air strip nearby). Finally she was able to get a recording at three a.m. one morning that was pure trees and natural environment. The resulting record was that you could hear what the tree hears (Do trees hear?). The wind being blown through the leaves, the water lapping at the shores, insects crawling around both on them and underneath their bark and water being drawn up the center of the tree through their root systems (resulting in a drawing, popping sound like sucking bubbles up through a straw). The clicking and croaking of bugs under the trees bark sounded very frog like as they went about their business. I'm guessing you would get very different sounds depending on the time that you recorded, day or night.

The hydrophone equipment recording all of this was buried beneath the trees base amplifying the sounds and vibrations that are outside of the normal human hearing frequency. I stood amongst the centians on this cool moonlit night soaking in the sounds emitted through the speakers hanging in the branches and pondered the significance of this. That there is all this going on that we can't normally hear, that is beyond our frequency, confirms to me that it's also most likely there is visual imagery that we can't see because it is beyond our normal range of visual perception. So just because we can't see (or hear) the different dimensions doesn't mean they're not there. I wish some naysayers had had this experience to open their eyes (and ears) to what they refuse to see (or hear).

Both are senses, therefore the same could be said for touch etc. I remember feeling my deceased father hold my hand once during a particularly stressful time for me. I was sitting on a train and he held my hand all the way to work, it was very comforting.

I was blessed to be the only one here at this installation at this time, the majority of the township witnessing a performance up at the Apollonian Hotel.[3] *Knowing this was a once off opportunity to take in the full installation undisturbed I allowed myself time to bathe in the whole experience which was very womblike and comforting, I didn't want to leave. I'll have to ask Lenni if I can get a digital copy of the recording. It would be great for meditation, de-stressing and soothing to sleep etc.*

After a long while soaking in the calming sounds of nature Lenni passed me some headphones that were connected to the trees in real time. She told me to tap the tree, scratch its bark and stamp my feet on the ground to hear the effect on and through the tree. Wow. The ramifications! The effect we humans have on trees and plant life without realizing it. The impact we have on our surrounding environment, the plants, the birds and fish etc. (depending on their sensitivity and ability to hear certain frequencies). How loud it is for the tree, our footprints as we walk by and I thought of all the children that had been down on the foreshore that day running, laughing and playing. Lenni told me about the detrimental affect the sounds from power boats on the lake had on the fish and marine life. It was a real eye (and ear) opener and I'm forever grateful for the experience.

I stayed as long as I could immersing myself in the whole experience but the crowds were starting to arrive. The performance at the Apollonian must be over.

Q. Do trees have feelings and emotions?

It reminded me of a book I once started to read at University but never got to finish. I wish I could remember the title. "The Secret Life of Trees,"? I'll have to Google it because now I'm fascinated.

(Having since Googled it's actually "The Secret Life of Plants."[4])

Q. Any perspectives?

Yes and this excites us. It is as you have been thinking since this day/evening that you will strike up your own conversations with the trees or centians as you like to call them. But it will be in your own manner and form. As you think you will start out with dowsing methods and speak to them this way. As you become more and more attuned to them the conversation will shift such that you hear the trees in a similar manner as you do us. In this way you will start building relationships with the trees and a few in particular. As suspected they are very wise and will have much to tell you and share. You will be astounded. The information they provide will be explosive.

From these conversations and experiences you will grow exponentially in a vast array of areas, not just spiritually but also botanically and more. The centians are great quiet observers and have much time to think, ponder and analyze the ways of the world. They communicate with each other and their surrounds partly by spreading their experience and wisdom through their seeds and discarded leaves but also their memory/thought that is carried on the wind. Thus they are great travelers and deceive with their supposed steadfastness. They are much much more than they seem and are highly knowledgeable.

The book you are thinking of would be well worth searching out as it is very comprehensive, loaded with research and analytical detail more than I can offer you here right now as that would be a book in itself. Just know that this book would benefit you greatly and send you in new directions of discovery opening up a whole new world and a whole new world of possibilities also.

What you learn you will eventually share with others taking them on adventures of discovery. You will not only communicate with trees from your area but once comfortable in your methods will branch out (excuse the pun) further afield and even use it on your travels. At this stage I cannot tell if it is for this reason you travel (your communication with trees) or if you simply choose to communicate while you are travelling for other purposes. I feel they will be somehow intertwined. I know you have already thought of sharing with others this communication once you have gained enough experience and if that is what you want it will be so.

Do not concern yourself too much with the botany sides of things that you are not an expert in that field. This is not necessary as everybody has their own area of expertise and one cannot know all and everything all at once. They have their area and you have yours and everyone can benefit from sharing with each other as you have just benefited from Lenni who was previously shown by someone else and so you all grow.

We are so excited to see this happen that we along with the centians will help guide you along the way, at least until you are confident with communing by yourself. So if you get stuck at all or are blocked in any way ask us what to do. As with anything it is important just to begin and let things develop naturally. Make sure your energy is right before attempting communication. It is very similar to talking to us. You must be well, well rested, hydrated and able to quiet the mind. Record your findings as you do with us. It will aid in your growth, give you reference for the future and you can watch your development. There will be useful insights and it will also make for interesting reading for third parties.

Go now and make plans to visit your first tree when this abysmal weather clears. There is one on the foreshore that you wish to speak to but fear others observing so go to Paradise Beach or the shores of The Valley of The Snakes and visit your first tree there. The right one will summon you. Take paper and pen and record everything. Report back your findings.

That is all — Nameless.

Thank you Nameless.

THUR 13TH JUNE

Good morning All. I'm in need of some help and advice.

The last few days I have been at work. Today I've taken a sick day, the reason being I was so angry and distressed I couldn't bear to go to work in such a state.

Working under the instruction of management and a change in resident's routines, I was yelled at by a resident who was (understandably) not happy with the changes. It seems we, the PC's (A.I.N's), being the ground staff bear the consequences of such changes. I work my butt off at that job. It's extremely stressful and we're all under such time pressure trying to please everyone across all levels of the facility all of the time (residents, RN's, management, family). The job pays barely above minimum wage. I literally wipe arses for a living! These people have been abandoned by their families and we're looking after them, you think they would be just a little bit grateful. It's distressing to be yelled at when we are all doing our best to help the residents whilst complying with management instructions. This resident knew I was following orders yet chose to take it out on me anyway, yelling her abuse. I was left absolutely seething and angry, in tears almost and wanted to walk out right then but chose instead to take today off. The problem is I'm still seething with anger and can't get it off my mind. I feel highly stressed and anxious. I'd love to just up and quit but I'm tied to this job to pay the bills.

Q. How can I get over this anger?

Firstly even though you don't want to hear this you must empathize with these residents. It is not all about you. Yes their families are unable for different reasons to look after them. To say they have all been abandoned is untrue and harsh. Some find themselves in a predicament where they have no choice and you should try to be more understanding. Most days you are and give a great deal of your time and energy to your charges, even becoming attached to a few in particular.

The issue is one of wear and tear. You are being worn down by the hours (your dislike for getting up at four thirty in the morning) and the physical and emotional strain and stress you are under. It is time for you to take a break, a holiday and this would refresh you enough to manage a little longer. It is true you are not long for this job. It is not for you. You are destined for greater things. Helping people in a much larger way on a much larger scale you could not possibly imagine. But it will be a much more enjoyable experience for you. One where you get great joy and passion from. One more suited to your constitution and energy levels at this stage of your life. It is unfortunate that where you currently work attracts people of a "Certain age" who themselves are starting to wear down physically and emotionally. The younger ones would carry the job with less guilt and worry and this is a down fall of yours, is that you do care and do worry and bring it home with you. What to do about it? Well when this happens as discussed first see from the other person's perspective. What it would be like living in their situation having to ask for bathroom assistance every time they wanted to go and for those that are cognitive enough the humiliation they would feel. It does not diminish the hurt/pain that you feel for being yelled at however and so this we need to address. Talking with us helps and yes they do need to have an onsite counsellor for staff to debrief but money is the issue there.

If you had a bath I would say go soak in it but your mind would still wander and it is the mind that needs healing. Options are keeping the mind busy with things that bring you joy. A movie, shopping, flicking through your art books, a trip to the gallery etc. but more than that we recommend you work on forgiving yourself and this resident for whatever part you both played in the outburst. A healing meditation for yourself would be good, do a distant healing for her. As you don't have a picture write her name down above a human outline and go through and rebalance all her chakras. Both of your auras have been disturbed during this energy exchange and so they could be worked on also. Once you have done this you will be feeling much better about yourself and also your next meeting with this resident.

Take a walk in nature also, sit amongst the centians for a while. Ask one of them for a healing energy transfer. Sound therapy is also good. Play your crystal bowl CD nice and loud in the house for a quick retune of your vibration. All of these things will help bring you back into alignment. As you do these a few more may come to mind. Write these down for the benefit of yourself and others to use at times of such stress, anger and anxiety.

As a last word this happened for a reason. To spur the new enterprise on, to move you forward into newer more positive directions. For this be thankful. You will not be long for this job. Six months tops so take some comfort in knowing this. But only you can take action in your life for change to occur. It is time to change now. You are on the precipice of your new and wonderful life. There is much joy coming your way. START NOW.

Forever watching and guiding over you — Nameless.

Wow, that channeled through fast and you are always such a great help. You're right. I'm tired, worn out and overdue for a holiday. This probably wouldn't have affected me so greatly and I would've been more empathetic and less harsh in my judgment if I wasn't so drained. I'm grateful always for your level headedness, help and advice. Thank you Nameless.

SAT 15TH JUNE

I was doing the dishes this morning and wondering about my first clients, what kind of questions I would be asked and if my guides or theirs would come through when I instantly got this message…

You will see a red heart either on the person or somewhere prevalent in the room. This heart is sent to you from us as confirmation that you are in the right place at the right time following divine guidance. See this heart also as a symbol of our love and commitment to you and all that you are doing and also as a reminder to love yourself, give yourself more love and kindness and show yourself forgiveness for any wrong doings as to be human is to err sometimes. Love yourself nonetheless for you are of *Light and Being* and in that respect and on that level can do no wrong. That is your true being, your true essence of who you really are and should be celebrated daily, hourly and minute by minute. Hence brush all bothering's aside and celebrate the good in you bringing love and joy back into your life. Take this gift (heart) in your memory to be carried with you always.

I wondered who was talking.

It is Hoyan

Thank you Hoyan. (Obviously he was aware I needed comforting and some sort of absolution given my recent distress.)

▫▫▫

I've gone to The Valley of The Snakes to finally catch up with Marikahee. It's been a while since my last visit and as I traverse the marshy entry I'm reminded why I haven't been able to come here for so long. It's been raining almost nonstop for a few months now, the rains came late this year. This would have made entering The Valley of The Snakes near impossible as the entry into the valley would have resembled a large swamp. As it is I have to travel carefully and sideline the muddy path, walking amongst the long grasses and fighting the plague of mosquito's to get there.

Once there it is pure bliss. I am completely alone on this small private beach surrounded by brackish waters and dense bush land. Sitting on the foreshore of Lake Cootharaba it's so peaceful, picturesque and serene I decide to meet with Marikahee here, on the edge, instead of in the thickness of the valley itself. I take a while to absorb the beauty of it all, breathing in the fresh crispness and staring out at the water when I notice Marikahee is in the middle of the lake and floating towards me like Jesus walking across the water. I sat in awe of this moving apparition awaiting her arrival, apologizing profusely when she did for my lack of contact recently. She motioned that she understood that things had been difficult for me of late. Her eyes tell me everything as if we 'speak' through them and it's true as that is how we communicate. Her eyes are very wise and all knowing.

Marikahee started chanting "Hey ya, hey ya, hey ya," as she passed sage smoke over me with a large feather. This was to ward off the evil spirits and to cleanse my aura. She drew in ever closer and even lifted up the hair around my nape to cleanse underneath. I could smell chewed tobacco on her breath and the campfire on her clothes. The chanting started soft and slowly got louder and more powerful. We were now inside her healing teepee but still on the beach and through the opening I could see the glass like stillness of the lake. Two Indian sentries stood guard at this opening, watching me and the ceremony taking place. I sensed the village life of the Indians was going on outside like normal, people gathering wood and food for their fires and it's quite possible we were in two dimensions at the one time… hers and mine.

When the chanting subsided she took a rattle out of her medicine bag and gently shook it around my aura all the while watching me intently with her hawk like eyes. She told me to acquire one for myself, that it is a great healing tool and a quick way to cleanse and protect oneself and others. She used the rattle much like I would a crystal, giving it a gentle shake and then smoothing over areas. Some areas that required more vigorous healing got a more vigorous shake!

Next Marikahee wrapped my feet in muslin that had been soaked in the central depths of the brackish lake (that's what she had been doing out there!), the salt both purifying and grounding. There was a white paste of unknown origin and with a harrowed finger she drew markings on my face, three diagonal lines below each eye and three dots in successive sizing from my third eye up towards my crown. This was more an initiation than anything, a badge of honor as I was welcomed into her tribe.

Satisfied the external had been taken care of Marikahee then offered me a small ceremonial bowl containing a sage concoction and three drops of deer's blood. The sage was to cleanse and purify the internal organs and 'being' and to clear and clarify the mind. The deer's blood supplied a person with vigor and vitality, a young and vibrant spirit. It was warm and inviting. There was no "ickyness" of the blood in such a minute dose, merely a passing on of its essence. Marikahee then motioned for me to bow my head and placed an eagles feather (my first) in my ceremonial headband then bent down to unwrap my feet of the muslin. Calling me her squaw yearling, she told me I was ready to travel my path.

Marikahee then took one last look at me, waving her hands across my shoulders in a final cleansing gesture and as she did so she leaned forward and 'whispered' a blessing in my ear. I closed my eyes briefly taking it all in, feeling the warmth of her breath on my neck and when I opened them again Marikahee was slipping backwards through the opening of the teepee and back into the middle of the lake where she stood for a while, looking at me… then slowly faded from view.

COMMUNICATION WITH CAABD

While I was here on the shores of The Valley of The Snakes I decided it was a good opportunity to communicate with my first tree. Even though I've been getting to know a particular tree at Paradise Beach I've only managed thus far to find its spiritual center and gained vitality through energy transference with the centians agreement. This tree often comforts me at times of distress, when I'm reaching breaking point and in dire need of recharging, rebalancing and grounding. I'm yet to engage it in conversation.

Now standing here on the edge of the lake I look for a willing participant. My eye is drawn to one in particular and armed with my pendulum, notepaper and pen I approach it. Using my pendulum, the first thing I do is ask its permission to communicate. At first "he" (I sense it is a he) says no which shocks me. Then I realize I didn't say please and ask again. This time I get a yes! I asked if he would only talk to people with polite manners…another yes. Are all trees like this? He said he couldn't answer for all trees. All trees are different just like all humans are different. Next I work on finding the spiritual center of the tree and it surprises me that like the one on Paradise Beach it is facing away from the lake and not towards it as I would expect, the reason of which I'll find out later. All communication is governed through this point and I start asking my questions. What he tells me is truly revelatory.

The tree is seventy-seven years old. His name is Caabd (pronounced like cupboard). Even though he is getting plenty of water he is not in great health. He is suffering from an insect infestation and concerned I ask him if it is threatening his life to which he replies no. He will manage eventually to rid himself of them. They will ravage him first and then move on to another tree. It will then take a long time for him to recover. He could do with my help. Not knowing a lot about the nutrition of trees but knowing enough that specific plants require specific nutrients I ask him if he is a Paperbark[5] to which he replies no. This throws me because he certainly looked like one to me. Before I can help I'll have to find out his species and consider consulting a professional. For now I try to find out more about Caabd himself.

He tells me he is sad, melancholy because his whole family are on the other side of the lake (five kilometers away). Every day he looks out at the water and the land on the other side knowing that he cannot ever see or be with them again. It is like a daily torture for him. They are all 'over there' and he is here all alone.

Apparently, as a seed, he was carried by the wind out into the lake where so small and tiny he thought he would surely drown. Then along came a bird gliding in the water and he managed to attach himself to one of its feathers, burying himself deep in its base. But instead of the bird helping him back to the shore and his family the bird took off in the wrong direction flying the full width of the lake and landing on the other side. By the time they got there the little seed was so exhausted from holding on tight for fear of drowning and was just glad to be on dry land again that he ousted himself from the feathers. While he sat on the shores recovering from his experience and contemplating his next move the rains came and buried him below the soil where nature took its course and he sprouted and took root. Now seventy-seven years have gone past. He cannot rid himself of the sadness over the loss of his family and the cruelness of having to face his reality every day looking across the lake and so he chooses his spiritual center, his core essence, to face the other way.

Feeling moved by the pain and anguish he is feeling I wonder what I can do to help and ask Caabd if he would like a hug. He says he's not sure and I ask if he knows what a hug is to which he replied, "No." This shocked me. I don't know why I assumed he would know what a hug was so set about explaining it to him and then asked again if he would like one. He still was not sure, telling me he didn't know me well enough and maybe on subsequent visits we would get to hugging.

The afternoon wind blew across the lake, the sun was fading and it was getting cold. I decided it was time to go. I asked Caabd if it would help if I came to visit again, say in the next week or so. He agreed and we said goodbye. I left totally gob smacked at the conversation I had just had and just a little thrill at the ease of it all.

But also I took some of Caabd's sadness home with me.

SUN 16th JUNE

Good morning all. It's official! I'm so excited. The new enterprise is now open for business! I decided it was time to stop procrastinating and as you suggested, just get started. Ok being desperate to increase my finances also had something to do with it. So Daughter and I having been to the movies on Friday night to see "The Great Gatsby," decided it was a good time to go pamphlet dropping and so we did. All around Noosa and Tewantin we pinned up advertising postcards and business cards and placed the advertising car magnet (duh) on the car. Woohoo!

I can't believe how long it took me to get to this place in time. I'd been expecting to start much earlier but you know, life gets in the way. I would have done all of this a few weeks ago but just as I was about to someone commented on my business card saying it was too sexy! The card had a very large depiction of my angel drawing titled "Being of Light," which I have to admit is rather busty, undoubtedly because the image was inspired by a swim wear model in a Jets catalogue. Not wanting to offend women who I assume will make up a large proportion of my clientele and not wanting to attract unwanted male attention (or weirdoes) I decided that I should change the business card even though I love that image. With no time to produce another art piece I had to quickly come up with another design so sourced something off the internet that will do temporarily. I couldn't put it off any longer. Of course every time I order business cards I then have to wait for delivery. Everything takes time.

On Saturday we drove out to Pomona and Cooroy dropping pamphlets and cards on those noticeboards and today we drove to an estate in Noosaville and letterbox dropped a hundred business cards. I'm both excited and nervous.

We also are exited and have been watching the shenanigans as you go about the earthly business of organizing such things. You see in our world because there is no time there is no waiting and things just are the moment they are thought of or desired. Hence our suggestion to just start. Just do. Just be. Because that is how it is for us. By observing you we are gaining an understanding of how exhausting all the planning, organizing and implementation is for you humans on earth and so we show much patience knowing that you will get there in your own good timing. We have encouraged you to manifest something and manifestation takes a lot of time in your world. There are so many obstacles to overcome and many give up along the way. Thus we are very proud that you have come so far in a relatively short period by your clock. If you could see us you would know that we are beaming. The fact that you are now displaying the new enterprise has made it real in your terms, bringing it out of the thought processes and into the physical realm. Celebrations and Congratulations are in order.

We embrace you — Nameless

Thank you Nameless.

FRI 21ST JUNE

Success! Or part thereof. I got my first client enquiry today, a phone call asking me how much I charge for readings. I've letterbox dropped about a hundred and fifty business cards and was starting to get disheartened as there hadn't been any response. When I did this years ago for a mobile hair business I would get three clients per one hundred letter box drops. I guess readers are not as in high demand as hairdressers, LOL and it's going to be harder to drum up business than I thought. She didn't make a booking but at least it's a positive sign that I should keep going and my first client may come soon.

Yes indeed this is good news and a good sign of things to come. More and more it is coming into manifestation due to your capabilities, hard work and dedication. You are not one who gives up easily but like to see things come to fruition especially if there has been a lot of work in the planning and execution. You are also not one to rest on your laurels especially where there is passion involved and we can see by your action there is a lot of passion aimed towards this avenue by your undertakings.

Things are travelling well and heading in the right direction always positive and in a forward motion and so it builds and grows until one day you wake up and are enveloped in the very being of what it was you were trying to create in the first place. You are there where you wanted to be all along. Hold this picture in your mind of where it is you want to be and everyday do something that sees you heading in that right direction even if it is something small. Thus it could be the delivering of pamphlets and business cards or the sitting in contemplation of what it will be like to be in the presence of your clients or perhaps preparing the physical body as well as the mind to be in that right space at that right time so that you are in optimal health and vibration to be of good service to others and this should always be your aim so as not to forget the self which is just as important a being.

All is right with the Universe. All is as it should be. Go now Marikai knowing that things are coming together and you are nearing the beginnings of your new life. In Light and Being—Nameless.

Cheers, thanks Nameless.

TUE 25TH JUNE

Hi All. I wanted to tell you about a fascinating program I watched on the ABC the other night called "Wonders of Life - Expanding Universe,"[6] a series which explores the formation of life on earth from a physics perspective. I love physics. I wish I'd been more intellectually advanced in high school as I may have chosen to go down that path. Anyway I tell you the following because it relates to the experience I had with Lenni Semmelink and the Hydrophones. How I had previously discussed with you the concept of our senses only picking up a certain amount of information that is surrounding us and how we are missing the experience of so much more because of our physical and sense limitations. The timing of this program really couldn't have been more perfect!

The narrator explained that when sound is travelling from air to water ninety-nine point five percent is reflected back off the water's surface. So ninety-nine point five percent of sound cannot penetrate water and this is why we can't hear or have trouble hearing surface noise under water. I remember playing these games as a kid in the pool and you had to try and guess what the other person was saying under water. It was more a test of your lip reading skills than anything because you couldn't hear didley squat.

So sound can't travel through water, eh? Guess what? Our inner ear is made up of fluid! We are only able to hear thanks to the three bones (malleus, incus and stapes) of the inner ear and their vibration which allows for the transmission of sound from air through the fluid in our ears so we can hear. I already knew this as do most but it's the figures and percentages which perked my interest, apparently this is only achieved at sixty percent. Forty percent of sound is still reflected back therefore we don't hear forty percent of what is going on externally around us! Also the human hearing range is between forty to one hundred and twenty decibels and anything outside of this range is beyond our physiological mechanism for hearing.

There is a lot on hearing range and frequencies of different animals on wikipedia.org[7] including how fish, dolphins and whales hear under water. Mice and rodents emit very high pitched ultrasonic sounds as a means to communicate with each other without alerting their predators as it usually falls outside the predators' normal perceptible range (including outside human hearing range). However I didn't realize that cats have an even higher frequency range than dogs enabling them to pick up these ultrasonic sounds and this is why they're such good hunters (Imagine if they could be trained!).

Why am I so excited by this? Because its scientific proof that there is a lot going on out there sense wise that we are not privy to and as I mentioned previously just because we can't see it, touch it, and feel it doesn't mean it doesn't exist. I know there are a lot of people who can't comprehend communication with guides or the experiences of clairvoyants, clairaudients and other mediums. Just the other day I was telling some people about my channeling forgetting that they were your average 'Joe Blow'[8] and they couldn't stop laughing and asked me what brand of weed I'd been smoking. I'm sure they walked away thinking I was totally loony. The same would go for anyone who knew I talked to trees. In the old days I would have either been committed or burned at the stake.

At one stage I thought I was going deaf. I had a lot of trouble hearing people who were right next to me as they would be drowned out by more distant noise. One day Daughter and I were at the beach and I couldn't hear her talking to me because of the sound of the waves crashing on the ocean floor (I can pick up this sound from my house at night even though I live five kilometers from the beach!). I went and had my hearing tested and was told the opposite, that I had such acute hearing I was very sound sensitive and picked up too much audio around me which was blocking out nearby sounds. This also explains my annoyance with my teenage daughter having the T.V and music up way too loud, amplified even more by my acute hearing and why I prefer silence (no T.V/music) when she is not around. I've heard of some people having such acute hearing they can hear their own blood travelling through their veins.

Q. Is that how I communicate with you? Does my particular hearing range allow me to communicate with you? What about Caabd, how do I communicate with him?

Although this is all very interesting it has nothing to do with our communication with you. Our communication is far beyond the travelling of waves and frequencies. It is instant. If you open yourself to it, it is there. But only in the silence. It is true all these sounds only serve to block and get in the way of communication. We have always said the way to communicate with us is to empty the mind. To be of no mind. This opens up a void, a portal to allow other worldly knowledge to be acknowledged. It is always there waiting for your grasp whenever you choose to attune yourselves to it. You understand this as telepathic. In telepathic communication there is no time delay. There is no processing, no sending of, *it just is*. The only time delay comes from you then attempting to externalize it either verbally or by writing or thinking about it. We are trying to explain to you the mechanism of how it works.

We are one. You, the planet, humans, animals, rocks, the Universe are all one and the same. Therefore you do not need to communicate with a perceived other but are essentially communicating with yourself. For when you speak with me, I am a part of you as you are me and so we are one and the same. It is for all as it is with us. Remember that humans perceive things, objects to be separate and this is not the case. Think of the image you saw of the 'beating heart of the earth'[9] on the internet the other day. Ask anyone and they will tell you that a tree is separate to a lake is separate to a grain of sand, an elk, a gem, a fish and so on but it is not so. They are all connected. They are all one. The image you saw of the earth, the planet (and everything on it) was as if it was beating, pulsating as one entity and it is so. The same can be said for the planets in the Universe. Each beating to the one rhythm so that the planets as a whole are beating to the one *Universal* rhythm. This is then mirrored in the galaxy and beyond. It is infinite. Thus you are all connected to each other, to fish, trees, rocks, grains of sand, the planet as a whole, the galaxy, the Universe and beyond.

You humans put such limitations on yourself! Think about the ramifications of what I have just said. That it is possible to communicate with all living (and supposedly nonliving) things and this extends out into the galaxy and Universe such that it is possible to communicate with life on other planets and in different galaxies. When I say other life I am not necessarily suggesting alien life but intelligent life as all life is intelligent from the smallest amoeba to the stars and even the Universe itself.

There are no boundaries to where this form of communication can take you, only the limitations you set upon yourselves. We are all pulsating as one, we are all made from the same intelligence. This is how you communicate with us and with Caabd and indeed the ant that crawls across you as he passes by. You can communicate with cats, dogs, dolphins and other marine life, rocks, planets, stars, galaxies, everything in such a manner. All you must do is to let go of preconceptions. Still the mind and in doing so dissolve yourselves of the physical body. Noise only serves as a distraction to hold you to the physical earth plane. Think when two people are talking to you at the same time it is very distracting that you are unable to concentrate on either one. Therefore they must take their turn and one must sit quiet while the other speaks. It is the same for us. We sit quietly waiting for your readiness.

Communication is achieved through the absorption method. You must open yourself to it for the information to be absorbed or bought into your consciousness, into the here and now. This can be likened to making boiled rice. The rice sits in a pot of water…

1. **You can think of them as separate entities. A pot, some water and some rice.**

   or

2. **You can think of them as one entity… A pot *with* rice *and* water.**

If you sit them on a cold stove nothing happens, they remain the same. If you turn the stove on and the water begins to boil (increased energy) the rice opens to the water and begins to absorb it. The rice and water become one…boiled rice. Now you have…

3. **One entity…a pot *with* boiled rice**

   or

4. **Two separate entities a pot *and* some boiled rice.**

The constituents have not changed only your perception of them. A scientist would look at the chemical structure of the uncooked rice as being different to the boiled rice. But if the biochemical structure is broken back down you come back to rice and water, nothing has changed. They *both* just took on the information of the other to change their shape, form, identity and information contained therein. I hope I am making sense in your world.

Another analogy could be the lava lamp. The lava lamp is one entity. Inside is different blobs of color. One such blob is you, another is me. At one stage we come close enough to exchange matter/information, enough to change our shapes. I now contain a little bit *more* of you and you a little bit *more* of me. I say *more of* because if you actually look at us as a whole we are part of one, the lava lamp. Holographically each individual part contains all the information of the whole. We were always one and the same each with free access to the information of the other. But during our interaction we have openly and visibly merged and communicated with each other, exchanging information before continuing on our paths. I hope this is enough of a visual to explain adequately to you the concepts of your experiences with us and with Caabd. Not wanting to overwhelm and confuse we will leave it here for today and let you ponder at your leisure.

Lightness to your Being — Nameless.

Thank you Nameless, I'm always grateful for your insights. That one was magical!

FRI 28TH JUNE

Not really a channeling today Nameless I just wanted to share with you my experience from a recent night out. I went to an event put on by a very well-known Australian psychic medium. I can't really divulge anything from the show as we were all required to sign privacy contracts on entry. I went armed with my note paper and pen hoping to pick up any tips that I could and must have looked very strange madly scribbling away in the audience having just signed the above but I assure you it was all for my own personal use.

The night was very enlightening and I was bought to tears at one stage as this person relayed some similar experiences to me and I suddenly didn't feel so alone. She enthralled me not just by her communication with those passed over but information from her guides and what we should all be looking out for or doing in the future. Shame I can't mention any of it here. Instead I'd like to tell you about an experience I had with this same psychic medium many years before and indeed I was sitting in the audience hoping to high hell she wouldn't remember or recognize me.

Roll time back quite a few years ago. This woman is already famous having been on the T.V and in magazines. I'm working in a salon a few days a week mostly having the shop to myself while other staff enjoy R.D.O's. Having rung up a few days earlier for an appointment she waltzes into the salon with a regal air about her and straight away I can tell her barriers are up. Who can blame her really? She must get accosted with all manner of questions everywhere she goes and is probably right sick of it. I understood immediately and keeping my professionalism got down to business.

She wanted a spiral perm. Only problem was her hair was already highly bleached meaning I was not sure it could take it. Added to that perms are not that popular these days especially spiral ones and I didn't think we had enough rods to do it. Plus she was under a time constraint having to catch a plane up north for a conference this very afternoon and spiral perms can take the better half of a day. I advised against it. Her hair was not in good enough condition, we were lacking in rods and the time frame was against us. She was steadfast in her reply demanding that it be done right now this minute and I wouldn't exactly say in anger but firm enough that I was too scared to say no to her and so for the next five hours I worked under silent duress all the time stressing if her hair would fall out, would I have enough rods to finish the job or would she catch that plane in time?

For five hours she hardly spoke to me as I toiled away at her head in silence (understanding she wanted to be left alone by how deep her head was buried in that magazine she was pretending to read) and just got on with the job feeling very uncomfortable and tortured. She must have been reading my mind however as at about the halfway mark she told me not to panic, that she knew it would be done in time and she would catch that plane and if not, well "...It's possible to time travel."

Time travel? This was the first I'd ever heard of such a thing and she went on to recount a few stories of how she had done just that, willing herself to be somewhere at a certain time when in our reality it would have been physically impossible. As quick as she spoke to me her head was back down in the magazine. Even though I found it quite fascinating at the time I brushed it off as impossible for us mere mortals. Perhaps she could do it but isn't she special? Now having read our conversations over the last months Nameless I realize this is what you have been alluding to all year, that it is possible for all of us to time travel only I'm just not sure you mean in the physical sense as she did.

It took me three hours just to wind but the perm got done and she was out the door in the nick of time and no tip I might add for my troubles. I thought (hoped) I would never see her again but two weeks later she was back and her hair was a disastrous frizzy mess! It was the biggest abomination of a perm gone wrong I had seen in my whole life and I was absolutely mortified and embarrassed. Did I do that? She told me she had had to contain it with large amounts of gel and a tight ponytail the whole time she was away.

I had warned her but felt stupid for allowing myself to be bullied into something I knew was against my better judgment. To make it worse she demanded I cut all the front short, leaving the back long in some manic over exaggeration of a Suzi Q haircut on steroids. She was not one I could argue with so I gave her what she wanted, my mortification growing by the minute.

Ironically she didn't blame me but said it could have been old perm solution as she knew we didn't use it that often. Her psychic instincts were correct, the perm solution was off proven by the next few perms that succumbed to the same fate and so it was not my fault after all. Phew!

Anyway I can tell you on this night her hair was back to its full glory and there I was still mortified every time she looked my way, head buried deep in my writing trying to send her a clear message… do not disturb!

9

JULY 2013

FRI 5TH JULY

Good morning All. I really don't know what to talk to you about this morning. Its school holidays and so much has been going on, workshops, business card dropping, seminars, searching for a room to rent and other options. I'm behind in my writings with you and will have to back track to catch up. Things are askew because Daughter's at home and I don't have the usual time to myself. When I'm not in contact with you sometimes I feel like I'm losing my way and it's hard to remain focused on my path. I broke the chain on my pendulum so haven't even had that to consult with on the odd occasion I needed it. I don't want to rely on it fully but there are occasions that it comes in useful when I'm struggling to make decisions.

This year I'm committed to following divine guidance to see if it will help change my life for the better so today I will ask for some guidance knowing that even though I have not written you my current situation you are aware of what has been going on.

Q. What advice can you offer me today?

That you are indeed following divine guidance and in a timely manner to move you forward into greater changes that will occur in your life for the betterment of you, your daughter and all of those that you touch and come near to. Only it is not happening at the speed with which you wish it to and hence your impatience and struggle with the concept of time.

You thought you would be so much farther ahead in the planning and implementation of your goals and path. But we are here to tell you that these things cannot be rushed and follow divine timing *not* your timing. Better that you do them well.

We are also aware that you have supposedly started the new enterprise by handing out your business cards and posting them on notice boards. The true beginning is when the first client appears and you are able to pass on your skills, knowledge and ability in a form that suits them. This has been more difficult than you anticipated. Do not fret. You are planting seeds in people's minds. One day the seeds will sprout and grow. The seed will grow into a tree branching in all directions and it will bare flowers and fruit. More seeds will drop from this tree and spread in the winds and so it goes. Currently you are doing all the hard work. The digging, the preparing of the soil, the planting of the seeds, the watering and nurturing. It is hard work and may be a while before you see the new growth pop its head above the soil. On this day you will rejoice knowing that all your hard work is coming to fruition. This will be an exciting day and will spur you on to plant more seeds and grow a whole orchard. One day far into the future when your trees are all maturing and the hard ground work is done you will be able to sit back and look at what you have managed to create. That is not to say the work is complete but that largely it is self-managing. You will still need to water, feed and nurture but it will be less intense than you are feeling right now.

Thanks Nameless. You always make me feel better by offering your support and putting things in perspective. I guess for now it's just head down, bum up and keep plugging away at what I'm doing. I'm having real trouble finding a room to rent either casually or permanently. They're all so expensive and out of my reach especially still having dentist bills for the next month or so. I'm feeling stuck between a rock and a hard place with possibly my only option being the market but would dearly love a room to rent. I've been trying to think outside the square looking at different options as you suggested and found the local library has a great room to rent at a reasonable price but I'd have to add marketing on top of that so once again it becomes out of my reach. My brain fills with ideas a plenty but my pockets never seem to have the funds to follow through. Just surviving. AUUUGH!

I shouldn't complain. I watched an SBS program[1] *recently where every week they showcase the hardest place in the world to do a job. Last week it was a taxi driver in India, this week it was a (rubbish) bin man in Indonesia. They would take someone with the same job from a westernized country and put them in this harsh environment comparing the differences in work and living arrangements. The westerner worked the host's job for a week in atrocious conditions as a means to appreciate his own position back home and perhaps pass on any knowledge that may make the hosts working life that little bit easier.*

One particular Indonesian family of four lived in a room (yes one room) no bigger than my bathroom. There was no running water or hygiene facilities, basically the room was for cooking and they ate and slept outside. Rubbish was piled up directly opposite their 'house' two stories high by other people who would come and dump there because they were considered of such low class. The whole family picked through this rubbish looking for bottles etc. to recycle to pay for food as the fathers bin job was only enough to pay the rent for their miniscule kitchen. If they didn't forage in this rubbish they couldn't eat.

That was not the worst. There were hundreds of people living at the local tip in makeshift shacks. The tip was equivalent to ten stories high. It was so high it was unfathomable, I could only imagine the stench. The tip dwellers rummage through the rubbish like little ants dwarfed by mountains. They compete for the freshest rubbish as it's tipped and turned by giant excavators endangering their lives as they do so. The freshest rubbish has the highest recyclable content and this is their only source of income for survival. Some people had been living at the tip for longer than thirty years having been born there, others arrive after experiencing life's difficulties and with nowhere else to go. There are no funds to get out of this place once you are there. People live and die in this horrid place yet I was overcome by their ability to laugh and smile.

I think of these people and I'm eternally grateful for my life no matter how hard it seems at times, I still feel blessed. It also makes me appreciate my "shitty" (literally) day job. Sometimes my thoughts of them is the only thing that gets me through my day.

And so it is and so it will always be that there is someone worse off than yourself. This you would do well to remind yourself when you are at your wits end or feeling at the end of your tether. Yes you are one of the lucky ones. Carry this luck and share it with others always and as much as you can. Remember, aim to bring a smile to each person that you come into contact with, to uplift their vibration and enlighten their day in some way, even in the smallest of ways. They should leave your presence feeling better about themselves. In this way you are contributing what you can and that is all that we ask. In this way you are raising the vibration of you, them and the planet.

You are all *Beings* of *Light*. The rich, the poor, you are all the same. Show each other respect. Each has his own plights to deal with. His own path to travel. You are all equal in our eyes. All worthy of love, joy and pureness of being.

Pleasure to your day Marikai. We embrace you.

Thank you Nameless.

SUN 7TH JULY

COMMUNICATION WITH CAABD

Finally today I have an opportunity to visit Caabd. Even though it's still school holidays Daughter has gone to the beach for the day and the weather is fine enough for me to enter The Valley of The Snakes. I prefer to walk there from my house filling my lungs with pure nature as I go but today I drive expecting a phone call from her later to be picked up. With the car nestled close to the valleys entrance I retrieve my kit bag and head off to walk the rest of the way.

The area is still damp and muddy from the rains and I have to watch my footing as I go. There are three rocky 'bridges' to pass and on reaching the final one I feel the tears start to well in my eyes with the knowledge that with every step I draw closer to Caabd. This took me by surprise, I'd missed him more than I had known. It was the anticipation and excitement you feel when you're waiting to see a loved one as you come through the gates at the airport, struggling to contain your emotions only to burst into tears the moment you see them, all composure lost. A tingle shook through me. As I navigated the terrain the butterfly's lining the path parted their ways creating a breathtaking site. My welcome committee.

On arriving I was disoriented. It was such a changeable environment the merest drop or rise in tide could alter the shoreline completely. Then there were the ever moving shadow castings on the sand mirrored by the clouds above and the brushes dancing in the wind but today was different...SOMEONE WAS CAMPING THERE!

A huge dog bounded towards me and I froze, the hairs on my neck going into full alert. "Oh shiiitt!" I hate big dogs, massive phobia, my saliva went suddenly dry. The owner told me she was friendly and disguising my fear I extended a pat, said "Gidday" to the stranger and quickly made my way to the shoreline peeved that someone was in my space perhaps ruining my intentions.

Sitting on the sand by a fallen log whilst trying to regain my bearings I eyed the stranger from a distance. He seemed to be busy building add-ons to his tent from the nearby bush, there was a tinny[2] *parked on the beach and I wondered how long he was staying for. Hmm, he was certainly making himself comfortable, I noted his hammock.*

Time passed and realizing the stranger would leave me alone I began to scan the beach for Caabd. The energy of the place had changed. At first glance all the trees looked the same. Which one was Caabd? I remembered Nameless saying, "The right one will draw you to him." I took a moment to adjust my energy and scanned the trees edging the shallow waters. The sun shone through the shadows landing on one in particular, the delicate fraying bark sending arcs of glowing light up its bough and into the branches beyond. Caabd? I moved in and inspected the markings on the tree and just to make sure I placed my hand on his spiritual center and asked if he was he. Yes! And when he replied such the tears welled again. I had found my friend. I had walked through the gates. I had come home!

I apologized for my absence and asked if he was well. No. The insects were still there but he could sense they were slowing down. One day they will have their fill of him and move on. He tolerates them as best he can knowing that repair will take ten times longer than it did to do the damage. The word ash had been sent to me periodically over the last few weeks. Would ash be beneficial and would he like me to bring ash to scatter at his roots? He indicated yes telling me there was some nutritional value in it of which I will have to look up. Possibly phosphorous? Again I asked if he was a Paperbark to which he replied no. Getting to know his personality, that he is quite particular and prefers formalities I understood that he would rather I address him by his Latin binomial. Another thing for me to Google.

Q. Can I have a hug today?

No.

Q. Is it because a stranger is here?

Maybe.

Q. Because you still don't know me well enough?

Yes.

Q. Are you happy? (Silly question)

No.

Q. Do you know what happy is?

No.

Shock! Why was I so shocked? He had been sad his whole life. I tried to explain to Caabd what it was like to be happy, how we smile and laugh and feel such joy that you want to dance or sing but trees can't do any of that so how do they express happiness? I'd have to find a happy tree and ask it. For now I told him it was not feeling sad any more.

It turns out Caabd didn't miss me like I had him. He just got on with things. What things? Just 'being.' He did wonder if I forgot him and if I would come back. He wanted me to come back but wasn't expecting it. It was a nice surprise when I did. That's why he lit up when he saw me.

The afternoon wind extending across the lake was getting cold and strong. I asked Caabd if I could rest on his roots for shelter. There was one jutting out that formed the perfect seat and settling in I snuggled up against him for warmth. I lost myself there, letting go of all thought and immersing myself in feeling, the two of us melding into one. It was like we simultaneously opened our heart centers and in doing so drew back our impermeable membranes such that I 'fell into' him and he 'fell into' me so there was no beginning and no end and I couldn't tell where he finished and I started. We had become one. Complete Unification. A unification I had only ever felt with a lover before and so was this really possible? Could I be experiencing this with a tree? Then the tears started rolling down my cheeks and I wondered why I was crying and why I felt so sad when I realized they were not my tears, they were Caabd's. I was crying the tears he couldn't. I was feeling his pain. I gazed across the lake and let the tears flow allowing myself to cry until they just stopped flowing and a feeling of peace and calmness came over me. I had been able to release Caabd of some of his pain, some of his sadness, some of his agony like the extrusion of a festering boil about to explode. Relief.

I was determined to help Caabd find his happiness but what could I do? I remembered the stones in my pocket and asked Caabd if I could clear and charge his chakras.

Yes, thank you.

Still nestled in his seat I went about clearing my own first which didn't take long as I'd done it only yesterday, then I set about clearing Caabd's. This took much longer and seemed to go on forever, the pendulum doing multiple rotations and always coming back to the heart center trying to clear it. My derriere was getting sore and I tried to hold my position for my friend as long as I could but soon realized there was a lot of work to do and it wouldn't clear in one sitting. I asked the pendulum how many more sets of rotations it would take. Six! Mercy on my posterior, I'd have to do these by distant healing so stopped the clearing with the promise of continuing at home.

I placed my hand on Caabd's spiritual center and another on the exposed root next to me and we sat in silence for a while 'holding hands,' I watching the windsurfers across the lake to the east and he watching the sun go down in the west. It wasn't necessary to say goodbye. When you connect you just know these things.

THE STRANGER

I came to rest against the log where I'd laid my towel and pondered the significance of what just happened. After some time observing the clouds above my gaze was instinctively drawn to my left and there, right next to me, was a small Aboriginal Humpy (or Gunya).[3] How had I not noticed it before? Blending in with its surrounding environment so precisely as to barely be perceptible even when one was practically sitting on it was testament to the skill level involved! The humpy rested up against the fallen log which was large enough to create one side of the wall and branches formed an arc on the other overlaid with brushes to form a small protective alcove scarcely big enough for someone to lay in. I thought about all the insects that would exit the log at night to do their exploring and hoped whoever slept here kept their mouth shut. The thought of bugs reminded me that snakes also like to call logs home and my adrenalin lifted but today was too cool for them to be moving around, I could rest easy knowing they would still be hibernating. The humpy should not have taken me by surprise in this area home to the Gubbi Gubbi[4] people but I had not seen one here before.

A sudden change in temperature alerted me to the storm rolling in across the lake and I took to leave stumbling across another humpy along the way, this one a little bigger than the first. I took note of how they were built in case I ever found myself on the TV series 'Survivor' and went to warn the tent dweller of the impending storm. I couldn't see him anywhere and decided he had retreated inside his tent. Shame I wanted to say goodbye and let him know about the humpies.

As I exited the beach the large dog frightened me as she unexpectedly leapt from the bushes followed closely by her owner. I made to pat her once again trying to conquer my fear and asked the owner her name to which he replied, "Sunny." Stopping to have a good look at her I became aware of her unusual beauty finding out that she was a Native American bear dog the likes of which I'd never seen before. The bear reference was unmistakable and striking.

The strangers name is Jonah[5] *and I tell him about the humpies of which he takes ownership. He is a descendant of the Gubbi Gubbi with an Aboriginal father and German mother making his look as interesting as his dog's. He is a walker he said and I ask him what that means thinking it had something to do with the Aboriginal term "Gone walkabout."*[6] *It turns out Walker is his surname and now I feel really stupid. Jonah, though smiling, exudes an air of roughness and is covered in tattoos looking like a member of the Hells Angels. I eye the hunting knife attached to his belt and wonder if I should be worried for my life being out here in the middle of Woop Woop*[7] *on my own when he could easily set his dog on me if he should choose. I check my internal radar and ask Teku if it's safe and feeling no fear it seems Jonah just wants someone to talk to as he goes on to tell me his recent life's story...*

He was engaged and bought his betrothed an investment house. Something run down that they were going to do up together and sell for a profit so they could marry. The wood of the house wasn't treated and was infested with white tail spiders. Jonah was bitten by one and spent a few months in hospital, his body racked with pain and fighting the sepsis. Consequently he lost his job, the house and then his betrothed in that order. After being released from hospital but still in mild pain it was necessary for him to rest and recuperate so he went to his parents' house in Boreen Point. Being a couple of oldies they didn't see eye to eye so he had taken leave with his tinny, his tent and his dog and landed on Caabd's beach when he had run out of fuel. It was walking distance he said to town and there were two campgrounds three kilometers in either direction that would allow him to shower there for twenty dollars a week. I wondered how long he was staying as he seemed to be making extensive renovations with plans to build canopies from the bush over his tent as a camouflage. There were council signs on the beach stating "No camping. No fires." How long would it be before he was discovered?

He pulled a local waterways book out of his bag telling me he had spent his last few dollars on it. His plan was to go up into the Noosa Everglades and build himself a tree house on Como Island where he could live in peace, away from society, the material world and all the expectations. I envied him but I had visited some of the islands up there myself with the same idea in mind and the mosquitoes are in plague proportions. I couldn't get back on my boat fast enough!

Jonah shook my hand, told me he trusted me now that we had spoken in such great length and said he could count on me to keep an eye on things if he wasn't around. I warned him that others visited here worried that he would be reported and encouraged him to set his tent much further back in the bush where he wouldn't be seen. "Too many mosquitos," he said.

I wondered how he would go on Como and how he would get there with no fuel.

MON 15TH JULY

Hi All. I'm wondering if anyone would like to comment on the experience I had with Caabd as it really took me by surprise.

Q. If I can have such an experience with a tree then is it possible that I could experience this with other living things? And what of supposed inanimate objects? Or is it only that which possesses a soul?

Yes we hear you and what wonderful news. We did not realize you would achieve this so soon and feel the work you have been doing with your chakras has opened you up to such possibilities.

The feeling of *Unification* you felt with Caabd is indeed possible not just for you but for all mankind. This is what it feels like to be *'at one'* with another being. It is possible to experience this with all beings, all beings meaning trees, cows, dolphins, rocks and the like. The next Holy Grail would be to experience this sensation with *all beings, all at once* (simultaneously). This would be the penultimate and bring you closer to *Nirvana,* closer to *Light and Being.* This is the ultimate aim. You have felt it on such a small scale, first with a human and now with a tree. Each time it has felt grandiose to you but we are here to tell you that even though you revel in the enormity of what you have experienced and felt it is but a small drop in the ocean of what is to come if you allow yourself to open and experience further. Fear stops many on their travels. Fear of the unknown. Fear of the all-encompassing joy of it all like no other experience they have had and therefore find very hard to process and put into context. Fear of letting go. Fear of losing themselves (or the ego's fear of losing itself).

If humans could manage to get past the ego once again and embrace such experiences as a normal part of their life how different your world would be both personally and on a much grander scale if this was to catch on. Imagine if people were regularly in such communication with trees, animals and the like allowing a different perspective on things. Perhaps this would put a halt to growth degradation, animal mutilation and cruelty if one was more in touch with a trees/animals feelings and intellect and the consequences of human's actions forced upon them against their will.

Traditional Aboriginals and other tribes speak to the spirit of the trees and animals asking their permission first, if they are willing to sacrifice themselves for sustenance or give themselves up to provide necessary materials. They only take what is necessary never more and ensure there is no wastage, always giving thanks and giving back what they can. When they themselves were ready to part this world they would walk out into the desert wild and give themselves back to the earth and wild life from which they took. Mass population and grouping in confined areas prevent this occurring as resources are destroyed and used up. People need to remind themselves to only take what they need and find a way to give back even more. In this way the resources would grow instead of being depleted.

If your best friend was a tree would you want to see him ripped from his home, stripped of his dignity along with his bark and made into matchsticks just so someone could light their fire when there is another, better way? What a waste of a beautiful being, a beautiful soul.

If more people had experiences such as yourself it would open their eyes to the world around them that bypasses them every day without their knowing. Oh how they are missing out. How they are devastating their worlds. The beauty that they do not see, the feelings of bliss they don't get to experience. And the poor tree has no way of crying out, no way of making you hear, unless you are prepared to stop what you are doing and listen.

The answers come in the silence.

When I talk of trees I am talking about all things/beings. Dogs, elephants, birds, rats, tigers, ants, dolphins and yes rocks and supposed inanimate objects. It is not the soul they have in common but life force and energy. The rocks life force and energy is denser and slower and therefore may be harder to communicate with as you vibrate on different levels. There would need to be a great energy shift on your part but it can be done. Some would find it easier than others if they are already adept at playing with their energy fields. As you are aware everything is energy even the table you sit at and the chair you sit on. Try it one day if you can, communicating with a chair. What does it want? What does it need? It sounds crazy I know but its answer may surprise you.

The possibilities from here are enormous and as previously discussed the penultimate aim is to experience oneness with all beings all at once. By talking and communicating with such beings it puts you in that *feeling* space. Empathy. Where you can understand things from their perspective and *feel* what they *feel* and if you are able to 'let go' you will fall down the rabbit hole into that space of *Oneness*, of *Unification*.

NIRVANA is *Unification with the whole Universe*, simultaneously.

LIGHT AND BEING is *Unification with the Whole of Existence* (the Universe, past, present, future and everything in it all at once).

We aim to guide you towards *Light and Being* every single day. Blessings to your day Marikai — Nameless.

Thank you Nameless. I'm trying.

THUR 18TH JULY

OMG, I had my first channel client! Woohoo! It didn't pan out how I'd expected at all, taking me by complete surprise. This was a few days ago and I'd just finished my morning shift at work when I got a call from a gentleman. He wanted a channeled reading this very day and I explained to him my working process of how I operate through the computer and T.V to provide material verbatim and already being in town I didn't fancy driving sixty kilometers to retrieve my laptop. Could I do it tomorrow? No, he was desperate and anyway he didn't want me to come to his house as he wanted to keep it secret from his wife who didn't believe in this stuff and would probably mock him.

We agreed to meet up at the Noosa library where we had a coffee and a chat discussing his issues and the questions he wanted answered. I told him I'd channel his reading remotely from home later that afternoon and then email it to him. It was mainly around work and life direction and well you already know that because it was you who gave me the information. I hope we helped. Being a guy he didn't give much feedback. I guess I should be more excited but I'm feeling more nervous than anything because I'm not really sure how I went.

Q. Any comments any one?

Just that all is happening in right timing and divine order. It manifested this way so as not to make you nervous from the beginning having no forewarning beforehand. You were just thrown in the deep end so to speak and it was sink or swim. There was no time to think but just to act and this was more beneficial to the outcome as it prevented any subjective thought on your part also. You handled it very well as we knew you would. You should be very proud of yourself as are we. You have come very far from your first beginnings and foray into this field. Remember it is one step forward each time that will see you grow and at a comfortable pace that is workable for you and so as not to overwhelm. Hence it will be a steady climb upwards to where it is you want to be and having now stepped onto the path that is your new life journey congratulations and celebrations are in order. We celebrate with you Marikai.

Always watching over you, always loving you — Nameless.

Thanks Nameless and all of you for your guidance and loving support, always.

SAT 20TH JULY

Good morning All. There's been changes to my shifts at work with the end result being I'm now another two hundred dollars a fortnight worse off. Just when you think things can't get any worse they do. It's only spurred me on towards giving the markets a go to try and make up the shortfall. I've ordered a gazebo for the Pomona markets, an easy pop up and good quality Oz trail one that set me back two hundred dollars! A big commitment for someone who is struggling to make ends meet and I'm hoping it's delivered in time for the next market which is the Pomona King of the Mountain, an annual international race meaning the town will be very busy .I'm writing to you this morning with actual pencil and paper. I miss communicating with you in this way as I feel more strongly connected to you than when using the lap top. I'm not sure why that is but I felt a need to be closer to you this morning.

Yes indeed the energy shifted a great deal at your workplace. Not just for you but for many others who are also unhappy with how things are panning out. We say hold on to your position as best you can as it is too early for you to take your leave. Try to go with the flow and make the most of a difficult situation. This has given you a jolt and made you realize that as unhappy as you are there, you really need it to pay the bills. If you try and fight it things will only get worse. Approach it from an observer's point of view and *non-reaction* to shift changes and negative energy going on around you. You have been doing a lot of chakra work and this is necessary at this time to help you clear and get through it. Remember all of this pushes/directs you towards your true path in life.

We are ecstatic at the manifesting of the market stall. These are humble beginnings but exiting nonetheless and necessary to start with partly due to your lack of funds and partly because it will be a gentle introduction to you of the healing as a profession. It will give you great grounding and experience to draw from at a later stage. Each person that comes to you for a healing or even asks a question will be your teacher, your guide. Imagine my face on their body (if I had a face). So it is as if I am coming to you for a healing and I am the client but also the guide that will guide you through my own healing. Thus do not worry or concern yourself that you will be stuck not knowing what to do...

This is intuitive healing

- ***Stop* and *listen*. *Quiet* your mind as you do when talking to us and *listen for guidance*.**
- **If none is forth coming *ask*!**
- **Failing that *feel*! Scan the body for subtle changes of energy shifts. You can use your hands as you do for crystal healing. Using your hands scan the body and you will be guided where to stop and hold them. It could be that you pick up on areas that are hot, cold or tingly or that you are being directed towards certain places.**
- ***Listen* for any attached messages also.**
- ***Don't concern yourself if you feel nothing* as the healing may be more on an auric and etheric level and not on the physical level at that time. I say at that time as the changes on the auric and etheric level will eventually manifest on the physical level.**
- **Remember that all energy healing is designed to be *subtle, gentle* and *gradual* so as not to shock any of the levels. This is the ideal way.**

- **If you want confirmation that changes have occurred you could do a chakra analysis both before and after the healing but this will add to your time factor and you may find this unnecessary or unworkable. A different scenario if you were working in a clinic or working from home.**
- **Have trust, belief and faith in yourself that you (as are many others) are a natural born healer.**
- **If your intention is pure then you can do no wrong.**

Your biggest difficulty will be in explaining to people *how* energy healing works. How can they know it's worked if it is something they cannot see or feel at the time of healing? This you should work on over the next week so you have an answer clear in your mind. Develop a handout sheet that can also be displayed. This way people can read it for themselves instead of you having to repeat it many times over.

- **How does energy healing work?**
- **How do I know if energy healing has worked for me?**
- **How many visits do I need? Etc. etc.**

These are probably the main ones but write down any other questions that are put to you at the market and develop answers for any common ones that you find. Your willingness to communicate these things is what will help set you apart from other healers. You are part healer and part educator/teacher. That is your path. You have spent a lifetime accumulating knowledge. Now is your time to share it. There are many who will benefit from your knowledge and skills. I say this not to overwhelm you as you cannot be *everything and all* to all people and you are not *all knowing* but you do possess skills and knowledge that can aid many and even set them on their own path of discovery.

As with our communication. You will always feel closer and more connected to us using pen and paper as there is less interference. When using the laptop and keyboard you are having to stop periodically to think about typing and what you are doing. This creates little breaks in communication with us similar to a mobile phone going in and out of reception. Each time you stop to think, the action of thought has stopped the stilling of the mind. Remember it is the stilling of the mind (absence of thinking) that allows reception/communication to flow through. As writing is automatic and you know it well enough not to have to think about what or how to write, the information flows through much faster and with more ease as it is doing now and you can barely keep up. We have enjoyed this session also because there are less barriers and it is easier to communicate with you. Whichever way you choose it is always a joy and always a pleasure. Enjoy your celebratory dinner with your daughter.

In Loving Light—Nameless.

SUN 21ST JULY

OMG, I'm fifty-eight point eight kilos! That means I'm only two or three kilo's off my goal of losing ten kilo's by years end, Woohoo! That vibrational and life force eating really does help.

Today I'm going to work on some distant healing, mainly cleansing and balancing chakras. I promised to do Caabd's, a girlfriend of mine who is currently unwell and the client I channeled for offering the chakra work as an extra. I'm very drawn to the shamanic, guided, intuitive form of energetic and vibrational healing but recently my attention is also being drawn towards Reiki. I think currently westerners are more familiar and trusting of Reiki knowing a bit more about it and the fact that it's certified. I've been reading a few books on the subject and doing some research on the net. One book called "Reiki Shamanism,"[8] by Jim Pathfinder suggests the two are linked. I'm wondering...

Q. Is Reiki a more powerful form of healing as the book by Diane Stein[9] suggests? Should I become certified in Reiki to both enhance my healing but also to offer clients a different energy method? Would becoming certified in Reiki instill a greater trust in potential clients in my healing ability?

I'm drawn to these ancient worlds but in different ways. The traditions of the (American) Indians, their shamanic rituals, stories and myths along with my avid collection of feathers but only those that are 'sent' to me. I also have a fascination with Japanese art/design/pattern and cloth, shibori, sashiko, and the little Amigurumi dolls I make and photograph. I like the idea of Shamanic Reiki and bringing the two together.

Q. What's your take on it? Should I become certified? Is one better than the other? Can I blend the two together?

No. One is neither better nor worse than the other though they do offer different things energetically. Just like different crystals heal different aspects and work in different ways energetically… fast, slow/gentle, on different etheric levels etc. The healing comes in the belief, the thought and the intent. The pure *intent* to heal, the *thinking* of where the healing will occur in the body, where it is warranted or that the body will take what is needed and the *belief* that it is so. That the healing *will* occur. Each ancient belief system has their own ways, their own methods. This does not make one better than the other only different. They are two pathways towards the same journeys end. It doesn't matter how you get there as long as you get there and the goal is reached in the persons own divine timing.

You are right to think that people will place more trust in you if you are certified. It's funny what a piece of paper can do. This places your energetic healing into the physical manifest where people can see it, touch it, feel it and pick it up so it is tangible and becomes *real* to them. It is in the physical world. People are naturally trusting if they can do this, see and feel a physical form and find it difficult to trust something that is not experienced by their normal five senses. There is no harm in becoming certified if that is what you choose to do and indeed will only add to your repertoire of skills and abilities giving you a greater knowledge base and set of skills to draw upon. It is not only the clients who will trust you more but you will trust yourself more also because you have been conditioned the same as them, that to be certified is to 'qualify' you and make it real.

You are already highly capable and as we have said all along it is only your confidence that is lacking. If you attune yourself in Reiki you will add the skills and knowledge but also importantly you will gain confidence in yourself. Once you have this confidence you will be feeling more comfortable in using your intuition and Shamanism to guide you, listening to your inner guidance for what works with an individual at any given time. It is not one size fits all style as this would be robotic and not healing or transformative at all. Remember the client is the healer and will guide you towards their preferred method of healing and what works best for them. By broadening your knowledge and skills you allow them choice instead of just one way. And so we say any learning is beneficial to you and to all. However we do caution that you do not take on too much too soon or in too short a time frame and you allow yourself due process to integrate what you have learned into your memory and your healing practice before you then take on more. Three to six months is a good time frame depending on the amount and depth of what you have learnt. You will know when it is fully integrated as you will no longer be consciously thinking about what you are doing it will just seem to naturally flow.

You are a Shaman. You are a Reiki Master. You are also an apprentice, a scholar and a teacher. You are all these things and more. Remember they are just words, labels that humans have attached to define and compartmentalize and make sense of their world. The truth is in the experiencing of the client who is healed. Trust, have faith in yourself and know it to be true.

Guidance and Light — Nameless.

THUR 25TH JULY

Good afternoon everyone so unusual for me to be talking to you this late in the day. Well my gazebo for the market only just arrived yesterday and I almost had heart failure thinking it wasn't going to fit in the car. I've had the most wonderful day today doing a practice run and setting it up in the butterfly room.[10] *I couldn't put it up to its full height but managed high enough for me to place the massage, pendulum and crystal tables and a few chairs underneath, hanging all the sheets, my banner and a few smaller signs. Then I sat in there and made a list of a few little things that I'm missing and need to purchase. Now I feel confident in managing to put it up by myself at the market if no one comes to help me. I really wanted to do this weekend's market at Pomona but they've rostered me on at work so now I'll have to wait a whole fortnight for the next one.*

Q. Any advice? Is there anything I should be doing right now or concentrating on?

You seem to be going great guns. Don't concern yourself that it was not manageable this weekend as it all would have been a bit rushed and stressful and this is not a good state to practice your healing from. It is better that you have the next few weeks to plan your market day to your liking. All those little things that will make the day special both for you and for your customers.

Don't forget the incense, white sage or sandalwood. I know you would prefer aromatic oils but this is a fire hazard in outdoor windy areas. In the future if you continue, once you can afford it you will invest in a diffuser. The incense and sage stick for now though heavier than you would like is necessary to help keep things clean and clear. A possible alternative is a scented candle inside a hurricane lamp. Complete the work that you are doing on the chakra handouts. Aim to have all seven done and copied by the fortnights end. Prepare your laminates also and any other handouts. Don't forget the general information on energy healing that you can display for all those inquisitive people. Sit down with yourself during the week and get clear in your mind what healing sessions you will offer, the different types and how much you will be charging. Think about different seating for the seated crystal healing. A stool or ottoman of some sorts would be better than a backed chair. Thus you could leave one of the chairs behind. Throw in a few practice sessions over the next two weeks and time them. This will help you with timing on the day. Add a hanging clock to your list. Write down anything else that comes to mind as you become aware.

Don't fret if it is all not perfect at fortnights end. Remember it is important just to get out there and begin. The (Pomona) market is a very relaxing starting point. No one is going to be too bothered if you are not so highly polished. The expectation is coming more from you rather than from others. You have a high expectation of yourself and for everything to be just so. It can't and won't always be like that (just so) and you will learn to be flexible especially in that environment. Decisions to change things can be made as they arise. You will undoubtedly be thrown a few 'curly ones' in the beginning. These are questions postured by others that even though you may know the answer to for yourself have never had to communicate and so may find yourself stymied and having to think on the spot. Do not alarm. Tell them so. As long as you are honest you can do/say no wrong. If you're not sure say so. If you are having trouble communicating an idea say so. I know if this happens you will likely offer to email an answer to them later having had time to think about it. There is nothing wrong with saying, "I don't know." Let them know about your own experiences and how it is for you. As you begin seeing clients more knowledge will be gained through practice. A working apprenticeship so to speak.

You are heading in the right and honorable direction. Always moving forwards. One step at a time. We would say pleasure to your day but the day is almost over and so we wish you to enjoy your evening. Guidance always—Nameless.

Thank you Nameless and All. I can always count on you to keep me centered.

WED 31ST JULY

Fifty-eight kilo's, two kilo's to go, yippee! I don't want to bore you or anything with my problems but I'm in dire straits and don't know what to do. I need your help and guidance. The shit has hit the fan at work. All the rosters are changing. It seems I no longer have my permanent shifts and find myself in a dog fight trying to regain the hours l've lost. All of us without shifts are competing for any vacancies on the roster and with over two hundred staff between both sites and a first in first gets basis, if you're not there exactly when the roster goes up you've got 'Buckley's and none.'[11] It's a sixty kilometer round trip just for me to access the roster and we never know exactly when it's going to go up. I was only given twenty hours last fortnight and applied for four other shifts which I missed out on. Another staff member told me that when the roster went up at least thirty people milled around applying for shifts, anyone who arrived after them had no hope. Now due to the shakeup we've been told that permanent part time rosters will be set at three days (Sat-Mon) and four days (Tue-Fri) and we have to choose which we prefer and apply for any vacancies such.

I don't want to work weekends because of Daughter, it's the only time we get together and If I work the four full days during the week I've rejoined the rat race and can kiss the new enterprise goodbye as I'll have no time for seeing clients, no time for channeling and no time for running classes. If I do the four full days per week I'll be stuck on minimum wage forever and a total slave to the system that I work in. The whole aim of this year is to follow divine guidance and try and better my life. I have the option of applying for the Tue-Fri evening shift and only if there is one available. It should see me home by nine p.m. and I feel Daughter is now old enough to look after herself until this time. My only other option is the uncertainty of casual shifts and just hope that I get enough hours but I find this really stressful being the sole provider. Will I be able to pay the bills or wont I? (Oh yeah I just got a four hundred dollar electricity bill, so much for it increasing by twenty-two percent because of the carbon tax, it almost doubled!)

I'm in a quandary, I just don't know what to do. Should I even stay here or should I be looking for another job? I've tried to stay calm and not react like you suggested but really, UUUGGGHHH!

I just asked the pendulum what I should do with regards to work...

1. *Revert to being casual and apply for shifts each fortnight.*
2. *Apply for permanent evening shifts Tue-Fri.*
3. *Look for another permanent part-time job.*

Q. The Pendulum opted for number two, do you agree?

Yes. We think this is the most rational though it is likely that you will need to use a combination of all three. First let it be known that you would like the permanent evening shifts even if none are currently available. Your daughter is indeed capable of looking after herself and will actually enjoy this time on her own especially as time ticks by and with age she becomes more independent. Her safety is paramount however so if at any time you feel her safety is compromised you will have to review the situation. She has her head screwed on and even though she may get up to a little mischief as teenagers tend to do it is nothing really outlandish or dangerous or stupid. You can trust her is what I am saying. Also you can trust the environment that you are living in.

Once you have applied for evening shifts and if none are available or forthcoming you will have no option but to compete for casual shifts. See what the coming rosters bring and if the availability of shifts and hours are not to your liking then start looking for a more suitable position elsewhere. Maintain any shifts you can get while you do this and hopefully the new enterprise will make up any short fall.

Remember all this is serving to direct you towards your goals not away from them so I agree, to go full time at work would not suit and you would only find yourself miserable and depressed. Thus we are trying to strike a balance here, of paying the bills and surviving while you aim to move yourself forward in more positive directions. We understand it is not easy and this is your current challenge. To make things work and fit with your future desires. Rest easy that you have always managed in the past even in the most difficult of times and you have always survived and pulled through. This is but a mere hiccup in the scheme of life. Give it the necessary attention it needs and no more. That is, follow the guidance above and take comfort that action has/is being taken and then you can do no more. To worry is only compounding the situation and the stress that you feel. We are here to tell you that even though this time is stormy calm waters will return. It will not be like this forever. You are uncomfortable because you are being forced against your will to act when you were ill prepared.

Yes communication is a problem at this company. There is an 'us' and 'them' division. Things will never change and may only get worse. Luckily for you your future here is limited. Hold onto that thought when times get tough. Still try to operate from a place of *calm* and *non-reaction* if you can. Keep your nose clean, opinions to yourself and try to ignore any negativity about the place. Meanwhile continue with your plans for the new enterprise, you have come so far and are so close to everything manifesting. We embrace your heart with much love at such troubled times and draw ever nearer to you. You never face these things alone.

We are always by your side, watching and guiding you towards *Light and Being*. — Nameless.

Thank you Nameless. I always feel calmer after talking to you.

10

AUGUST 2013

SUN 11TH AUGUST

Hi Nameless, more of a catch up session for you today. As you know last week was my fiftieth birthday. I had planned (more wished and hoped) for a big celebration jetting myself off to Hawaii for a week or twos' worth of luxury and R and R. Sadly it was not the case. Even if I could afford to send myself I can't leave Daughter at home by herself until she reaches sixteen which is another two years away. I certainly couldn't afford to take her with me as even though a teenager I would be paying airfare and accommodation for two adults plus spending money. I was highly disappointed (actually pretty peeved) that my milestone birthday pretty much came and went fairly unnoticed.

Instead of Hawaii I decided to treat myself to a shopping trip for some much needed clothes with the grand sum of three hundred dollars. You'd be amazed at what a bargain hunter I am and came back with bags and bags of stuff feeling like I have a whole new wardrobe including shoes (Target of course) which uplifted me no end. I know some people would think nothing of spending three hundred dollars or even three times that amount on one dress or a pair of shoes or jeans. Oh to be so extravagant!

Last week I treated myself to a John of God crystal healing session[1] and the host also read my cards for me. Apparently there is more friction coming at work, money, travel and a mysterious man who comes to help me in some way. I wonder if the traveling will ever come to fruition or is this just something they tell everyone? Another treat I gave myself was the gift of the Reiki I class that I've booked and am really looking forward to.

Today was Daughter's birthday and I took her and a couple of friends to Aussie World[2] for the day. The girls pretty much went off by themselves and having to pay an entry fee myself I decided to have my own fun and go on all the rides solo. I spent the whole day doing the rounds and I must say I scared myself shitless on a few of them but it was a fun scary and I was having a ball. I should do that more often just to blow all the cobwebs out. The girls were coming off the giant slides and spotted me on the dodgems having a rip-roaring time, being so shocked to see me (an oldie) having such fun they stopped to take photos! We went on a few rides together too as our paths crossed. Mainly the ones where the girls wanted to see me get wet (read drown me) or if they thought I might shit my pants, LOL. Be warned though, never enter a simulator with ten year old boys who think it's funny to let off their stinky farts! Other than that it was a wonderful day and we all left with our vibrations on a high.

SAT 17TH AUGUST

Good morning. It's very early for me on a Saturday morning when I usually lay in recovering from the hectic week. Indeed it's been extremely hectic this week in particular having worked every single day, getting up at four-thirty a.m. Everyone has had colds/flu all around me which I've been desperately trying to avoid and finally succumbed a few days ago probably because I've been too busy to 'protect' myself. On top of all this we have a rental inspection on Tuesday so I've been coming home from work flu ridden and madly cleaning and gardening so really I've been doing twelve to fourteen hour days all week, am totally exhausted and have not had time for much else such as catching up with you.

I bypassed human resources at work and went straight to the big Kahuna and put in an application for the new rosters as you suggested. She said they're working on them and it could take a month before they're finalized. I gave her five options that I'd be happy with and she said she should be able to accommodate at least one so that was an enormous stress off my shoulders. Meanwhile I applied for as many casual shifts as I could thinking I wouldn't get many like last roster but this time I got all of them and now I have too many! I somehow think you had a hand in that because I was so stressed. Oh well, better to have too much than not enough and it's such a relief knowing that I'll have money coming in and so much that I can even probably splurge on a new bikini. A good quality one from a real swimwear store and not from Big W! I priced them the other day at about a hundred and seventy to a hundred and ninety dollars. Totally outrageous but oh how good will I feel in it?

All this working has reminded me of what a scam it all is. Especially for someone on minimum wage. You bust your gut all week to barely scrape by and pay the bills and there's not much left over for anything else, any enjoyment. It all goes on the rent or mortgage, food, electricity, phones, petrol, car, insurance, dental bills… the list goes on. We still can't afford a decent holiday where we get to stay in a hotel or apartment and will have to tent it once again this coming vacation. We build all these so called necessities of life all round us and then spend most of our waking time working to pay for it all. Even though I whinge at not having enough moula I still think I'd prefer to work less and have less. If I ever had to work fulltime in a job I dislike again I know I would just be a depressed zombie. Really, you work and then you die…what's that all about? What's the point? Where's the fun and the 'real life' experience? I'd much prefer the tribal or nomadic existence but we're all stuck in one point mainly so we can educate our kids. Why, so they too can follow our paths? I certainly hope not. I hope Daughter has a much freer life than I. I project myself three years into the future when she's finished high school and I'm in a position to travel. How awesome it will be. I'm really a Gypsy at heart and all of this staying in one place is just torture.

Sorry Nameless about the venting. I guess at my age I'm still trying to get the (life) balance right. I thought I'd have it all sorted by now. Perhaps I never will.

We hear you. We hear the distress and frustration in your words that things aren't what you expected them to be at this life's stage. You are in the midst of what we would call a glip. A short term speed hump so to speak or bump in the road that has served to slow you down. A hiccup. Do not fret as sometimes these anomalies are there to serve the purpose of making you look at and re assess your life so that yes, you decide that you do not want to go in that direction but instead would prefer to take a different route. So we would look at this honorably as a good thing. That you are not just following blindly society and their expectations of you, but are courageous and brave enough to follow your own true path.

It's true what they say about money being the root of all evil. If only you humans had stayed with the barter system then your lives would have been much simpler and I think this is what you hunger for. A simpler existence with the emphasis on *experience's* rather than material consumerism. This is your challenge and your struggle. How to make this happen in this current world that you live in. It is possible and we know that you will find a way. That in the near future you will find your bliss on earth as it will all finally fall into place and when it does life will seem so easy in comparison to what you have been experiencing. It will be like the newly discovered band who suddenly finds popularity and with it increased wealth but what people don't see is all the years of hard work that lead up to that point in their lives.

Your real work is yet to be discovered. Your real work has been a life's work in progress and is yet to be bought into the light for all to see. It is at this point you will be able to finally breathe a true, deep and invigorating breathe. It is at this point you will truly come alive. You know what this is.

(This book of channeling and communication with Nameless etc.)

You work towards it every day. As yet you share it only with us. But one day you will go public. And then you will blossom into your new life as if you were re born. It will be a completely different existence to the one you experience now. It will be so vastly different it will be like two worlds, like you have lived two lives. The hard life is coming to an end. The new and exciting life is in its infancy, a cell in the womb of life that with each division draws one step closer to drawing its first breath. We are here to encourage and support you along the way. To remind you that it is possible, to not give up, to stay focused and on your path. It is important not only for you but for the betterment of the earth and of all mankind that you spread the word as what you have to say will spark thoughts in others that will set them on their own life's discovery and adventures.

Your struggle is because you are a unique soul. Not all are willing to listen. Discount these and offer yourself to more ready and likeminded souls. This is not about preaching your beliefs but merely sharing your experiences so that others can ponder for themselves. It is all chicken soup for the spiritualist's soul. There are many more others out there like you. You just need to make the connection. Reach out. This is why we suggested getting involved in groups as you are yet to do. Again we remind you. Here you will find a great deal of support and encouragement and recognize that you are not the only one. We highly recommend it. Perhaps when the busy work schedule settles back into normality for you. But it wouldn't hurt to touch base if you can find the time.

You are travelling well my friend. All is good with the Universe. We support you with courage and strength always. You are never alone. Always with love — Nameless.

Thank you Nameless.

SUN 18TH AUGUST

Good morning everyone. Yesterday Daughter and I took a picnic lunch and climbed Mt Cooroora in Tuchekoi National Park. Mt Cooroora is a huge majestic mountain that stands tall guarding the little hinterland town of Pomona like an ancient god. The mountain is subject to an annual race called the Pomona King of the Mountain where contestants from all over the world race from the township to the mountain peak and back, the winner usually doing it in around twenty-three minutes. The hiking sign says it takes an hour to climb and an hour to descend. In the two years that we camped through four states and the numerous difficult bush walks I've been on, this would have to be the hardest walk I've ever done. About half way up the mountain it ceases to be a walk and becomes a rock climb with strategically placed chains to help pull you up the mountain. Some areas are so steep I could barely stretch my legs from one footing to the next.

The last time I climbed this mountain was ten years ago. I was forty and on the precipice of a breakup with my partner. He got me stoned then took me on this climb and in my paranoia I really thought he was trying to kill me, it was that difficult. After climbing it yesterday I wonder how I ever managed it stoned. Daughter and I climbed to the peak in an hour and ten minutes but I continually had to stop and catch my breath and rest my aching legs. I didn't do too bad considering most people I saw going up and down were under thirty and I the only one carrying a backpack full of goodies, a picnic for us at the top. Someone asked if I was in training thinking the backpack contained weights as the mountain being so steep most people only took water bottles.

OMG! Once we reached the top it was sooooo worth it! We had picked the most perfect day, the bluest sky, a gentle breeze and barely a cloud in site. The view from up there is spectacular, breathtaking. Directly below is Pomona township, to the left about six kilometers is Cooran and in the distance you can see the Kin Kin ranges, Boreen Point, Lake Cootharaba and the sand flats of the Noosa North Shore National Park. There was a fire in the distance creating a smoky haze over Noosa itself. I could hear a distant lawn mower and the train toot its horn as it journeyed through Cooran Station. It was like being up in heaven looking down on everything. I remembered a mountain climb from way back when Daughter was little. To entice her up the range I told her she could touch the clouds at the top. There's a photo of our hands reaching out to do just that but today there are no clouds.

We settle on some rocks and enjoy our lunch having philosophical chats while we take in the sights. It's so beautiful I don't want to leave and we idle a few hours. I think about how wonderful it would be to have a wedding up here and we discuss the idea of a giant waterslide as an easy descent. Then she gets some teenage bee in her bonnet and we have a tiff ending with her storming off down the mountain without me. I don't know if I will ever climb this mountain again and want to take this opportunity to talk with a tree so search for a likely candidate finding one set back a little from the edge of the path. Its spiritual center is facing the view of Pomona.

Q. Can I sit with you a while? (I'm already sitting next to the tree)

No.

Q. Is it because I'm blocking your view?

No.

Q. Is it because I'm stifling your roots?

Yes, you are preventing day to day life, ants moving and carrying about their business. Everything comes to a stop.

You have an awesome view. (I stand)

No.

Q. I don't understand. I think it's awesome and your spiritual center is facing the view, did you want to be closer to the edge?

No.

Q. Then what?

Lots of people come and stand in front of me blocking the view therefore half of my life all I see is people's backs and I can't see the town from here due to the trees on the other side. So really all I do is look out onto more trees and grass down below.

Q. You say half of your life, how old are you?

Thirty three. Young compared to some others who have been here much longer.

Q. I'm curious. How did you get here? It's so high up I've noticed there are no birds around, it's really quiet.

Actually I originate from a little further down the mountain and as a seedling landed on a mountaineers backpack. When he reached the top and set his bag down the bump tipped me off and here is where I landed and stayed. Others have been bought up by the up draughts of strong winds and yet more through the excrement of scavenging animals. Birds do occasionally drop by but during the day they hunt lower to the ground. There is a small colony that nests here at night.

Q. What is your name? What can I call you?

Afllugh. (Ah- flew)

Afllugh goes on to tell me that he likes watching the lizards run and play when there is no one here.

The sunrises and sunsets are just beautiful especially this time of year. I'm lucky because I face north I can see both.

His favorite part of the day is when all the people have gone and he can just listen to the sounds. The rustle of the leaves in the wind, the hum of the cars in the distance, the occasional kookaburra and dog barking.

I love to watch the moon rise in the sky and bathe its glow on the land down below.

Q. Do trees have emotions?

Of course they do, I'm insulted that you ask.

Q. Are you a happy tree?

Most of the time. Except when people are here all day long. I get tired of their chatter and noise. I try to shut down and ignore them. Mostly they bore me. It's always the same. "Look at that amazing view." Occasionally there will be cross words spoken such as the argument you just had with your daughter. That's way more interesting. A bit of action that's what I like. I wish there was more action around here. It can get a bit boring, same old, same old. I like watching a good storm go by. Everything whipped into a frenzy, the birds below all scattering. Oh and the twinkling of the town lights through the trees on a clear still night with a full moon is my favorite. That's when I'm most at peace.

Q. Can I talk with you from home? I really have to go my daughters waiting.

No.

Q. Can I hug you?

No.

Q. Am I disturbing your peace?

Yes.

Hmm, Afllugh is not a very friendly tree. He just wants to be left alone in peace and everyone else is long gone so I make my way down the mountain. My legs have turned to jelly and are shaking as my hamstrings go into spasm. I can't believe my daughter left her fifty year old mother to climb down this steep mountain on her own. I'm met by the p.m. shift, the runners who are bounding up the mountain in the cool of the late afternoon. I think of them reaching the top and commenting on the "amazing view" and how annoyed Afllugh will be staring at their backs. They bound up and they bound down reaching the bottom before me. At one stage I think my legs are just going to give way. I wish for a walking staff and one instantly materializes, lucky me. I don't know if I could have finished the walk without it. I don't know if I will ever be able to climb this mountain again.

WED 21ST AUGUST

Morning All. Finally I have a day to myself to rest and recuperate from the hectic week. I'm feeling quite exhausted and am in desperate need of reenergizing. I've been working Monday's of late and can't go to Lotus Light for a much needed healing, it'll be at least two weeks before I can return. Both you and Lotus Light have been my saviors' this year supporting me through difficult times, stress, exhaustion and illness. I'm so grateful.

We have a front veranda room that is as big as our kitchen/dining and lounge room combined. We call it the butterfly room because it's totally enclosed in fly wire and resembles a butterfly enclosure. Sometimes I use this room as my art studio and sometimes I set up my massage table for healing but mostly we use it as an extension of the house. The open plan living/kitchen/dining area we call the rainbow room as when the sun shines through the glass slat windows rainbows are thrown throughout the entire room on the walls and floors.

This morning I came out to find one such rainbow on the floor and in desperate need of some energy I kneeled down and cupped it in my hands aligning it with my palm chakras. Then I noticed there were five more little rainbows scattered along the floor and realized if I lay down they would align with the chakras of my body so I lay there for a while giving myself a rainbow bath, topping and tailing to bathe all seven chakra's until the light faded. As beautiful as it was I feel I need more (yes I'm that exhausted). Clearing my chakras with the pendulum can take at least half an hour or longer especially when I've been working in a toxic environment and I don't always have the time to sit and do this.

Q. I'm wondering, can anyone can give me a quick way to clear and reenergize myself?

It is I Hoyan. We understand you are aware there are many ways to reenergize but you are asking for a quick fix. This is sometimes necessary but not always recommended for at times these may be enough but at other times they will only suffice to get you through until you can manage more comprehensive methods.

If it was warmer we would suggest you go down to the lake for a quick swim. The brackish salt water being cleansing and purifying as well as refreshing. A quick cold shower with some vigorous skin brushing using salt would also suffice if you are brave enough on a cold morning such as this. If not what to do? You need to raise the vibration not only of yourself but the air around you so that your intake is more pure and energized. Put on some loud music that you can dance to and go for it. Sing along and really let yourself go. Blow off all the cobwebs and shake off all the negativity. You could have a large glass of cool water and smudge yourself prior to doing this. Remember water is a conductor of energy. Clap your hands. Sounds silly but it works. Clap loud and clap hard. Clap all around your aura. Clapping increases your endorphin (feel good) hormones as does any form of movement. So running, jumping, swimming all of these are good. If you had a pool you could do a few laps. A trampoline is a good way to shake off negative energy. When you've finished dancing put on your crystal healing CD to retune yourself. This way you can go about your business while it works in the background.

If you can spare at least fifteen minutes go for an earth walk barefoot in the sand or in the bush, forest or park. While you are there hug a tree and ask permission for an *energy transference*. On your walk smell any flowers that you pass by breathing in their essence. Glory in their color and form, bring one home if you can. Also pat any dogs (you will automatically get energy transference) and wonder at the wild life. It is likely you will enjoy yourself and linger longer taking at least half to one hour

Re polarize yourself using magnetic therapy and practice the vitalization stance.[3] You don't have to do the full treatment if you don't have time. Just the first two steps will increase your wellbeing, ridding any negativity or dark energy you have picked up and opening up the channels for chi life force energy to flow freely. Take a fifteen minute sun bath. Sit in a warm sunny spot and look at the sun through squinted eyes. This stimulates the pineal gland rebalancing your hormones. It also activates your chakras and dissolves negative energy from your aura.

Prahnic breathing. Circulating pure life force energy through your system and purging all toxic material and negative energy on the out breath. This is not to be underestimated. A quick crystal cleanse of your aura with your selenite wand. Finally a warm Epsom salt bath at night will see you better by morning.

These are just a few to get you started, as you become clearer you will no doubt think of more. Add them to your list to share with clients.

Q. This is all great physical and external stuff I can do but is there any quick internal cleanse and reenergize I can do? For example if I'm in transit after I've left work or have crossed paths with dark energy and am not in a position to do any of the above?

The Prahnic breathing stated above coupled with visualization is your best bet. A complete meditation would be too long but something to get you by until you are able to manage more is what is required here. Try previously learnt methods like the vacuum cleaner meditation[4] followed by a quick rainbow bath[5] and/or a complete body rub. These you could do sitting in your car by the side of the road if necessary but always better if you can sit in nature (the beach or a park).

Thanks Hoyan, much appreciated. I love the visual of the internal vacuum cleaner picking up all that sticky mire and expelling it down into the earth.

SUN 25TH AUGUST

I'm sitting in the beautiful afternoon sun down at Paradise Beach my feet buried in the sand, the cool wind tickling my neck. The Brahminy Kites are circling above me hunting their prey. I love hearing them call out, it's a home like sound to me signifying this is where I'm meant to be. I look out across the lake and can see a lone windsurfer and five yachts tacking with the wind a few kilometers away. Apart from that I'm alone and reveling in the peace and quiet bar the Kites and the waves constantly breaking on the shoreline. I breathe in the salt water air and purify my lungs, my cells, my very being whilst eyeing the clouds pillowing in the distance. For the first time in ages I'm feeling quite relaxed.

I went to the Pomona market yesterday. I won't say I worked there because I didn't attend to one soul, the whole day nearing disaster. Except for one gentleman early in the morning no one came and even spoke to me the whole day. At least last time I had a few interested parties and enquiries. This gentleman wanted my opinion on a Chinese herbalist he was thinking of seeing down in Brisbane. We had a brief discussion and then he left. That was it, I saw no one else all day.

Word around the market was that it was very quiet generally. I sat and watched the healers opposite me, two Zen Shiatsu masseuses and a Reflexologist. I watched them work and the people who stopped to browse their signage and their stalls. I realized that Energy and Crystal Healing not being very mainstream is going to be a harder 'sell' than I thought. It's a bit out there for some people and they don't understand it, thinking it all gobbledygook and airy fairy. Thank god I booked the Reiki course as I feel this being better understood will help draw people to me so at least I can explain what else I do. Really it's all working with energy and chi life force just like Acupuncture, Zen Shiatsu and Reflexology so I don't understand why people have trouble comprehending (or believing) it.

The whole day was not an entire loss. I scrutinized the set ups opposite me and realized how simple and streamlined they were with simple matting and scatter cushions on the ground and storage ottomans for seating. Very simple and Zen, very tropical and Bali. Also quick and easy to set up compared to my tables chairs and massage table. I spent the morning sketching and making lists for yet another shopping expedition. How much money am I prepared to throw at this?

I won't be able to do this market again until October as next market day I'll be doing the Reiki weekend and then Daughter and I go on holidays. Before I left I went to visit Ray's crystal stall and purchased a large feather and crystal wand I had coveted for weeks to accompany my abalone shell when smudging. I left happy but wondering…

Q. Is taking my energy and crystal healing to the public going to work? I don't think they are ready for it.

You have only just begun. Do not think about quitting. Do not allow this to even enter your mind. It is exhausting we know, all the work you have done to get this far and yet there is still more work to do. Again this is only the beginning. It would be remiss of you to think that just to open your doors, your arms that patronage would flood your way. We reiterate you are an educator and it is up to you to bring into the light an awareness of the type of healing work you do. Remember that at the moment you are planting seeds/ideas in people's minds. Even though you speak to no one all those that pass by and read your signage are embedding their consciousness unconsciously. We are aware of the money situation but you must find ways to market yourself and spread the word. Brainstorm and make a list, choose at least five. Give your all and saturate the market as best you can. Also you may find that this market is not the right one for you. Don't limit yourself. Experiment with different markets, different marketing strategies, different stall set ups. This is all a learning process. Remember we discussed earlier that how you begin is not how you will carry on and you will change and adjust as you experience and grow. Yes Reiki being better known and more mainstream will be beneficial to your practice. Also the idea of having things to sell at your stall as the Reflexologist did is a good one. This will aid in drawing people to you. Be ready for pamphlets for those that drop by. A tiger never gives up. A tiger is courageous even in the face of death.

Oooh, that's a bit strange that last bit Nameless, that doesn't sound like you at all. Sounds more like a Reiki guide coming through, there's even an accent.

Q. Who's speaking?

I am your Musta (Master), Shozimishun. I teach you listen. Be good student we get along velly (very) well. (Laughs)

Shozimishun is sitting on a mat cross legged laughing. I get the sense he can be tough, serious but also humorous. I'm taken aback by this unexpected presentation (of a new guide?). Perhaps my Reiki guide making his presence known but he is not what I expected in a Reiki guide at all. I sit there a little in shock and a little afraid of his masterful aura and feel like the naughty school kid who just got caught with their hand in the cookie jar.

You go now catch big bear and bring me the craws (claws).

He shooed me away with a wave of his hand, dismissing me. What the hell does he mean?

□□□

I'm reading over my notes and glancing out of the corner of my eye I spy a dark shadow running across the sand towards me. Jumping with fright thinking it's a large spider I look to find a feather at my feet. Marikahee?

SAT 31ST AUGUST

OMG! I've had the most horrendous week at work having worked five days in a row this week. Most people would say so what? They do that every week and often more. Some might even think me a bit of a bludger never working a full week but it's the getting up at four thirty a.m. every morning and they're nine hour days not eight and you're so busy you barely get time for a piss break and the A.I.N's often don't get lunch until an hour before they go home and the RN's sometimes not at all. Not that you go home straight away as then you've got to go and pay bills and pick up groceries, put fuel in the car etc. Living rurally it can be a twelve hour day before you even get home and then it's cook dinner, do dinner, do dishes, put bins out, do laundry, get clothes, lunch and bag ready for the next day, teenage issues and drama's and now it's been a fifteen hour day and it's stressful to get it all done in time for you to go to bed early enough so you can get up at four thirty a.m. again the next day. Phew! And so it continues the same for five days when actually I'm a born night owl and this is all in opposition to my natural biorhythms throwing me totally out of whack.

Needless to say by day five I'm completely exhausted and doing my best to juggle the demands of eight residents all wanting something at the same time. I think I'm doing pretty well and am horrified once again to be yelled at and physically abused by a resident, having a meal tray thrown at me because I have to prioritize and with three residents in wheelchairs desperately needing my help to visit the bathroom (all at the same time), her request for a cup of tea is not first on my 'to do' list. Really? These people are eighty not eight. They don't care that other people need my help. They just want what they want and they want it now. "I WANT MY CUP OF TEA AND I WANT IT NOW!" she yelled as she threw the meal tray at me and stamped her fist on the table demanding her third cup of tea for the morning.

They certainly don't care about me and I've witnessed their total lack of concern or empathy for each other and it shocks me. I sit here thinking about the people most likely to get abused in their jobs. Policeman, doctors, nurses (especially A.I.N's who are less respected than nurses) and paramedics. They're all in caring positions where it's their job to help people because that's what they love to do. How revolting and unfair that they should suffer abuse while attempting to do good for others. I still can't get over it.

Today I have taken myself down to Paradise Beach in an effort to revive myself. I sink my feet in the sand and stand in the revitalization pose for ten minutes gazing out at the lake and crisp blue sky, filling my lungs with salt air. Strangely I can't feel any revitalizing going on and think I must be that severely blocked. I'm feeling a bit down, not quite depressed but feel I need some help/direction so decide to do a white room meditation instead. I lay back on my picnic rug, close my eyes and set about building my room…

▫▫▫

I decide on a beautiful white marble floor with the faintest of grey and cream feathering. The marble continues half way up the walls and turns into the most opulent white Paua shell. If you look closely the pearlite blue reflected in its sheen is actually a vision of a distant ocean so far away it's a mere hint in its surface. I look up at my creation of a milky white glass ceiling as it draws over the top of me completing the enclosure. Next comes the chair, always grand. This time it's a white lion also sculptured from marble. His head is large and ferocious acting to crown and protect me. Speaking of protection I summon Teku to come and stand beside me. Not that I feel like I need protecting but that it feels appropriate to have him here. He greets me with a warrior dance, a Hakka, all fierce to show me his power and strength then rises up afterwards and says comically, "Hey what's up bro?" in his cheeky delightful manner. I laugh, his smile is infectious. Already I feel lighter. Next come's the door. I make it a double and put a key code on the door handle then firmly command...

"Show me my bliss!"

Sitting in anticipation and excitement until I can sit no longer I vision the doors to open. They separate slowly to reveal a cascade of white feathers raining down which Quan Yin materializes through. She walks towards me and places a pink and gold pillow in my lap. On the pillow is a scroll. Unravelling the scroll reveals these words…

"Blessed is the one who sits on the hill of divine
guidance overlooking the truth of all existence and
reveling in the knowing of being."

Quan Yin speaks to me…

Take this knowing and bring it into *feeling*. For *feeling* is where the truth of all being lies. Draw this feeling essence into the very core of you and the core of every cell of you. You are about to shed the skin of old as a snake does in the spring of new life. You will discard the old life and step into the new, never to return. The key and the gift is in the *feeling*. That is your answer.

Quan Yin nodded to me a knowing nod then stepped backwards through the door as graceful as a geisha. The feathers blew up around her feet and body in a vortex and as she disappeared from view the doors quietly ambled closed.

I turned to Teku and thanked him for standing guard for me and did something totally out of character, I asked him for a hug. Big, strong, Amazonian Teku hugged me and I felt safe and secure, loved in his arms. I couldn't believe I was actually hugging one of my guides, I had never thought to and as Quan Yin had said I just concentrated on the feeling of this beautiful warmth and safety, this cocoon of caring and enveloping of protection. Bursting with happiness and appreciation I started to cry, the tears trickling down my cheeks. OMG, am I falling in love with Teku? But this seriously can't be! Just my luck, he's already taken and his love for me is more as brotherly protector. Also we only ever meet on the spiritual plane, LOL. But really I'm just feeling a great sense of BEING loved, which I haven't felt in a long time.

□□□

I pondered what Quan Yin had revealed and decided it reiterates Nameless's advice from the past. This is my interpretation…

- **Stop *thinking/doing and instead feel***
- ***Feel what it is you want/desire***
- ***Feel where it is you want to be and it is so***
- ***You can have anything, do anything, be anything. All you have to do is shut your eyes and feel it. Bring this feeling into your everyday existence***
- ***If you want to be happy feel what it is like to be happy (Remember we choose our emotions at any given moment whether it be happy, sad, angry etc.)***

It's not revelatory but somehow we keep needing reminding until it becomes second nature. Maybe this is what Quan Yin is trying to tell me. That to enter into relationship (or anything else for that matter) I first have to feel it, not just know that it's possible but feel it into existence. Or perhaps I've been living too much in my intellect and need to bring my energy back into my solar plexus which is the core feeling chakra and from there back into my body.

I know most of us are so busy 'doing' that we forget to feel at all, for ourselves or others. I know it in my heart that if we were more feeling towards others we would all be closer to Light and Being.

11

SEPTEMBER 2013

FRI 6TH SEPTEMBER

Yeeeah! Finally I've got my permanent short shifts back and today is one of my first free afternoons in months. I finally have my happy medium and don't have to stress about too little or too much work. Even though I still hate getting up at four thirty a.m. I know I have to make some sacrifices. Today I've decided to visit Caabd as I look back over my notes shocked to find a couple of months have gone by since our last visit. First I head down to the lake and pick up some ash from the public barbeques and as I'm already in the car I drive instead of walk.

At the entrance to the private beach I see a new extremely large "No Camping/No Fires" sign has been bolted to the iron gate by council warning of fines. No doubt the stranger was discovered possibly having been reported by someone. I did try to warn him. The good news is I'll have the valley, the lake and the beach to myself and as I walk the path I'm serenaded by an array of birds high in the tree tops. Arriving at the beach I inspect the stranger's campsite but there's no sign of him ever having been there. Even the humpies are mostly destroyed, looking like a bunch of dried up branches washed up by the tides.

Feeling tired I decide on a nap before meeting with Caabd, laying in a sunny spot and using a large log as a wind break. This time of year requires more caution, it's September and the snakes will soon be on the move if not already being unusually hot for the beginning of spring. I bathe in the complete silence. There are no sounds of boats, people, dogs, kid, cars or even planes overhead. Bliss! It doesn't take long for me to fall asleep but an hour or so later I'm woken by the cacophony of Black-Cockatoos arriving in the trees above and I hear the familiar Kites in the distance. An hour is all I needed and as I shake out my towel ready to visit Caabd, there graphitized on the log beside me in charcoal from a previous campfire are the words, "Rory pooed on Emma." "Nice one," I grumble looking around to make sure I hadn't slept in any!

Once again I apologize to Caabd for my absence and he suggests that whenever I'm able to visit is ok by him, no pressure. Caabd doesn't seem to stress, just taking things as they come. If I visit great, if not his life continues on regardless. He tells me the infestation is now over and I ask about the ash hoping I'm not too late. He still needs it thank god or I would've felt terrible not getting it to him sooner. His main worry is water, it hasn't rained decently for months and sixty percent of Queensland is currently classified in drought. It's hard for him to recover when he's not getting the required quota. I tell Caabd the weather report isn't bringing any good news, a trickle here and there maybe. We're back on water rations ourselves and half of Boreen Point has already bought their first load to fill their empty tanks. I know traditionally paperbark's drop their limbs to survive drought conditions and I look up to see that as tall as he is Caabd only has three limbs.

Q. Are you happy today? Ugghhh, why did I even ask that?

No.

Of course not stupid (I'm talking to myself not Caabd). He's not well and struggling to survive.

Q. Can I have a hug today? (Of course he'll say no)

Yes.

Yes! He said yes! I'm so shocked by his answer, I wasn't expecting it and ecstatic at his willingness to openly accept me I'm happily jumping with joy, I can't believe it. Then quickly composing myself I look to see if anyone has stepped onto the beach and is observing this bizarre behavior. I don't know why though I choose not to hug him straight away, instead saving it for later when we say good bye.

We discuss the recent burning of the ground cover by the council pre fire season. Caabd was concerned that if things got out of control he could catch fire. He says he's seen quite a few trees burn in his time and it's not pretty. He watches the fires across the lake on the Noosa North Shore every year. Last year was particularly devastating and he worries about his family on the other side of the lake, wondering if they're still alive. I rub his bark to comfort him and can't help myself, peeling some off. I ask him if it hurts expecting him to say no because he's peeling and shedding all over, that's what paperbark's do, that's their nature. He say's when I peel it off I take more than I mean to not just the dead layers but some of the newer, fresher bark underneath comes off or is exposed before it's ready. Kind of like us when we're sunburnt and peeling, the new skin underneath is pink and raw.

Q. Do trees feel pain?

Yes.

Q. Physical pain?

Yes.

Q. Emotional pain?

Yes.

He thought about this last one for a while before he answered. I don't think Caabd is very in touch with his emotions or it's just that he's not had to really think about them before. To him, he just is. But there is definite pain and sadness surrounding the loss of his family. I rubbed his bark some more. Some areas felt like velvet. We sat for a while in silence until I was 'woken up' by the fact that I had inadvertently peeled another strip of bark off his trunk.

"Oh my god! I'm so sorry Caabd. I'm so so sorry!"

I can't believe I just did that after what he just told me but it's automatic that when you sit next to a Paperbark you have this unconscious compulsion to strip away the layers. I rubbed the area and inspected the damage which was quite deep and surprisingly damp underneath given the drought situation, evidence that Caabd had managed to store some water and was not as parched as I had originally thought. Feeling quite bad I offered a healing and set about 'putting in.'[1] *I couldn't sense any anger from him, it was minor compared to what he'd been dealing with and he knew I didn't mean it.*

The healing over time came to leave and I drew in for my hug, fidgeting until I found just the right nook and position and comfortably lay my head down on his trunk, gazing out at the lake. "Ah this is the spot, beautiful." Now I could relax and let go, feel that falling feeling again. Only I couldn't mentally let myself go because I was conscious it was that time of day where people start bringing their dogs down for a walk before tea time and someone might see me hugging this tree. Trying to enjoy my first physical hug with Caabd I kept an intent ear out for strangers entering our zone and so the whole thing was rather spoilt because I allowed myself to feel guilt and shame for sharing with this beautiful being. I left feeling a little bit sad that I had let both of us down, that Caabd's first ever hug was not the free enveloping and sharing of unabashed love that I had wanted it to be.

WED 11TH SEPTEMBER

Hi Nameless. Not really a channeling today I just wanted to let you know about some research I've been doing online.

I looked up the Latin Binomial for the Paperbark tree and its formal or scientific name is Melaleuca Quinquenervia.[2] *A swamp loving, coastal hugging, very fire and drought resistant species that is part of the eucalyptus family. Apparently the seed casings can contain up to two hundred seeds each, can fall as far away from the tree as one hundred and seventy meters and the seeds themselves can survive for up to ten years and can even germinate underwater (if the bottom is soil based) so a very hardy tree and one well adapted to the harsh conditions found in Australia.*

I'm sure any gardener would know the properties and benefits of ash on the garden but being a flat dweller of many years and with little garden experience I turned to Wikipedia for help (http://en.wikipedia.org/wiki/Ash) and found the main constituent to be calcium carbonate (twenty-five to forty percent) with only one percent phosphate. The calcium carbonate increases the soils PH by acting as a liming agent to de acidify it. So Caabd needed the ash to improve the quality of his soil. Smart tree.

Speaking of trees while I was online and on a whim I decided to google 'talking with trees.' Was there any one else out there doing it too or was I the only nutter? To my relief there is a whole community of people who believe in or have experienced communication with trees. I've barely scraped the surface but in my narrow search came across Fran Sorin who is an avid gardener and author. In her blog[3] *Fran suggests posing a question to a tree and then stilling the self and waiting for an answer and that trees, rivers, rocks, leaves and all of nature can help us open to previously untapped wiseness. There's also interesting comments from people who've had experiences with trees, one man having received psychic visions from a tree he accidently collided with. Fran's also got a great project going called 'Give a flower, get a smile.' I love, love, love this idea. Giving a flower to someone (a friend, family, a stranger) for no reason, taking them by surprise and bringing a smile to their face and yours thereby lifting the spirit, soul and energy vibration of both giver and receiver. She suggests starting with just five flowers and they don't need to be purchased but maybe from your garden or elsewhere.*

When Daughter was little she used to bring me a flower nearly every day picked on her way home from school, sometimes a beautiful hibiscus and sometimes a weed from the side of the road but it made my day that she had thought of me enough to do it and carry it all the way home with her. What a great way to raise one's vibration and the vibration of the planet! Next time I'm feeling down I'm going to try this as my remedy.

MON 16TH SEPTEMBER

I've just experienced the most wonderful and interesting Reiki workshop retreat. Arriving at the entrance to find an extremely long and steep driveway I decided to park my car on the street and walk to the house. I'm glad I didn't drive down, not only for the fact that I didn't think my car would make it back up the driveway on my exit but because I experienced the most beautiful walk through a mini rainforest which helped set the tone for what was to come and eased my mind and physical body into that healing space before I made my entry.

I rang the large bell and was greeted by my Reiki Master, a small petite French woman, an artist like me…it was meant to be. I immediately fell in love with her, I had chosen well. Reiki Master summoned me through the house and introduced me to the others. We shared our stories and reasons for coming before being guided through the introduction in our workbooks whilst all the time I was taking in the visual appeal and ambience of the house.

It was very Zen which surprised me for an artist who are usually clutter bugs. The whole living area was surrounded by floor to ceiling glass windows and doors that opened to invite the caressing winds wafting over the decking, tinkling the wind chimes as they passed. Across the vast lawn was a pool and a Balinese shade house. An Indian day bed resided in the lounge area along with a large bamboo coffee table. The furniture was not overdone, a few key statement pieces sitting amongst large areas of wooden flooring all very natural and easy on the eye. All sorts of crystals were placed throughout the rooms but not overbearingly, more like you would catch them with a passing eye but only if you were paying attention which I did. A little fountain trickled in the central court yard which could be seen from every room. The whole setting was very calming and my house in comparison looked like some chaotic explosion. I would love such a place. Oh the peace and the bliss of it all, I would never want to leave such a house. Next to the office, itself very open and airy, was a smaller lounge area which currently housed the massage table. There were floor to ceiling bookcases embedded in the walls and I was pleased to see she was an avid book collector like me as I noticed the Mark Rothko edition reflecting her painting style. Speaking of paintings her large Zen like abstracts were on all the walls with just as many resting on the floors in all sorts of spaces somehow never adding to clutter the place. I was in awe of her private art studio dreaming of the possibility that one day, hopefully, I may have my very own.

After a tea break Reiki Master gave us our first healing demonstration. I was excited to see her use crystals and a pendulum! The pendulum she explained had been utilized more in her first year of practice but now she mainly used it as a visual tool for her students to recognize the activity of the chakras. I was extremely surprised to note that Reiki was very similar to the process I had already been using, working to clear and re-energize the chakras and any blockages. I had expected Reiki to be something completely different to what I already knew though unsure of what that would be. Nameless had told me that I was already a healer and that I was only lacking in confidence. Attending this workshop has given me the realization that I do actually know what I'm doing and served to cement the knowledge and practice I've gained thus far. Having said that it was great to receive the power symbol and its many applications. Reiki Master bestowed upon us many beneficial tips, insights and knowledge that only comes with years of practicing and mastering. To me this cross pollination of experience is invaluable and I was extremely grateful.

We broke into groups of three and set about practicing our group healing. One by one we were summoned by Reiki Master to a room upstairs for our first attunement. I was glad to practice a healing before my attunement as a comparison for afterwards. My 'before' healing surprised me with its accuracy and I was already feeling sensations through my hands, possibly because of previous polarity work. My turn for attunement came. I climbed the stairs to the temple like room at the top of the house and sat in the leather lined chair. A large bowl of crystals sat in front of the open window which revealed the tree tops and the bluest of skies. A subtle incense atomized the room. Reiki Master guided me through the attunement as I closed my eyes, felt the breeze caress my face and listened to the chimes down below. Her soft flute like voice enveloped my very being and her breath awakened my spirit. The tingle activated in my hands extended all the way up to my elbows. This was the hot hands I had read about. I was now attuned to Reiki and thanked my Master!

Upon alighting the stairs it was my turn for a healing of which I felt nothing (this is not to say that healing has not occurred) for all I could feel was the strong tingling in my hands and forearms. Reiki Master said this was the gift I had been given that day (others possibly would take something else from the day). I know some complained they felt nothing with their hands but we were all told it would come the more we practiced.

I drove home on a positive high. It was such a beautiful drive and I was feeling empowered. I realized I was a beautiful, vibrant, playful being, vivacious, loud and happy but that I had been hiding myself away for such a long time because I knew I could be overpowering with my boldness and this repelled people. I had stopped interacting as myself and toned myself down to suit others. Mainly I did this at work as I had stopped interacting with people socially a long time ago. At home I can just be myself. The same goes with partners. I had always toned it down to be accepted. It has been a long time since I've been the real me, in my twenty's probably. I vowed to be more true to myself and who I am.

Here comes the dilemma…The second day of the workshop I felt a very different vibe. The energy had shifted. Three people had stayed overnight and I sensed there had been talking and among the subjects was me. I suddenly didn't feel welcome. Not by my Reiki Master and two of the others but by all the rest. There was silence at the table. Every one sat there like dead mullets. My revelation from the night before that I be my true bright and vivacious self went out the window. I could tell if I spoke animatedly like I wanted to I would annoy quite a few people at the table and one in particular who seemed to want to argue with me every time I opened my mouth of which I did the least possible because of the animosity I sensed. It was a shame as it clouded my whole day and experience. I was torn.

Q. Can someone help? Do I be my true self and to hell with other people's perceptions or do I sacrifice my true self to accommodate their feelings?

Yes there is much to discuss here and there is no easy answer as this is a complex issue. Firstly you owe it to yourself to be your true being. Who you really are. Otherwise you are falsely representing yourself to the world and this is deceit.

Having said that there is not just one aspect to you but many aspects to you. The 'you' that toned yourself down to accommodate the feelings of others is the thoughtful and kind you. You are learning the lessons from the Master given the day before. That is not to anger and to be kind. It was a key observation exercise and shows how highly attuned and observant you were to your surroundings and the energy at that particular time and place. Possibly you (and everyone else) may have had an even worse experience if you had ignored the signs and only served to rile this person up even more perhaps even spilling into an argument. Kudos to you for recognizing the situation so quickly and choosing to observe and come from a place of non-reaction. This was the very lesson that was imparted to you the day before at the lunch table. Many people were present at the same conversation but not all were listening or have yet to put into practice what they are learning. It is true what Master says about it being a lifestyle choice that these practices are to be bought into your everyday life to bring about positive change for you and for others. There is time to be the vivacious outgoing you and the time to be the quiet observant you. More than anything you were showing respect to your fellow students and teacher.

However it is now time to express your more outgoing self and this we have been saying all along. That it is time for more fun in your life. The more you give yourself to experiences that make your spirit shine the more you will attract the same to self. Thus if you want to meet likeminded souls who are bright shining lights just like yourself then go where the bright shining lights go and do the things that they do. By locking yourself away your soul withers and dies a little bit every day. Greet the world with a smile and if it scowls back at you you're going in the wrong direction. See this as a warning sign on the path of life. Nothing else. Just a sign that you are going the wrong way and this is not the path for you. You are looking for smiles to be reflected back at you. These are your green lights. It's like playing bumper cars. You get a bump, no matter, you change direction and keep going. It's both scary and fun. That is the journey. Don't take life too seriously. Don't let others bring you down. You may choose to temporarily accommodate in certain situations but you want to be your true self a large percentage of the time, always coming back to self. Otherwise you are living someone else's life, not your own. Your challenge, your quest, is to find the right balance.

When you leave such a situation give yourself a cleansing and a healing and walk back into your true life.

Lovingly — Nameless.

Thank you Nameless.

WED 18TH SEPTEMBER

Good morning everyone. I got a phone call today from one of the Reiki class attendants. I'll call him Gem because he seems like such a gentleman and we warmed to each other immediately. During the class practice sessions, while Reiki Master was attuning upstairs, Gem asked my advice because he was concerned he wasn't feeling any sensations in his hands. I reassured him that it would intensify the more we practiced and in the beginning of my healing journey I too felt very little. I asked him to follow me outside and showed him the vitalization stance, a bio magnetic therapy tool to increase ones chi and the Universal healing energy. To show him this I needed to find out which way was north and so asked my pendulum. Some of the students had not seen a working pendulum before the Reiki demonstration and he asked me about it, was I moving it and so on? The pendulum had obviously left an impression because the next day he told me he had been discussing it with his daughter, both mine and Reiki Masters use of it. Except for a brief overview and demonstrating its use, the pendulum was not really the focus of our studies that weekend, our concentration being guided more towards the channeling of Reiki healing energy through our hands which was what we were all seeking. I offered Gem to spend a day with me when I return from holidays to teach him everything I know about the pendulum and all its applications. I told him it would be my gift to him but also my gift to the Universe because I know he would go on to incorporate it into his healing sessions with others and so many people would benefit. I felt exited that I could do this for him and the planet in general. Gem was very keen and we exchanged contacts. As I drove home that second day I realized he would be my very first pupil. This would be a test of my teaching ability. Can I pass this knowledge on to others in the gentle and humble way that Reiki Master passed on her knowledge to us? I sincerely hope so.

I sent Reiki Master an email acknowledging her warmth and generosity and the kind and calming energy she exudes. I thanked her for the knowledge and expertise she had bestowed upon us, ever grateful for sending me on my new life journey and told her she was something for me to aspire to. Gem rang me and asked if I was going to do Reiki Masters next class which was Reiki Crystals, incorporating crystals into the Reiki session. Oh yes and I'd been exited to see that she ran this class because it was exactly what I was looking for, combining both the Reiki and Crystal Therapy and I was blown away that this was acceptable with Reiki which I had envisioned as being more strictly disciplined. We had to book early as spaces were limited to six. As soon as I got off the phone I booked online. An hour or so later Gem rang me back and told me he'd rung Reiki Master and booked and paid for both of us. It was his gift to me because he said he was so taken with my kindness and generosity in offering to teach him what I know for free. I had to laugh as obviously we were both practicing the precept of kindness and after making sure he didn't feel obligated I accepted. He said he had wanted it to be a surprise but realized after he paid that I would probably go ahead and book online without speaking to Reiki Master directly and so she would send me a refund which she did. How's that for quick Karma? I'm sure Reiki Master would have been very amused and happy watching her students bestow kind gifts to one another.

One thing I've been struggling with is a decision regarding my birth name. When I introduced myself at the Reiki class I found myself once again apologizing for my long hyphenated name. It sounds so pretentious some times and I'm always having to explain its hyphenation to new people I meet because it's so unusual and sounds like I'm saying my first and last name at the same time. It's been the bane of my life and when I turned fifty I decided I wanted to break free from this constraint and have something easy to carry me through the journey of my next half century. Out with the old me and in with the new, reinvent myself. At first I thought of my nickname but that's just as unusual. My spiritual name, Marikai, whilst I like it is also too formal and so for every day purposes I thought of reducing it to Kai which is short, sweet and easy.

Q. What does everyone think? Should I drop my long hyphenated name in favor of Kai?

It is I Hoyan. Once again we are talking labels here. What's in a name? Yet you humans put so much emphasis on names and labels and it does cloud people's perception of things. We are inclined to agree, only as we have witnessed the degree of difficulty you have experienced with your name all along. It has been a heavy burden to carry which has only served in weighing you down. You have chosen well, a new name, a new label that is light and breezy but also not intimidating. Your previous given name served to mark you out as different and some may see this as a good thing but it has also, unknowingly to you, put a target on your back by those who might easily feel threatened because it makes you seem different to them. Kai is a much less threatening and approachable name. It fits well with your future life and who you aspire to be, lighter and more free-spirited.

It does not concern us what you are called as you are all one and the same, *Light and Being*. Names only serve to differentiate and separate out and so you all identify as individuals when really you are all the one

Universal energy system. Partly your communication system is to blame. You have developed methods of communication with each other that require names to know who is being addressed. For example letters, emails, business cards but even simply verbal communication. Where we come from there is no such need for these things and so communication *just is*. It is a *knowing*, an acknowledgement, the telepathic passing and sharing on of information without the need to address individually. It does not matter to us what you call yourself as you just *are* and always *will be*. However as discussed we can see the need in your society and so whatever makes you comfortable and is the easiest both for you and all individuals is the one we recommend.

Blessings — Hoyan.

Thanks Hoyan, then Kai it is. Nice to speak with you.

SAT 21ST SEPTEMBER

Today is the first day of my holidays, the first break I've had in eight months. I should be happy, ecstatic but I'm highly stressed, anxious, worried and nervous.

The shit hit the fan at work again yesterday and this time I've had enough. Nameless you told me to try and hang in there for another six months but I simply can't do it. I'm too exhausted from the stress of it all. I feel like it has put a real dampener on my holidays. How can I rid myself of this stress, worry and anxiety? I thought about doing a healing and Reiki but I'm too stressed to heal myself. I thought of Reiki and the five precepts "Just for today I will not worry, will not anger...," but easier said than done. My Reiki notes suggest chanting 'OM' twenty times to reduce anger and change your vibration in peak times of stress but I think this is beyond that. I now know I can't work there anymore. I got on line and looked at some possible job prospects like community care which I wanted to do all along anyway having only set myself a three year plan to work in a facility to gain experience. Now it's been three and a half years it's time to go. Daughter said I should do something completely different like working in a pub or the RSL, a happy place.

Q. Can you guide me Nameless? How can I reduce my stress, anger, worry and anxiety? What shall I do next with regards to work? Should I hand in my notice straight away never to return from holidays, wait till I go back after holidays or wait till I've found another job?

Yes we understand your feelings of stress, worry and concern having been put in such a precarious position but it was always going to eventuate. You are not meant to be there and this latest event has only forced your hand. We were hoping that maybe you could eek it out until the new enterprise was up and running at least enough to compensate for your loss of wages but you are right that working there is no longer viable. It is not healthy for you. Thus why wait? Why procrastinate? You have already made up your mind that you can no longer work there. You are just delaying the inevitable and serving to torture yourself in the process. Let it go. It's time to move on. You tried and did the best you could do under the circumstances. It is a highly stressful environment and people say and do things they wouldn't normally because it is such an environment.

Your decision now is do you hand notice in straight away or wait till your return? I feel doing it in person though hard is more appropriate and to do it now you would have to mail it to them. If you hand in your notice on the day of your return it is likely that they will pay you out those two weeks anyway which gives you opportunity to have a longer rest and recuperation time before looking for other work. You will need this time as you have not been the real you for a long time and need time to rediscover your true self. Who you really are. Which is not this angry, stressed, anxiety ridden person that you are experiencing right now. This is what you have become because of where you have been and the stresses that have been placed upon you. Your true self is a *Being of Light* and ultimately you should aim to position yourself where you can exhibit your true being, the essence of who you really are.

We understand that you are concerned about finding other work but now you have the necessary skills to back you up it will not be that difficult if you put yourself out there. However this type of work is more casual based and requires flexibility on your part. We suggest you try the community care work and see if it is for you. Give yourself six months to settle into the job and if it is not for you then look elsewhere. We say six months because we see other things coming on the horizon. Something that will take you in different directions entirely. This is exiting and something to look forward to. Something to keep in mind as you go about putting food on the table, that there is more to life than doing things you hate simply to survive. Also six months is a good projection time. It's easy for someone to envision themselves doing something for only six months knowing they can re assess things from there. You are, as always, concerned about money. Don't be. You have always managed to pay the bills somehow and you will continue to do so. You may have to pull in the apron strings for a while but this is nothing new to you and only temporary.

As for your anxiety and worry… we remind you that all is right with the Universe. You are being sent in a different direction for a reason. Unfortunately it was quite harsh but possibly because you would not have left of your own volition otherwise being tied to the security of the weekly income even though you felt dead inside. Remember with death of the past comes new and exciting beginnings. Look excitedly forward into the future. Do not dwell on what happened in the past, yesterday or the day before but grasp the reins of what is to come. Looking at the whole life scenario this is but a small glitch in the scheme of things. This latest episode is not your whole life, merely a minute part of it only to be a faint memory in five years' time. So really what does it matter? And yes things were blown all out of proportion but again what does that matter now? Only that you take this opportunity for growth and forward movement, grasp it with both hands and run with it. You are one of the lucky ones that are escaping the nightmare that company has become. *Feel* lucky! Look upon it like this. You are blessed. You have been given a gift. You have been given an out. That is what you have wanted for a very long time, what you have been seeking and so the Universe has bestowed it upon you. No more four thirty a.m. wake ups. Your time there is done. What a blessing.

Give it no mind while you are on holidays. Deal with it when you return. If you do think about it at all concentrate on your future position with excitement. What it will be like, how different it will be. Write a manifestation list to describe your ideal position. Dream up your new job. The future is in your hands.

We support you in all your endeavors with Guiding Light. — Nameless.

Thank you Nameless. I'll take on board your advice. Once again you have helped put things in perspective. I'm already feeling more positive about things.

FRI 27TH SEPTEMBER

What a glorious day and kick start to my holidays as I sit on the edge of the pool at Southbank in Brisbane having just cooled off with a nice swim. Daughter is at a NIDA[4] workshop for the day as she has been every day this week. Meanwhile I've been busying myself at GOMA,[5] the Art Shed, the Paddington op shops, Reverse Garbage,[6] The Crystal Cave[7] and Queen St Mall indulging myself in books, fabric and art supplies and am feeling my bliss return.

I must confess Nameless I didn't take your advice and handed in my resignation the day before I left for holidays. I knew I wouldn't be able to relax or enjoy myself with that hanging over my head knowing I'd have to deal with it when I return. It's been so long since I had a vacation I wanted to really enjoy it. What a relief! It took about three days before I felt my body and shoulders start to relax. It's only when you let go of something like that that you realize the stress you were carrying around in your body not to mention your mind.

Anyway I've been having a lovely time pottering around Brisbane and one of the first things I did was visit incube8r[8] in Fortitude Valley, perusing all the artist's cubes. There were some beautiful handmade art dolls on display and a young woman sitting in the corner making 'Felties.' I spoke to the owner about my Amigurumi and Redbubble store and enquired about renting an art cube. Could I have such things as my iPhone covers if they were produced elsewhere even though they had my art work on them? Their ethos is predominantly handmade goods but I was told this could be accommodated if I'm also responsible for the photographic and design work and have some of the original art work and Amigurumi either for sale or on display. My excitement overtook me and I asked her to send me an application only to deflate once I left the shop. What have I done? How can I afford this? I had to remind myself I have no cash flow.

This got me thinking. Maybe this could be the beginning of a whole new business. Stuff working for someone else. I could get an Etsy store and link it all up to my Redbubble site and I could produce art and make things to sell online, on eBay and in my little cube. I'm getting all exited with everything going around in my head, what I will create and how much to sell it for when deflation hits again. This is my dream job if money is not an option but it is and I have to think about paying the bills and putting food on the table. I often read about artist's who quit their day job to pursue their dreams and passions, becoming successful entrepreneurs but behind each one of these is a supportive husband (or wife) who is not only paying the bills but building them art studios to boot. I don't really care about being successful and rich if only I could do what I love and make a decent living from it. It's all so torturous, like the carrot dangling just out of my reach.

So that's my dream job… to paint, collage, make art dolls, design fabric and anything else arty I can obsess over. Nameless, you have guided me to put my art aside for six months while I start the new enterprise but it's all I ever think about and obsess over. I'm wondering if my life is unsuccessful thus far because I HAVEN'T pursued my art. Now that I've left work I'm in a quandary...

Q. Do I take this opportunity and a small sum of money and try and make a go of my art selling my originals and Redbubble wares on eBay, Etsy and incube8r or do I continue to stay focused only on the healing and look for other part time work?

You have no choice as your contractual obligations to receive family benefits will require that you be looking for work. Having said that this is a window of opportunity and whilst you are looking it doesn't hurt to put a few feelers out there to see if you get any bites.

You may be surprised by what you find with this exercise and the type of items people are likely to purchase. If you find that a few items are selling this could be encouraging for you to invest more time and energy in the process. Test the waters first to see if it is worth it. Pick a few choice items to put on eBay and Etsy and see if there are any takers. It's not to say that your items won't sell at all but will you be able to sell enough of them to make a living out of it. Only the response of the public will tell you this. Vary the items that you choose so that you can easily see which ones are being looked at most or bought. If you flood with one item it may not be the item that people would normally purchase. This won't take up much of your time to begin with and requires no great monetary investment either. Follow up with the art store it is good grounding experience for you and each can bounce off the other. Again test the waters with the minimum quarterly contract and if it's not working little harm done. Any spin offs you make from items prepared can be sold online also.

Many entrepreneurs start this way. The women you described above are a rarity. There are a lot of others out there like you who have to juggle to make things work and this tests their commitment. Focus and discipline is your main issue here as you know you are drawn in many different directions to the detriment of each other as one never gets fully realized before something else grabs your attention. We understand it takes time to find your niche and you are still in the experimentation and playing process. When you find your focus/niche in the art business, what you are good at and what you are driven to create is where and when you will find your success. Until then it may be a struggle but it is all part of the journey to get you where you want to be. When you find that *one thing* that defines you everything will explode from there.

We *always* recommend you keep up the healing for you, others and the planet. The ideal is to balance the two. Time is a consideration here.

The art is more of a longer term project to see it up and running before it can fulfill monetary commitments whereas the healing is more immediate. Unfortunately the bills are always your downfall and serve to distract you from your purpose but it will not always be this way. Have faith.

Encouragingly — Nameless.

Thank you Nameless. Yes I look at Reiki Master and she seems to have it all in balance… her painting, healing and teaching. I don't think it was an accident that I was drawn to her. This is what I'm striving for.

12

OCTOBER 2013

MON 7TH OCTOBER

Today is the last day of school holidays, Queens Birthday weekend and a beautiful sunny thirty-four degrees. We pick up one of Daughters friends before heading to the quarry. Surprisingly there's only us and another couple there, everyone else must be at the beach. After a few hours of cooling off in the crystal blue waters we head into Noosa for a change of scenery but main beach is packed full of tourists so we follow the boardwalk around to Little Cove which is only five minutes from Hastings Street and more secluded. There's only a handful of people here on this beach, one of the places locals go to escape the holiday invasion. I set my towel away from the girls who I'm sure don't want to be seen with me or have me listen in on their 'convo's.' After taking a sun bath and languishing in a salty dip we head back to main beach Noosa for an ice-cream while watching the light fade over Laguna Bay. What a glorious day.

And so it is that this type of joy is always there for the taking.

SUN 13TH OCTOBER

Yesterday I met up with a girlfriend at the Noosa Yacht and Rowing Club where we chatted for hours over lunch, downing a few beers and gin and tonics before going on an extended walk along the river. I informed her of my plans to change my name and we spoke of all our 'brilliant' ideas and how frustrating it is not being able to implement any of them for lack of start-up funds. What's even more annoying is the ideas don't stop coming. How many others are in the same boat?

Gem is coming for his pendulum workshop tomorrow. I've spent the last week writing and photocopying notes and pendulum charts in preparation and realized there's a lot to get through. I hope we can do it all in one day. If things go well I'll advertise the workshop out in the community. Gem rang last week and floored me with an admission of his enamor for me joking that he thinks he's met Mother Theresa in Elle McPhersons body, LOL. Apparently he can't stop thinking about me even waking during the night and having to stop himself from ringing and emailing so as not to annoy me. The truth is I know it would. I told him I found that rather strange (and thought to myself a little weird) considering we have only met twice before.

Q. Why can't I just meet someone nice, normal? They're either too full on and suffocating or totally absent. Whenever I show a man a little bit of kindness they seem to latch on like piranhas. This is why I keep to myself. What's wrong with this world? Or me? I was so looking forward to this class but now I have this extra concern which is spoiling it.

Q. Do you have any advice in preparation for this workshop tomorrow?

It is I Hoyan. Be kind but also keep it professional. You do not want to embarrass or hurt this persons feelings. Having just lost his wife he has lost his way and is grasping for breath, subconsciously looking for a bit of hope, a reason to keep going and something to occupy his mind to block out the trauma he has just been and is still going through.

Think of the five precepts and practice those…to be kind, not to worry or anger and to endeavor your work. Also be grateful that he is providing you this opportunity to practice your skills. Be as humble in your presentation as Reiki Master. You will need to find a nice balance of being friendly but not overtly so and professional at the same time. This is your challenge. Your quest. Ask him to stay focused on the task at hand as indeed you both have a lot to get through.

Pupils are often enamored by teachers and this may not be the last time you experience this. The challenge is going to be in how well you handle yourself. If he diverts away from the task it is up to you to gently guide him back without embarrassment. How you do this is up to you and something you will need to think about over the next twenty-four hours. We suggest you keep it light, if he brings his feelings up acknowledge what he has said without too much comment and discussion. Gently nudge him back into the present focus and reason for him being in your presence which is the pendulum course.

As for the men you attract, you are a born healer and thus attract people who need to be healed or counselled in some way. You are a magnet for them. If you can recognize this for what it is and keep a professional distance it will not disturb you personally but often these people cannot separate out their addictions and cannot see the bigger picture of what is going on. As the healer it is left to you to gently guide them on their way. In the past you have just completely shut yourself off from them, walking away completely. We ask is there another way? Can you support them while remaining friends? It might be worth a try.

Thanks Hoyan but I've tried this before and they don't listen to me when I ask them not to constantly call or come around unannounced. This irks me no end as they are oblivious to my feelings and needs for a certain amount of peace, privacy and freedom which I value highly. I find this disrespectful and so end the friendship.

Hmm. Not all are tarnished with the same brush. Judge each one on its own merit if you judge at all. So try with this one and see if you get the same response. Perhaps it is you that are not making yourself clear enough? Perhaps a different approach is warranted.

You could be right. I'll try again and see what happens. Tomorrow will be interesting to say the least.

We watch in trepidation. You only need to ask for our help and guidance. We are there with you always, listening and ready to help and offer our advice — Hoyan.

Thanks Hoyan for helping put things in perspective.

WED 16TH OCTOBER

Hey everyone. Well I thought the pendulum class with Gem went pretty well considering it was my first time presenting it. He came bearing gifts, flowers from his garden, a book and jewelry which was all a little embarrassing but he said the jewelry was for my fiftieth birthday and he'd just been to the Crystal and Gem fair which one can't really manage without buying something. He told me how two lovely ladies helped him choose the moonstone necklace and I envisioned he would have had a lot of fun doing it as they fussed about him. Not wanting to be rude or affect his karma I accepted graciously and thanked him.

We had a lot to go through. I had written over ten pages of information which was broken up with demonstrations, exercises and little games to help Gem program and get used to using the pendulum. After two hours we went to the Apollonian for lunch and then finished up down at the lake where we measured each other's auric fields and then back home again for exercises in using the body as a pendulum. I measured it as four hours overall, broken into two blocks with a lunch break in-between. I feel we could've done it over two days if I wanted to add more practice exercises showing all the different applications and uses. Also I only had to explain the chakra applications as Gem had already seen it in practice at the Reiki workshop but for anyone else I'd have to include the demonstration.

All in all it was a great exercise for him and for me with only a few things I might like to change. My two main difficulties where in explaining how the pendulum works and how the body receives energy from the Universal Energy Field through the auric field layers and into the body via the Chakra's. I know it in my mind but to explain it to someone else is difficult.

Q. Can someone help me out, explain to me how the Pendulum works?

It is I Hoyan.

I know, I felt you coming through. Where's Nameless? I haven't heard from him for a while. Not that I'm not happy to be speaking to you but just that I'm worried. Has he left me? I think I'd be scared not to have him in my life and I'm getting a bit teary thinking about it. When he doesn't come through for a while I get nervous. I miss him.

Do not worry little one 'he' is just busy at this time.[1] There is someone who needs his help more than you that is taking up a lot of his attention. He feels comfortable enough that you are travelling well that he can take leave to help this person and knows that I and the others are here with you also.

Ok thanks Hoyan. But it does concern me that it's quite possible one day Nameless could leave entirely. He's like my BFF. He, all of you, have been so supportive over the past year I don't know what I'd do without you all.

Q. Can you tell me how the Pendulum works?

Yes. It is as you know but are having difficulty conveying so I will try to simplify it for you. Think of a radio transmission which are electrical waves travelling through the air to reach their destination point of the radio. Remember electricity is a form of energy and as energy comes from *The Source of All Being,* within it there is knowledge/information. Think of each molecule of energy being programmed with its own information so an apple is an apple because each energy molecule contained therein is programmed or contains the information of being an apple. This goes back to your earlier instruction of what things become is dependent on how large, how dense and how fast they spin off from the vortex of *Light and Being/The Source* of *All Kind*. Why is a muscle a muscle? Because it contains that information. Think of stem cells and their ability to become any tissue in the body but the stem cell itself must first contain all of the information for all of the tissues for this to be a possibility.

So the energy/wave particle is Light and can travel at fast speeds and can carry with it a vast amount of information encoded therein. Thus a radio transmission can carry information from one point to another. The radio itself is just a communication tool for that information to become known to you auditory wise (a TV transmits visually) and this is how the pendulum works. It is using the electrical impulses from your subconscious mind (and Universal mind) to carry information to the visual tool that is the pendulum which reacts in accordance with your programming, allowing your conscious mind to read it and the information to become known to you. Thus the pendulum is an outward expression of your subconscious mind and Universal mind allowing you to tap into a vast array of knowledge that you wouldn't normally have access to on a conscious level.

The Universal Mind is just an extension of your subconscious mind linking you up with the *Light/Source of All Being* (which is *All Knowing*).

Thus you could look at it this way…

Light/Source → Universal Mind → Subconscious Mind → Conscious Mind

Or…

Light/Source → Universal Mind → Subconscious Mind → Pendulum → Conscious Mind

The arrows represent energy/electrical impulses and information being passed down the line. Interestingly it is a two way communication system. The arrows (information) can be reversed and this is how you can send messages/wants/desires out into the Universe and back to the Source. This is how affirmations work. You can also reprogram your subconscious mind this way.

Our world does not have so many pathways to travel and knowledge is much more instantaneous, an innate *knowing* and communication is more *telepathic* as we are closer to *The Light Source* and don't have your physical constraints.

Thanks Hoyan. You've explained it well without being too complex because some people have prior knowledge and others don't and I was looking for a simplified version. I'll try this or perhaps do a print out.

You're most welcome, I am always happy to help. Light be with you today. — Hoyan.

SAT 19TH OCTOBER

Houston we have a problem! Unfortunately even though I explained to Gem that I'm quite independent and value my freedom, my peace and tranquility and made it quite clear that even though I'm open to friendship I do not want someone calling constantly or coming around unannounced, it seems he has chosen to ignore this request which I'm very annoyed with as it's disrespectful of my wishes and obviously he wasn't listening to me.

The day after the pendulum class he came around unannounced even though I had stipulated the day before that I HATE this. Luckily for me I wasn't home having chosen that precise moment to go and fill up my solar shower and buckets down on the lake (we have run out of tank water and currently have no running water in the house). Thank god I wasn't home. I would have been furious. I only found out because he called me that evening and told me that instead of calling me prior to coming over he had consulted the pendulum like I taught him, which told him I was home and wouldn't mind him coming around. He forgot the bit about if you are too emotionally invested in the outcome then your conscious mind will overrule and it won't give you a correct answer.

He kept me on the phone for near an hour with an issue he was having. The next day he emailed me and told me he had rung and booked a water (tank) delivery for me the following Thursday which he was going to pay for. How rude. Where was the consultation? I have barely met this man in person three times and already he is taking over my life. He says he is just trying to be helpful and that may be so but I see it as controlling. It would be different if he was a long standing friend but I barely know the guy and feel it's out of line. Last night I went to Reiki Masters art exhibition and he told me during the week that he had RSVP'd on my behalf even though I wasn't going with him, I was going with a girlfriend. Really? Who does that? All this on top of the Reiki crystal class he booked and paid for without consultation as well.

Now I'm annoyed that I have to get firm with him once again and tell him to stop. He has created this issue that I didn't need where I'm feeling uncomfortable. If I didn't have the crystal healing workshop with him next weekend I would end the 'friendship' right now. All the suffocating signs were there in the beginning. Did I tell you that after we first met at the Reiki class he drove all around my village asking people where I live? The publican, the store owner, the realtor and when they didn't know he drove up and down the streets looking for my car. WARNING!

Why does it have to be like this? Why couldn't he listen to me? I'm doing the Pomona market next Saturday and I just know he's going to turn up unless I say something first as he's mentioned it twice already. I don't even know why I'm ranting about all this. I'm not sure if I even have a question for you this morning. Gem has just put me all out of sorts. It's a shame because I had hopes that we could be Reiki partners but he's just too overbearing.

Q. Do you have any comments for me?

Yes it is I Hoyan. You are feeling all out of sorts because this is your warning system telling you something is not quite right. Even though he comes across as a genuine nice guy he is a wolf in sheep's clothing. Trust your instincts, trust your intuition that is trying to guard you against harm's way. Your reasoning egoic mind is trying to justify his behavior and tell you that you are being overly harsh when this person is probably just trying to be helpful but it is the gut instinct that you should be listening to that is telling you to be wary of this person for whatever reason or reasons currently unbeknownst to you. Pay attention to how you *feel*, how this person makes you *feel*. If you are feeling uncomfortable then this is not a good thing and the alarm bells should be sounding. Tread with caution. It does not necessarily mean you have to obliterate him from your life forever but that you should proceed with caution and a keen observer's eye. *Observe* his behavior, really *listen* to what he is saying and constantly checking with your gut instincts and your *feelings* which is your innate security system.

You are right in thinking this person has control issues that he himself may not even be aware of. He doesn't see it like that and views it differently. He will always try to justify his behavior through self-martyrdom, that he is always giving and that is just who he is as a person but there are always ulterior motives attached even though he will never own up to it. He is not selfless but rather selfish and only gives with what he can get in return in mind. He tells you he is not trying to buy your friendship but this is precisely what he is doing even though he will deny, deny, deny. Perhaps he is lying even to himself or has convinced himself otherwise believing his generosity to be pure of heart but it is not so. Take the volunteer trip he is going on as an example. While a small part of him wants to do good for those less fortunate a larger part of him wants to be recognized for it also. This is a stroke to his ego. Underlying his conversation about it he is really saying, "Look at me, how great I am doing good for those less fortunate!" Those with completely pure intent do not talk of it at all. If he was confronted with this, again he would deny. Either he is lying to himself or is not fully in touch with who he really is and has not examined his motives fully. It is not a purely selfless act but is marred with selfishness. The same goes with you. He offers help but there is intention behind it. It is not one hundred percent unconditional. He is expecting payback in some form or another which may simply be friendship but I suspect is more. You are right in thinking it is outrageously close to his wife's death and this in itself tells you something about his character.

He is not to be trusted. Keep him at arm's length. Wolf in sheep's clothing! Trust yourself more and listen to your gut instincts and *feelings*. Observe with a keen eye. Guidance and Light always — Hoyan.

That's a bit of a sharp turnaround from before when you suggested I give him a go. I wonder if I should bother at all with someone who has ulterior motives and I can't trust. I'll get through the Reiki crystal class and take it from there. Thanks for your help.

WED 23RD OCTOBER

Fifty-nine kilo's. Hmm, I really have to watch my weight now that I'm not working. I must enter a new contract with my pendulum/subconscious.

It still hasn't rained and every day I lug buckets of water up from the lake to flush the toilets. Twice a week when I'm in town I fill up all the containers for drinking water and have a hot shower at the mall while I'm there, washing my hair and shaving my legs. Otherwise it's a cold shower at the toilet block down on the lake or a cold bucket wash with boar water again bought up by bucket from the lake. The stifling thirty degree heat makes it worse. The other day Daughter attempted to sneak into the Boreen Point campground for a shower. They've put electronic code devices on the doors to protect their water supplies but she was so lucky that someone was exiting a shower just as she arrived and held the door open for her. They charge twenty dollars a week per person for showering and not working, for the two of us, I just can't afford it. If you could see Daughter and her mass of long spiral curls you would know that a bucket wash does just not cut it.

I'm busy crocheting a few more Amigurumi for the incube8r shop and then I'll work on some collage prints on fabric. I've booked the Pomona markets this Saturday and have ordered my new Reiki signage, business cards, car magnet and also my incube8r art business cards which I pick up tomorrow. It'll be interesting to see if I get personage from the Reiki sign as opposed to Crystal Healing. I spoke to Reiki Master who said she gets most of her clients from her website though she was doing the Cotton tree market last week. I was hoping to hand out advertising for a pendulum class but realized I can't hold a full day class here while I don't have running water or flushing toilets and I can't afford a venue for an entire day. Same goes with seeing clients at home, just when I was going to put out a 'free Reiki' sign to get a bit of practice in. Why do I feel like the Universe is always conspiring against me? Now that I'm ready I still can't pull it off. UUGHHH, it's so frustrating.

I have the Crystal Reiki workshop with Reiki Master this Sunday which I'm not really looking forward to as Gem and I had an altercation after my avoidance of him at the art exhibition. I don't need the drama in my life. Now I'm not even sure if I will go to the crystal workshop.

Q. Do I go and sit through six agonizing hours of room filled tension? Or do I forfeit and go another time?

Again your *feeling* (gut) is your warning system here. You feel sick at the thought of going. It is not worth putting yourself through such stress and tension. Anything that you could possibly learn will be marred by your experience of having him present in the room. This will make you self-conscious, holding you back from asking questions, giving input and saying your piece. There will be a lot of information you miss out on because you cannot be fully present in the moment. If it was a large class and he was easily avoided it would be workable but the size of the class prohibits this and so the air will be very palpable making it very uncomfortable for all those in its presence, Reiki Master included. The class will be offered again at a later time and you can take it then gaining much more out of it as being relaxed your intake will be greater. He has paid for this current class so you are not losing out financially by opting out. You will need to inform Reiki Master, let her know what has been going on, his unwanted attention towards you and how uncomfortable you feel. You will find she will be accommodating. You may even find that he has opted out already and in that case you will need to re assess your feelings about attending.

Love and Protection — Hoyan.

Thanks Hoyan. Do you have any idea when it's going rain?

Yes you will get rain tomorrow as predicted but it will not be the amount you desire. It may raise the tank level enough to treat yourself a little but not enough to sustain you. I feel you have a few (at least three) weeks of hardship left before the tank is adequately filled.

FUCK! (Oops, sorry) Thanks Hoyan.

MON 28TH OCTOBER

Morning All. I received my first Reiki client at the Pomona market on Saturday, Woohoo! A positive sign considering it was apparently the quietest market day ever because of a garage sale trail running in town.

I informed Reiki Master about Gem as you suggested and she relayed a similar experience she had had with a person that spanned a two year period, several times having to get quite firm with him. She gave me a meditation to help cut the links and put the issue behind me so there would be no attachment. She also said she would energetically work on protecting me before, during and after the class and ensured me the class would be healing and peaceful. So I worked on the meditation, re assessed my feelings and attended the class which was as she said and I came away feeling wonderful and with much valuable information. Just being in Reiki Masters presence is healing in itself as she exudes such a beautiful, peaceful, calming energy like a walking safety cocoon, you feel like nothing can harm you in her bubble.

We received a small amount of rain as you said and I treated myself to a shower but again are back on rations. During the Reiki Crystal class we learnt about grids. I asked if it is possible to make it rain. The American Indians can do it because they are in tune, unison, and communication with the nature spirits and mother earth and only do it with pure intent. I was mocked in class by another for asking and was made to feel my request was selfish because perhaps it wasn't in Mother Earths' best interest for it to rain.

Hell I wasn't asking for the entire planet, just my backyard!

Q. Am I being selfish? Can I invoke rain? How can I do this without the right crystals? I can't afford to buy more.

To be honest there is an element of selfishness there. You are suffering and having to do much work to supply yourself with water. Something that you (and others) normally take for granted. This is a great and valuable lesson for you as exhausting as it is lugging buckets and collecting drinking water it makes you realize that you are at the mercy of nature. You are not as in control as you thought you were. At any moment disaster could hit and your test of strength and courage is how well you cope before breaking down. Yes there is a lot more work for you to do on a daily basis but consider yourself lucky at all that you are at least able to source the water you need albeit from some distance and that you can access clean drinking water. Think of all of those around the world who do not have this luxury and how they are suffering. Think of these people as you go about your daily gathering and give thanks and blessings that it is relatively easy in comparison instead of bemoaning the difficulties.

Giving thanks is where you begin, start with appreciation for what you have and what you have access to. Every day be grateful. Be grateful for what you can access and be grateful for the chance to experience even on a smaller scale what it must be like for a large majority of the world. If you truly take this lesson on board you will never be complacent again, always giving thanks and appreciating on a grander scale. Your society has become spoilt, everything at their fingertips but it may not always be so. This exercise in barrenness may prepare you for future escapades. It's all about survival. Air, water, food all of these things are taken for granted. When one or more is taken away from you, you realize the importance and what truly matters on this earth. Not the current arguments or the latest fashions or gadgets but that mother earth is looked after because it is a contingent relationship and you depend on her for your survival.

By performing ceremony and dedications to mother earth and the elements you are paying your respect and cementing this respect in your mind consciousness also and so it is when you perform such ceremony as when working with grids it is dedicating your intention to paying homage to and respect to mother earth and the elements. If this is done with pure intent and from true heart connection with no thought of selfishness then and only then is it possible to invoke rain. This is the connection that the American Indians have with nature. An experience of oneness, becoming one with nature, the earth and its elements.
As you know the crystals help amplify your intent. Remember you can program clear quartz to take on the persona of the crystal you desire but without crystals entirely it is as simple as writing their name and thus their energy property on pieces of paper and placing these as a grid. The magic is in the ceremony, the dedication, the pure intent and the consequent heart connection that links you to communication and dialogue with the earth and its elements.

The same can be done for any request. Be clear, specific and stay humble.

Love and Light — Hoyan.

Thanks Hoyan and thanks for your honesty. I'll give this a go.

13

NOVEMBER 2013

SUN 3RD NOVEMBER

Morning All. We've received a little more rain during the week, nothing really substantial but enough for me to do a couple of loads of washing which will save me a trip to the laundromat.

I'm yet to do the crystal grid, it seems my days are full and the week has just flown by with multiple phone calls, interviews and doctor's appointments resulting in a medical exemption from seeking work until the sixteenth of November. Instead I've started working on the fabric prints for incube8r, my sewing machine and over locker arrived from e-bay and I've been out sourcing fabrics and notions. It's hard trying to fit everything in to my day, Reiki and Shamanic Healing, channeling, writing the workshops, looking for work, art and the art store. It's no wonder I'm feeling really scattered. Why do I do this to myself? My girlfriend says it's because I have lots of passions whereas some people are passionless. I get the feeling these people have easier lives and I wish I was them. Sometimes I think something is actually wrong with me. My daughter thinks I'm a bit schizoid, LOL and you are all just my imaginary friends. The other day I was so distressed about my scatteredness and being pulled in too many directions that I was on the verge of tears with the frustration of it all. Why can't I just do one thing, love it, do it really well and get paid for it?

The aim of this year was to follow divine guidance and see if it changed my life for the better but I feel it is just adding to the complication of it all. It's just another thing I have to do and deal with. I wanted to go gung ho with the Reiki and healing as you suggested but a woman at the market who used to do kinesiology said, "Face it, it's just a hobby," meaning it will never amount to anything substantial that I can live off. This deflated me no end. Am I wasting my time? What she said really threw me. I know it could take a while but is it going to be worth it? Can I make a living doing this or am I just fooling myself, wasting my time when I should be getting a 'real' job? Sometimes I wonder if you're guiding me such for your own selfish reasons. I know you want me to heal myself, others and in doing so aid the planet but I need to pay the bills here, put food on the table. Also the average person isn't really aware of vibrational healing so I feel like I'm up against a brick wall.

Q. Am I wasting my time? Why am I so scattered? Can you help me?

There are a few things in particular holding you back from going gung ho with the Reiki and healing most notably the insurance aspect. You would have more working and job opportunities if you were able to be insured. You cannot be insured until you have completed Reiki II. You cannot do Reiki II until at least January when it is on offer. Also you need to practice Reiki I as much as possible before this point to adequately prepare for Reiki II. You will also need to have the funds to pay for Reiki II and then pay the insurance fee.

Once you have all of this under your belt the possibilities open up to you like a blossoming lotus flower. You have already thought of taking your practice out into the local resorts, day spas and eco retreats. This is not possible until you have insurance and insurance is not possible without Reiki II. These are just formalities, society's stipulations and expectations. Otherwise you would be ready now. This is all part of the journey. Take your present knowledge and skill and practice what you have learnt thus far as much as possible. This is not to say you are not currently qualified but that society has rules and you have to play the game. Aim for one to two clients per week, offering it for free if you have to or by donation to begin with as it is more important at this stage that you get the practice in.

So you see you are still in the preparatory stages and are being somewhat impatient and unreasonable with time aspects and how long it will take before you can draw adequate funds from this practice which won't be at least until you complete Reiki II. This is all part of the necessary journey to get you to that place and so nothing is ever a waste of time. Also remember it is not about money alone but the fact that you are helping another being and in helping them you are helping their surrounding others and the planet in general and this should be your focus, not the money.

UGGGHHH. You are so frustrating, I get all that, healing me, others, the planet but YOU don't have to pay the rent and put food on the table and I DO!

Yes and this is why we suggest you continue to look for supporting work as with the art it is going to be a longer term project before you can draw adequate funds. How much and how quickly depends entirely on your effort and the time you dedicate to it so in that respect the ball is in your court. We cannot do it for you. It will not just happen. As with everything else we can only guide and advise but you must *make it happen,* if you so choose it. This requires work and effort on your part. You reap what you sew. What you put in you get out. So the rewards will be testament to your level of dedication. Do not expect overnight success, this would be unreasonable and if you are feeling overwhelmed break it down into small more manageable easy parts. Write a manageable plan. Not just with the healing but with all aspects of your life. You know you work better with lists. Work out your current goals trying to limit yourself to the most important, pressing three (work, healing, art in that order). Then break each one down into manageable steps. Write it on a board that you see daily. This will help prevent you from being overwhelmed and feeling scattered. It is your current life plan. For example healing…

- **See one client a week (paying or otherwise)**
- **Attend the market every second weekend**
- **Once a month hold a class (e.g.; pendulum, channeling)**
- **Advertise (car, community notice boards etc.)**

Do this for your other two goals, work and art and you will have an achievable format. Make sure they are balanced, each one not asking more than you can give. Also remember that they are fluid and changeable depending on patronage, new ideas or circumstances that arise. They are an outline only but one that will give you more peace of mind than your current state. Also in this respect you will be moving (your life) forward which is all that we ask, always going in a positive direction. When this is occurring you are doing well my friend and all is right with the Universe.

We encourage and support all your endeavors.

Nameless, Hoyan and the others.

Q. Nameless? Are you here? I thought I'd been feeling your energy the last few days.

Yes I am here, as with All.

Oh thank god, I missed you! I'm so thankful and happy you're back, the tears are welling. I have to tell you I love you Nameless! You are my BFF and I'm so grateful for all your help, guidance and friendship. You're such a blessing in my life! I appreciate all of you.

And so it goes that we are just as fond of you, the love extends both ways. Be not so harsh of yourself. You are of the Light.

Thank you, I'm feeling much better and more focused now. Work, healing, art. In that order.

THURS 14TH NOVEMBER

Morning everyone, it's been a long ten days since we last spoke. I've spent those days madly fabric printing and finishing preparations for incube8r even though you had specified that work, healing then art was my priority I had to honor this commitment. I went down to Brisbane on Tuesday and set up my little art cube and now that's done I can refocus on obtaining work and the healing practice. Even though I've already written the pendulum class I think I'd like my first class to be on channeling.

I've been watching a few programs on SBS of late about healthy aging…STOP, OMG!

As I started writing this I had the TV going on in the background and noticed Shirley MacLaine was being interviewed so tuned in. She's just written a new book[1] on a series of questions posed to her guides during channeling sessions about all sorts of topics! She said she'd sit and channel for up to five hours at a time asking about questions that were running through her mind, everything from serious and pertinent (politics and economics) to seemingly shallow (vanity issues). UGGHHH! Just when you think you're doing something good, worthwhile and original someone always beats you to it. Also because she's famous not only for her talented acting ability but also her experience of channeling and past book accomplishments people will naturally be drawn to her work.

Q Why would someone buy my book, me a nobody?

At first I was excited about her book, excited to read it but now I'm also depressed and feel like crying. I thought I'd found my channeling/writing niche but now I feel guzumped. Something I've been working on the WHOLE YEAR and it's November and I'm almost at the end. I'm so frustrated, all my hard work, a years' worth of labor, is it all for nothing? I can't not continue, I'm so close to the end, so close to finishing but now I feel like my balloon has been popped. All the shine has been taken from it. I'm in tears.

Q. Is all this work worthless Nameless? All the hours, the conversations, the commitment? Should I continue with my quest to finish and attempt to get it out to the public, my year of divine guidance?

There is much to discuss here. Firstly you are not a 'nobody' but we know what you mean. You are an unknown. Also you are a regular person, an everyday 'Joe Blow,' not famous like Shirley MacLaine but rather than this being detrimental it is actually to your advantage. People are more able to relate to you and your experiences because they operate more 'on your level,' having similar problems and issues. The fact that someone is considered of fame can put them out of reach of the average person. They might like to read about them and their lives and their experiences but do not necessarily feel like they can relate or follow their paths, have the same experiences because they are living such different lives. Thus though interesting to read about is it as accessible to put into practice in their own lives? Can they see themselves doing what Shirley does? Probably not, even though they admire what she does the public has put her on the fame pedestal. She has been marked as different, special, and unique because of her background. Even though it is quite possible for them to follow her path they see it as unlikely but that is their belief system at play preventing them from following a path they might desire.

You on the other hand are considered to be average, 'normal,' the same as them. If you can do it why not they? In this respect the channeling becomes more accessible to the average person. If we were marketing this would be your selling point. It is your normality and averageness that makes it readable, believable, and achievable! Also in your questioning over the last year the reader can see the journey that has taken place, the story that has played out over the year and how you have grown, matured and developed. It is the accompanying story that also differentiates you from Shirley. This is your story, your journey and how it's been for you and how it could possibly be for them. There are valuable insights you have learnt on the way that you are willing to share with others so they may follow their own journey, their own paths and development.

Another point is saturation. Some might say it's competing with an already saturated market but your approach is unique to you (a year of divine guidance) and the message you convey is both the same and different. Saturation is not necessarily a bad thing as it is all planting seeds. Sometimes someone has to hear the same message many times over conveyed in different ways before it sinks in, is embedded in their consciousness. Enough for it to become part of or played out in their reality. It's the same for other ideas and concepts such as health and science matters. It may take many different health experts to convey the same message in different manners before the public takes it on consciously and acts upon it. If more people from different backgrounds are saying the same thing, delivering the same message then there is obviously merit in that. Perhaps enough for the individual to investigate it further or try it for themselves to see if they can benefit also.

Remember everyone has freedom of choice. Those that choose to ignore or denigrate are either not ready, have not gathered enough information or have not sufficiently analyzed it without bias. Is it possible? Yes anything is possible until proven otherwise.

One day if enough seeds are dropped one of them will sprout and grow into a tree. The truth is in the *experience* and for this people need to give themselves the freedom to experiment. Experiments take time. Various methods work for different people or differently for each person. Trial and error should be employed over a period of time. People don't try to lose weight and diet for one day and say it didn't work. You would usually try several different methods over a period of six months to a year or even longer before you found the right one for you, an individual, perhaps even pooling your knowledge built up over that time to personalize your own unique method that works specifically for you. The same goes for channeling. Shirley's experience and method used is unique to her, yours is to you. The public gets to read both (and others that are out there) to build on their knowledge base and develop their own unique approach. The more they read about different experiences and methods, the more they learn, the more confident they become within their self-development. Is this not how you got started? That over time you read many books and then one in particular which triggered this whole process? You were collecting seeds. Then one sprouted and grew. Now it is your time to share, spread your own seeds.

Nothing is ever lost, no time spent is ever worthless. Even if you decide not to publish you have gained much but another way to help heal the planet is to share what you have learnt and your experience with others which aides their own guided journey and thus helping to heal their hurts, pain and anguishes, surrounding others and the *Planet Being,* Mother Earth. Thus we encourage you to continue on with your quest to publish for the betterment of *All Kind.*

Thank you Nameless. But what about Shirley's book? I really want to read it but I'm scared it may influence me, what should I do?

Don't worry *(Nameless has a little chuckle).* It's all part of the journey.

I gather that's a yes then.

And enjoy as I know you will. Blessings — Nameless.

Thank you Nameless.

WED 20TH NOVEMBER

Ten a.m. and I'm sitting on the couch still in my PJ's, what luxury! Once again a whole week has gone by. We've had a rental inspection and I've been madly cleaning and scrubbing all week and trying to get the yard under some sort of (impossible) control. This time of year heading towards Xmas always seems to speed up and the year is going to be ended before I know it. I'll have to think very carefully about the questions I want to ask you before years end as there's not much time left.

I'd like to continue our last conversation at the point before I was interrupted by Shirley MacLaine. I was talking to you about the healthy aging programs I've been watching on SBS. One in particular that discussed intermittent fasting, not only as a way to control weight issues but to also lower blood pressure, blood glucose and cholesterol levels etc. I found it all very interesting and in an attempt to lose my last two kilos and reach my goal of losing ten kilo's by years end I thought I'd try one or two of the methods, either alternate day or 5:2 fasting. Both being advocated as more of a long term lifestyle approach rather than a 'diet.'

It also got me thinking about the meat issue. I've read and been told many times that if you want to channel and work in the Higher realms (psychically, healing or otherwise) that you shouldn't eat red meat because it causes a certain density of the tissues weighing you down energetically, lowering your vibration and preventing you from accessing Higher realms. Many spiritually inclined people become vegetarians and vegans for this reason (and animal cruelty issues). I've tried being vegan and vegetarian before but never lasted more than a year as I found I became very weak and cognitively challenged. However now that I do eat meat I find that I can channel without issue whereas before I would've found it difficult to concentrate or focus and been very lethargic and unmotivated. There's always conflicting reports from different camps regarding such things and I'd like your opinion on it.

Q. Do you think it's wise to fast intermittently for both weight loss and health reasons? Does fasting heighten spiritual awareness like the Sufi's and the Buddhist monks believe?

Q. Does red meat or meat in general have a deleterious effect? Does it really affect ones energetic being and their ability to transcend, to channel, to heal and access other dimensions?

It is impossible to speak for each and every person, everyone being an individual in the human body concept though the same energetically. It is the body you are feeding first before the spirit and if the body is not functioning adequately yes this will have a deleterious effect on the spiritual plane for how can you access it if the body/mind is not working to its optimum level. So there is no one food program designed that will accommodate all individuals. In this respect it is up to the individual to fine tune themselves and discover what is their premium fuel that keeps their motor running at the most efficient levels, while, at the same time producing the least amount of physical damage but instead providing added protection from external damage. In this case every person is an individual as even though you are all one and the same on an energetic level you are all housed on different bodies. What works for one will not work for another and vice versa. You must trust your own instincts and experience of what works for you. This is trial and error over different periods of time.

It is good that you are consciously aware enough to care about this issue and always thinking, listening for new discoveries that may fine tune the physical self so that you can delve into Higher and Higher realms. Yes you have no issue talking with us but that is not to say that you are perfect, nor would we want you to be. You are you and are where you need to be right now at this point in time. If that means you feel you need to eat meat to function adequately then listen to your gut feelings regarding the issue. A time may come when you will no longer want or desire such a thing. It is not for us to say what is good or bad for you as we are not in the human form and do not fully understand the strong desires that you feel. Having said that gluttony is never a good thing and as long as moderation is taken into account then there can never be too much damage done that the body can't repair itself given that all other health areas are balanced (not too much drinking etc.) and that regular healings can be attended to.

It is more your spiritual desire, dedication and hard work that will see you transcend into Higher realms rather than any earthly fasting of meat or other foods though we can see the health benefits to the physical body and it would not hurt for you to try this out for yourself. One can only discover these things through your own self experimentation. Does it work for you? How do you *feel* on it? Do you *feel* healthier, better? Is your cognitive function clearer or worse?

You are well aware of the vibration of food, how to test its vibration, how to raise its vibration before consuming it. If you deprive yourself of something that your body is craving what does this do to you on both a physical and mental level. Remember we are talking moderation here. There are others out there who have lost their souls to gluttony which is another topic entirely. Rather we are discussing the merits of fasting over not, meat over not. There are no hard and fast rules. Personal experimentation is the key.

The spiritual realm is open to all who want to enter. Once entered you will receive guidance and insights into your own personal spiritual journey. When and if the time to give up meat is warranted you will be guided thus. To you it will become just a '*knowing.*' The timing will feel right. You will just *know*. You will lose all desire for its consumption. That time is not now. When and if it happens you will not have to think about it, discuss it and ask for advice. It will just happen. You will wake up and it will be so. Like a switch has been turned on. For now you need not worry. Your portions are not out of control, not detrimental to your health and certainly are not constraining your development.

Those that expound the virtue of going vegetarian or vegan... good for them. There are definitely health aspects for and against. They have chosen what is right for them. If they try to push their beliefs on to you look at the connection to ego. No one can argue that a beautiful ripe melon is not better for you than that steak that you crave, you only have to check the vibration of each but balance is the key. You are human having a human experience. That means you are not perfect, will not always make the most perfect choices or in the words of your daughter you "Would all be Angels." It is all part of the journey, all part of the self-discovery and learning process. Don't be too harsh on your choices. Everything is fluid and changeable. Nothing need be static or set in stone.

You are wiser than you think. Trust in yourself always — Nameless.

Q. But what about the Buddhist monks and the Sufi's? Have they got it wrong? Some isolate themselves and fast in search of spiritual enlightenment. Is this not necessary?

The spiritual enlightenment is a direct result of their *desire* and *intention* rather than the isolation or fasting which is more ritualistic than anything, putting them in that quiet space allowing communication and insights to come through. It is their *belief* system that these two open the doors that actually allows it to occur. The dedication and time they give also helps.

What we would like to make clear is that it is not necessary to be a Buddhist monk to access the Higher realms, contact your guides or receive enlightenment. You do not have to go and sit on a mountain top, live in a cave, become vegan or give away all your earthly possessions. Guidance is open to all and everyone who seek at any and every point in their lives be they living in the slums of India, on a farm in outback Australia or even on death row. All that is asked is to quiet the mind and ask for guidance, to *believe* that it is possible and *trust* that it will happen. So it is desire, intention, time dedication, belief, trust and a quiet mind that will see the connection and information you seek come through. I do not want to take away from the monks, it is their time dedication that makes them so wise but everyday people need to know that they have free access to knowledge that could help them so much in their lives. You do not have to be special or unique. You just have to ask. And then sit still long enough to listen.

Whoa. Thanks Nameless. That came through really fast today. I felt your passion behind this topic, even felt that you could have said so much more but

I get the picture. Thanks for your perspective.

In love and Light, enjoy your day.

SAT 23RD NOVEMBER

Q. Good morning Nameless and All. Last time we spoke you mentioned the word Angels, do Angels really exist?

Yes in your mind's eye. It was referenced to a phrase your daughter uses. There are so called 'Angels' but not as you perceive them. However whatever works for you on your planet that is beneficial and helpful is always acceptable and a good thing. When we say they exist they are not of the winged variety that you so often depict in movies, paintings and your own thoughts and visions. Rather they are formless guides just like us that omit a pure energy. Humans have added form themselves as a way to make them more accessible, have given them human form and shape so they can perceive them visually and this brings them into their reality making it all the more believable because on your planet unless you can see it/touch it/feel it, how do you know if it exists? The physical form you give with your mind's eye is just another label, a visual label. You are so governed by your sensory perceptions to quantify things. This is your conditioning.

The 'Angels' you perceive are High guides, pure thought and energy. They watch over and guide you, even protect you and comfort you. They help raise your vibration and listen to your troubles and woes. I myself am an Angel in this regard yet you do not see me in this physical form for I do not allow it. I do not want perceptions to cloud what I have to say and thus I choose to show no form at all. I am formless and nameless. Thus you are more inclined to listen to my words and feel my energy using your lesser known sensory attributes.

In your world you have job specifications. Different people do different jobs with varying levels of skills. So it is for us also. There are different types of guides as you already know and have met. 'Angels' (a label humans choose) are just another level of guide, no better or worse than any other guide but are job specific. They are usually very good listeners, are very loving patient and kind, very forgiving of your virtues and are comforting and warm. They have a great ability to transcend their warmth through the energy waves to your level of vibration so that you can feel their energy and warmth. This is what comforts you in times of trouble and need. It is a very warm blanketing of energy that feels like a safe cocoon. That is why people are so drawn to this type of guide. They are great communicators at getting messages and energy through to you (meaning people in general). They are highly invested in the human race showing a large amount of forgiveness and compassion. They understand how harsh it is in your environment and it is their mission to ease some of your pain. This is the work they have chosen to do. It gives them great satisfaction to be able to offer themselves up to you in this type of service and thus it is not selfish on your part or one sided for they benefit greatly too. So by you asking for their help it is not a selfish act for you are giving them a purpose, a reason for existence in their realm. They are natural givers and this is what they like to do. They receive joy from helping you and seeing you do well in life. That is their reward.

That is not to put pressure on you that if you are in communication with these souls that you feel you must be good, do good or achieve for their benefit as this is not what they seek. Rather they are there to comfort you, raise your vibration and energy levels. Thus you naturally feel better about yourselves and your lives and can move forward, taking steps towards *Lightness and Being* and sharing your increased joy, energy and light with others. Not by preaching but that it happens naturally in your daily life, it is the rub off effect. You know what it is like when you are around someone who is always happy, uplifted, joyous and how infectious that can be. Imagine you 'catch' some of that and then like a virus it spreads from person to person. That is what we are trying to achieve. A global uplifting of the planet. If you could only imagine what it would be like if and when the whole planets vibration is raised, what the possibilities could be. Literally 'out of this world' and 'off this planet.'

We 'Angels' know that there is a lot of work to do to even imagine reaching this point. But this is our relentless aim for we have absolute faith that it is possible that one day this will occur. It may be eons from now but each step, each person we reach and affect in a positive manner is another step forward to reaching planetary ecstasy for that is what it would be like...like a giant earthly orgasm! Can you imagine how explosive that would be? And the repercussions for the Universe? The human orgasm is a mere tip of the iceberg. Imagine that a gazillion fold and you start to get the idea of the experience of *Light and Being*, though it is not transient but everlasting!

Far out you just blew my mind even talking about it. I have to ask though as some will want to know…

Q. Do the archangels Michael, Raphael, Uriel etc. really exist?

Yes they are High guides. What you call Masters. There are guides and High guides that are generalized (that is they are accessible to everybody) and there are personal guides that are only particular to that person. Each guide has his own specific quality, area of expertise and body of knowledge as you do here on earth and this is how they can be differentiated out. No one guide is considered better or more knowledgeable than the other just different, unique. When I talk of High guides I am not saying they are of a higher quality rather that they work from on High, High above so to speak, are coming from a particular level of energy if that makes sense. Guides are grouped in specific levels of energy or realms particular to their likeminded qualities or exhibiting certain aspects. Remember we are all the one and the same... Light and Being but we show different aspects of ourselves. So no one realm is considered more superior to another, merely accommodating those of certain aspects.

Q. So who or what is governing all of this?

There is no governance. It is like when you have been doing your job for a long time and you know it so well that you can perform it to a high level without instruction or interference from a higher body and so you just go about your business. It is thus so.

Q. *You mean you don't answer to anyone?*

Only to ourselves.

Q. Cool, can I come and live where you live?

And it will be so one day but now is not the time.

Ah well, back to the 'real' world. Thanks Nameless that was really interesting.

Then I have served my purpose for today. Enjoy your long hot shower and take pleasure as always.

(Nameless is referring to the fact that it has now been raining regularly and I can have a non-stop three minute shower!)

SAT 3OTH NOVEMBER

There's an opportunity today, a window of time, where I can fulfill a long awaited for wish to speak to possibly the most recognized and known tree in Boreen Point, The Wedding Tree. This tree is in the most prominent of positions in a popular area of town making private time with it difficult but it's been plaguing my mind of late and on waking I just knew I would have to visit it this day and make an attempt at communication.

THE WEDDING TREE

The tree is situated half way up Paradise Beach (officially known as Dunn's Beach) that edges the campgrounds on Lake Cootharaba. It's the longest stretch of beach in Boreen Point hence its popularity with both campers and locals alike, the latter of which use it as an exercise run for both themselves and their dogs. Due to the shallow waters it's a safe area for kids to splash about so a popular spot for families and a launching place for small boats and canoes. There's a decent width of sand for the kite surfers to stretch out their gear in preparation for takeoff and many others bring their chairs down at twilight to enjoy a barbeque and sip wine as they watch the sunset over the lake. Thus you can see my difficulty in starting up a conversation with a tree in such an exposed area but I'm spurred on by the fact that it will soon be school holidays making my quest near impossible and so it's now or never.

Rumor and myth has it that the Wedding Tree is called thus because anyone who sits in its branches will soon be wedded but I've tested and debunked this theory having sat in its branches many times while taking in the afternoon sun and lake breezes and even been kissed while embraced in the crevice of its boughs with another. Yep, still single.

The Wedding tree is one of the largest Paperbark's of its kind and the only one actually sitting on the shoreline of Paradise Beach where it rests on the lakes edge, its gnarly roots extending out into the water. A prominent landmark from all angles, many photos have been taken of this beauty over the years and even some capturing the very essence and energy of both the tree and the lake during auspicious times have won competitions. An acquaintance of mine renowned for his ability to capture nature spirits on film showed me a photo he took of the Wedding Tree and in the water at its roots was the clear and unmistakable face of an Aboriginal man. Entirely awesome.

Now having walked down through the campgrounds and setting foot on the beach I'm absolutely devastated to see the Wedding Tree is a shadow of its former majestic grandeur. Slowly over the years I've watched it age and degrade at a snail's pace but today there is a large amputation and displacement of a major bough which is resting half way up the trees trunk and the other half in the brackish waters below. A feeling of sadness comes over me as I look up into its branches grasping for signs of life. There is one large sprouting of green matter at the very tip of its most skyward aspect, otherwise the tree looks dead but with Paperbark's being somewhat grey in nature they never look very much alive anyway.

There are people on the beach, a group of young Germans, backpackers I presume but ignoring them I approach the tree with my pendulum and set about finding its spiritual center. I'm surprised when I find two spiritual centers one facing north and the other facing south. I've never come across this before. A closer inspection reveals there are two trees joined at the base and bifurcating at the lower limbs. Siamese twins! The twins are twisted around each other such that it's near impossible to tell which part belongs to which tree looking like just one rather large one overall. They sure fooled everyone, no wonder their former majestic size.

I make an attempt to speak with South first…

Q. Can I speak with you, are you still alive? I follow the branches upwards. South is the only one sprouting greenery and showing any signs of life.

Yes.

The pendulum hardly moves indicating the tree is barely hanging on.

Q. Are you Siamese twins, two grown into one?

Yes.

Q. What is your name?

Davinagh.

Q. How old are you?

Forty-two.

The information coming through is not strong so I shift my placement and turn my attention to North.

Q. Are you Siamese twins, two grown into one?

Yes.

Q. Can I talk to you?

Yes.

Q. What is your name?

Leif.

I love that name!

Q. I see you've lost a large limb, can you tell me what happened?

{I move again trying to make myself comfortable but now I'm sitting on a root belonging to Davinagh and communication with Leif is lost. I decide to try again with Davinagh.)

Q. Tell me, its clear Leif is breaking down what's happening with you?

There is a symbiotic relationship going on here much like the Siamese twins in your world. Its true Leif is degrading but is still able to draw on my strength and this is the only thing keeping him alive for he would surely be dead by now if it wasn't for me. Not that I'm trying to say that I'm any better but that's the way things panned out. That is his fortune and this is mine. I'm glad I can help in this way as it's my turn to pay back what I can, he having helped me when I was much younger and struggling to survive myself and if it were not for he, our connection to each other, I myself would not have survived past yearling. The day today being one of beauty and absolute calm, a delight but the conditions here at times can be very harsh. You don't see that side being cocooned up at home.

Q. What of your future? It doesn't look good, I'm so sad to see you both in this state. You look like your suffering.

Everything must break down eventually. Everything has a time and place in this world. This is our time. Our time to enjoy the last days, year (or years if we're lucky) of this time in existence. We sit and watch. Watch the boats go by, the canoes, the windsurfers, the people frolicking in the water. We oversee everything, the comings and goings, night, day, the seasons, sunrise and the sunsets. Things of beauty, things of pain, storms and great winds. We've seen it all yet we never tire to see more and this is our experience, our life, to sit and observe and take it all in. We are the silent ones. The steady and the strong. You can always count on us being here, our vision on this beach you cannot miss from any angle and iconically we stand until one day we can stand no longer.

Q. My friend took photos of you awhile back and on developing the film discovered the clear image of an Aboriginal face resting in the waters at your base... what do you know of this?

Yes, there are many souls connected to our presence. We were once a thing of beauty and grandeur exuding a great aura, a spirituality. Many were drawn to us with ceremonies performed beneath and around us on the beach.

(The most recent ceremonies belonging to Floating Land and the indigenous performing artist group Gubbi Gubbi Dance[2] during opening and closing ceremonies and the firing of the kilns on the lake, a sight to behold.)

What you see is memory. Memory of those that felt a soul connection to us and so they left a part of themselves behind, an imprint. You leave imprints everywhere you go that you find a connection to. Thus when you leave this earth, you have not really left as your imprints are all over the place, wherever you have been in your travels that have spoken to you, your heart, your soul in some manner or form but only those with the gift of seeing will notice these imprints unless of course as you said they are accidently caught on film. We will leave our own imprint one day when we cease to exist. Thus you can visit this place many decades from now and given the gift of seeing, we will still be here. You, yourself are leaving an imprint that will remain with us as you get up to take your leave. Know that a little part of you will always belong here too.

Ooh, I'm fascinated by what you're saying about imprints. I'd love to know more and I don't want to leave but I promised to take Daughter to the movies and I have to go. It's such a gorgeous day and I could sit here forever talking to you and taking it all in.

Then take in the peace and serenity that is this beautiful day into your heart and carry it with you always.

Thanks Davinagh, thanks Leif.

Many people stop by to admire but very rarely does one get to speak. For this we thank you. It's been a lovely surprise and one that's made our day all the more special.

14

DECEMBER 2013

SUN 1ST DECEMBER

Inspired by my readings on Shamanic Reiki I decide it's time to take a journey to find and meet my power animal. Here I recount my adventure...

FIRST JOURNEY

Walking through the forest singing and humming while rambling along the serpentine path I marvel at the ambient temperature and the suns ambition, twinkling its way through the thick foliage above. It's not a difficult walk but the forest is quite dense, the aroma of dew laden leaves arousing my nostrils and awakening my other senses. Oh how I love being in nature. The divine aroma coupled with peace, tranquility and birdsong serenades. After a while spent lost in thought I'm jolted back into awareness by an increase in light filtering through the canopy and unfolding ahead is a rather large grassed clearing which beckons me forwards.

On entering I realize I'm surrounded by a circle of trees, one in particular drawing my attention is majestic in size and probably eons old. I've seen such trees before in ancient forests, the hollows in their trunks large enough to house several people all at once. It's no surprise to me that this hollow is where my journey begins given my affinity with trees and removing my backpack and belongings to the ground I wonder if I should take the water with me but instead decide anything required will be found along my travels.

Taking one step back from this giant centian I prepare for the journey ahead by performing a small Reiki ceremony. Connecting with my guides and invoking the power symbol I inject it into my aura, draw the Chokurei[1] with the palm of my right hand in the air directly in front of the hollow and sing the Kotudama.[2] *This is the key that opens the door.*

Satisfied the safety aspects had been covered and all my guides were on alert my first step is more of a small leap down through the hollow of the tree onto a small earthy ledge. It's much darker down here and I wonder what I'll do for light when a small glow worm appears at my left shoulder. He may be small but he is very powerful, I thank him and together we continue.

We come upon a circular stair case made of iron, very ornate looking like it belonged in some grand manor from antiquity. The muddy earth was compressed up against its rails creating a naturally rendered wall and after descending every hundred steps or so towards the planets core we would stop to check our surrounds, now having travelled way beyond any root systems and instead water was starting to trickle at its sides. Underground springs? The wet walls are starting to concern me but needn't when turning the next corner reveals a second ledge and the opening to an underground water slide. Suddenly I feel like I've jumped down the rabbit hole. It looked both scary and fun but where would it take me? "Oh well I'm committed now," I thought out aloud, not fancying climbing all the way back up those stairs.

Not sure where it was going to lead me I took a giant leap of faith and exerted myself from the slides opening. Everything whizzed passed me so fast, the walls constantly changing colors and they lost all their solidity as the ability to transfix ones gaze on any one point was totally lost. "Is this a vortex?" I was enjoying myself but petrified at the same time fearing what was at the other end or how I would stop as my momentum picked up and I was 'flying' at great speed. I needn't have worried though and if I could go back in time I would have enjoyed it more, safe in the knowledge that I was well protected.

The motion started to slow and everything came back into focus when suddenly and without warning my bottom unceremoniously came to an abrupt stop on the end of the tunnels slide and I found myself deposited in a giant underground cave the size of a huge amphitheater with enormous cathedral like ceilings, the beauty of which was overshadowed by a deep emerald green lagoon. It was not dark down here but lit with warm gold courtesy of the glow worms making the lagoon glint and shine as if in bright sunlight and with a sparkle that would emanate from any gem of sound quality. My little glow friend encircled me to ensure I was ok then went off to join his clan.

The lagoon was enticing and venturing to the water's edge I noticed a little wooden boat with a sign that said, "Ride me." Laughing I thought, "That's very Alice in Wonderland," and deliberated against it for a while but after assessing the possible dangers and realizing I had no other options I obeyed and stepped into the boat. It took off immediately in a gentle rocking motion, heading towards a narrowing in the cave reminiscent of those rides I took as a kid at the fair ground that were named something like 'Majestic Mountain' or the 'Underwater Love Caves.'

On entering the tunnel like caves the walls become narrower and the boat started to rock and bump against the sides when I came across my first display. A black bear standing on its hind legs, growling and sniffing at the air as he sensed my arrival. The recognition came over me that I had reached the animal sanctuary and this is where I'd find my power animal. Just at that thought a wolf dog jumped into my boat and sat beside me, not communicating but just staring silently ahead. I felt it was offering me protection on my journey through the cave. Strangely it was not solid but ghostly in appearance. "No, you can't be my power animal." "That would be so cliché," I laughed.

I continued on my search, the boat drifting further until we came upon a python. Slithering and writhing up to head height it hissed at me as we ambled by. "Nup, definitely not the snake,"

How bizarre. The next display was a whole African scene with elephants, wild deer and zebra's all far off in the distance. It was clear they didn't want to be associated with me, looking more annoyed by my presence than anything. The elephant looked up at me with disdain then ignoring me went back to eating his grass. So no, I couldn't recognize anything here either. After that came a sole lion regally sitting very close to the edge, unperturbed and snubbing us as we cruised on by. He exuded that sense of aura and satisfaction, like he'd just eaten something!

The little dinghy was coming to a corner about to veer sharply to the right when the wolf dog again jumped into the boat, this time at the front sitting and facing directly in front of me. I checked to my right and the wolf dog was sitting there also still staring straight ahead. It was the same wolf dog but there was now two of them in the boat. I knew these to be two different aspects but still refused to believe the wolf dog could be my power animal. He sat wisely, silently and knowingly in my boat. "It can't be, it's too obvious a choice," I muttered doing my best to ignore him.

The boat scraped the edges as it rounded the bend giving a little jolt and I wondered if there where piranhas in the waters below when my thoughts were intercepted by the vision before me. The most beautiful of all the displays, a tree laden full of owls, all dark woody brown except for one pure white one. It was so breathtakingly beautiful and fluffy and I was rather drawn to it as it looked at me with its big wise eyes but no, I sensed that was the one that belonged to Harry Potter. That was not my power animal, though why he was down here watching me in my little boat was a mystery.

I decided the search for my power animal was taking too long and growing impatient asked all the animals to gather in one place, the field from the African display. Hundreds gathered. It was a veritable Noah's Ark with all the chaos and cacophony that goes with it. The elephant is kicking up a fuss, he doesn't like everyone moving in on his territory and is taking a while to placate. The quicker we get this over with the quicker he will have his field back he is told by the others. I want to tell him to calm his farm but think better of it.

Once things quietened down and regaining everybody's attention I asked my power animal to step forward and show itself. Suddenly, absolute silence. I held my breath in anticipation then slowly one by one all the animals parted ways either to the left or to the right like Moses parting the red sea. There, left seated in the middle, was the wolf dog with his back to me (the third aspect), this time showing himself in solid form.

I stared in awe as if for the first time at this beautiful being, part husky part wolf, his snow white coat flecked with the smallest of black. The wolf dog turned his head to look at me and I knew it to be true. Here was my power animal, strong, gentle and wise. He picked something off the ground and walked towards me with his knowing and placed it at my feet. It was his prize possession, his only possession, a small and delicate bone from an unknown origin that he had been saving just for me. An offering and sacrifice to show his dedication and unwavering commitment, surrendering his service so that I may grow. I asked him his name and immediately the wolf dog jumped to his heels and standing as tall as I, placed his paws on my shoulders and howled, "Arooooooon," which I understood to be Ronan. This display was an unusual gesture for a wolf dog as they're notoriously shy of humans and it took me by surprise. Face to face we stared into each other's eyes, his being the most piercing blue, loving and kind eyes I have ever seen and I instantly fell in love. How could I not? "He looks like a 'Coju' to me," I thought so I tell him I will call him Ronan Coju. I place the bone in my hair as Ronan Coju steps down, nuzzles my leg then heals at my feet. "It's time to journey," he tells me telepathically.

For some reason I'm expecting Ronan Coju will carry me on his back and I stand stock still wondering how this will happen as even though he is quite large not nearly enough for that. My thoughts are disrupted when I feel a tug on my pants leg and Coju jumps into the water taking me with him. I desperately cling to the fur on his neck and paddle madly in an effort to keep up as he drags me along the caves river to the other side where we scramble ashore. Strangely as we exit the water we are instantly drip dry. "This feels totally weird," I murmur patting myself down and looking at my clothes, my jaw agape. Coju has already taken off through a hidden path of large boulders and is steadily climbing a rocky cliff face signaling to me which ledges are safe to travel. Panting I struggle to keep up such is his pace like he's on some sort of mission. This is hard work and I can't help but complain as I beg for him to slow down which he doesn't and I have no choice but to keep going and keep up. Finally, exhausted, we reach the top of the cliff and after taking some moments to catch my breath I notice Ronan Coju staring silently out over the valley below.

Following his path of vision reveals a scene of horror. Below in the valley is a large Indian reservation. There are people, men, women and children screaming and running everywhere in chaos. The animals are doing the same and I realize they are being attacked but by whom I cannot see. Everything is moving so fast and there is a lot of dust, or is that smoke? Yes smoke, the teepees have been set on fire. Cemented by shock this is not what I expected to see on my journey and feeling helpless to do anything I ask Ronan Coju if we can go now. I don't want to be here watching this, it's too distressing.

Coju, "We have something to do first, stay close."

Horrified I follow him as we sneak down into the village invisible amongst the chaos but so terrified am I that my heart pounding in my chest is enough to give me a sudden headache and I fear I might faint. Grasping for an exit away from this turmoil I know it's possible to think myself back to earth's reality but I'm curious to see what Coju is doing and it outweighs any fear. Knowing that I'm petrified Ronan Coju hands me the reins of a riderless horse for me to shield behind and instructs me to calm him and make ready to escape. My safety in his hands I do as he says then watch in earnest as he stealthily makes his way to a nearby teepee which is clearly on fire and he disappears inside. Is he mad? Does he have a death wish? Time seems to go on forever as he fails to emerge and I start to panic. What should I do? I can't leave him. I'm still deciding on my next move when again unnoticed by the murderous mob around him Coju finally escapes the flaming teepee not a moment too soon, dragging with his teeth a swaddled infant. Marikahee? Have we gone back in time?

Ronan Coju reaches me and explains, "This baby is motherless, homeless and soon to be tribeless. It's time for us to go."

Gladly obeying I mount the horse and we flee at lightning speed taking the attackers by surprise, being so fast they have little time to react. Once beyond any danger the pace slows yet neither of us speak, both with thoughts of those who have and still may be suffering back at the scene. I wonder what we are to do with this baby that is oblivious to any occurrence. We meander along the path not speaking for an uncertain amount of time but I know I'm getting hungry. Suddenly Ronan Coju stops and my heart sinks. "Oh no, not another cliff top," I couldn't take it. "This is turning into a nightmare."

Coju motions for me to look up and there, high on the cliff above, stands a young Indian warrior. Absent from his tribe during his initiation into manhood the young warrior was sent forth to discover his tribal name and purpose on the eve of his fourteenth birthday with instructions only to return after retrieving visions of his quest, however long that may take. Coju feels my tiredness and instructs me to rest and watch from afar. He will deliver the infant to the young warrior and ask him to care for it which he does. The young warrior is saddened by the news of the loss of his village but has received his own messages during his vision quest and was expecting us. He thanks Coju and sends me a distant nod acknowledging my presence. He will take the infant to a satellite tribe three days journey from here and has amassed enough skills and knowledge over his few short years to keep them both safe until they deliver themselves and the sad news to their cousins. He takes a handful of his hair cutting it at the root with his knife and placing it in a small pouch hangs it around Ronan Coju's neck. It's the only thing he has to offer in gratitude.

Coju nuzzles the baby in a goodbye gesture then turns to me and signals, "It's time to go home."

He knows a short cut and with this he morphs into a larger version of himself simultaneously sprouting the most expansive set of wings which propel him off the cliff face and flying in my direction, slowing down only enough that I may climb aboard and once again I find myself clinging to the fur on his neck as we take off in the clear blue sky.

As we travel Ronan Coju tells me that the baby's mother was down at the river collecting water when she was one of the first to be ambushed, her screams ripping through the forest waking the others. The father on hearing his wife emerged from his teepee only to be executed himself soon after. It was not their intention to leave their child defenseless and it was the fathers spirit that alerted Coju to her plight that she would either suffocate or burn to death, defenseless, helpless and innocent. "Was it Marikahee?" I ask. Coju doesn't answer. We've arrived back at the tree and land in the clearing nearby where I dismount, dusting myself off while checking everything is still intact. Realizing I'm without my backpack I spy it at the base of the tree and retrieve it.

Coju shrinks back to normal size, "Well Shozimishun, what shall we do today?"

There's that word again. What ever could it mean? Master, master in training perhaps?

"What, you're coming with me?"

Coju, "Yes we are bonded, connected, one and the same."

"Then welcome to 'The Circle' Ronan Coju."

We set off back through the forests path together as I reflected on the journey which was like nothing I ever could have imagined.

WED 4TH DECEMBER

Yeah, I've done it! I've gone and booked my very first channeling class at the Cooroy Library. I'm so excited. Finally I feel like I'm living my purpose and now realize what Nameless has been saying all along, how good it feels to be doing something worthwhile for myself others and the planet in general. I'm cutting it a bit fine for years end but it's taken me all year to get to this point. I didn't think it would take this long but looking back now I can see I wouldn't have been ready any earlier. I've learnt so much over the last year with all the conversations I've had with Nameless and The Circle and my confidence in my knowledge has grown enormously. Yes I'm finally ready and it feels great.

I had two dates to choose from and asking for guidance chose the twenty-eighth of December just scraping it in before the end of my year of divine guidance and indeed that is what helped spur me on. It could be likely I'll get a few people as often that Xmas New Year week businesses close down and people are free or I'll get no one as they're all on holidays and spending time with family. I made up pamphlets and spent the day driving all around town dropping them on community notice boards at Cooroy, Pomona, Noosa and Eumundi.

Whilst putting up notices at Eumundi I bumped into "Z" who owns one of the local healing centers. I find her very intimidating both in her personality, how she comes across and also the fact that I imagine her to be much more knowledgeable than me. Eyeing my pamphlets she asked me what I channel and commented on how I should get a few people attend because I had priced my class so cheap. I wondered if she was taking a dig at me always feeling judged in her presence or is that just my own insecurities? I told her I wasn't pricing it for me but for the people who would attend as I know many times over I've wanted to attend a class and haven't been able to afford it, hers included which

I personally think are outrageously priced and wonder if she gets any one attending at all but I didn't tell her that. She turned and walked away I felt in mid conversation and I was left wondering who was learning from this crossing of paths…her or me. Probably both. She is the one person in town I didn't want to bump into, something about her makes me feel uncomfortable, her air of superiority. I tried not to let it put a dampener on my excitement but left a little deflated.

Q. Any comments any one?

Yes firstly we are ecstatic of the new developments and the unfolding of your first petal. The blossoming and unfoldment has started as you put your teachings into motion and bring them forth into your reality. We all look on in pride that things are going to plan and in divine timing. That is your timing as you are right in saying that yes you are finally ready and if you did not take this step you would only stagnate and perhaps give up altogether. For that we see you as being very brave and very courageous for even though you have had our support all along we understand how hard it is to manifest such things alone in your human world without support from your fellow man. For this we commend you.

You both received a message that day. Take note for how this person makes you feel and how she comes across though she probably would be shocked to find out her effect on you, she does not mean to be this way. You are finely tuned to subtle energies of people and are picking up signals that perhaps others wouldn't much like a dog who can hear high pitched sounds that humans can't. Take these signals as a message. You have already ascertained how they make you feel. Learn from this and be wary not to exude the same type of aura onto others and put them in your position. That is always keep your own sense of superiority and ego in check. Stay humble and open.

We are all students, we are all teachers. Everybody has both something to learn from others and something they can pass on. You/we are all of equal footing one no better than the other, just unique with something unique that you can share so that others may learn, grow and benefit from to make their lives that much better and joyous.

So your lesson is one of humbleness. Think of the Dalai Lama and his nature and this is what you are aiming for. Wise, humble and joyous. Always helping always loving, kind and nurturing, never judging for it is not for you to know what another person is going through or dealing with. Remind yourself every day until it becomes your conditioning. To receive smiles and joy in your life you first need to project and then it will be mirrored back to you. So if you are lacking such things in your life work first on how you can honorably share these with others. Then watch your life change before your very eyes. It's taking that saying "What you think about, you bring about," that one step further into manifestation.

As for the other person she too received a message that day. Yes she is charging too much. Perhaps her business is not going as well as she thought it might. Her pricing among other things could be adjusted. Also you reminded her of the very core of why she chose this vocation in the first place. To help others. It is not meant to be for the wealthy and the well-off alone but Universal wisdom to be shared equally and among all for those who choose it. By overpricing you are creating divides between those that can afford it and those that cannot. The idea of "pay what you can afford," or as some restaurants do "pay what you think it is worth," could be an alternative option as could offering scholarships as some Reiki Masters do for those that require it. It is trying to find that balance of your right to be paid an honorable service fee of fair payment without abusing the needs of those you are offering to. Always keep this in mind. Having said that do not undersell yourself either. You have sacrificed much over the last year to attain the knowledge that you share. You deserve adequate compensation for this as would any one of any skill.

You are being interrupted. Your daughter is vying for attention. We have said what we wanted to convey for now. Mostly we are excited, watching in trepidation. Know that the right students will be sent your way. Bliss be your day — Nameless.

Thank you Nameless.

FRI 13TH DECEMBER

I'm so excited! I had my first student ring and book the class a few days ago and yesterday a few more booked so it's all systems go. Finally fruition. Yippee!

Today I walked to the valley to meet up with Marikahee and sitting back from the shoreline to shelter from the winds I made myself comfortable amongst a bed of leaves where I had laid down a protective circle of crystals to ward off the snakes and all that would do me evil. I closed my eyes silently chanting an (Native American) Indian mantra requesting Marikahee's presence until she showed herself to me…

▫▫▫

Marikahee was in a boat, a canoe, paddling upstream in an expansive river that was bordered on one side by steep mountainous cliffs and the other by deep wooded forest. Her canoe was one of many each containing at least three to four members of her tribe. Mainly women, children, the very old and all their possessions. I asked what was going on and she motioned that I was to stay silent and hidden, to only listen and observe and she would tell me the story. The rest of the tribe would not be happy if they knew I was there. They were fleeing the white man (being forced deep into Indian Territory, sacred land) and well, I was one of them. The tribes' men are travelling through the forest by horseback carrying supplies while their wolf dogs scout ahead for any danger and the best paths to travel. The two separate packs meet up before nightfall on the third day with four more yet to travel. This is no picnic but serious resettlement.

Observing from a distance I watch their reunion and gathering at a clearing on the rivers bend. The vibe is good. Everyone is happy knowing the other has made it safely thus far and I get a sense of the hierarchy and order of the tribe, that there is never or rarely confrontation or argument because everyone knows their place and just abides, no one stepping out of line.

They set up camp here for the night and with important matters to attend to an elder meeting is called in one of the wigwams. Marikahee performs a cleansing ceremony as they gather in a circle, infusing the tent with sage and sprinkling her panacea at the entrance to the teepee and around the circle of occupants as a whole. She chooses the elder who will govern the meeting by the placement of a ceremonial neckpiece. Each elder has their specialty and the chosen one is the most appropriate to deal with the matter at hand. Ultimately the chief has final say but wisely he considers the advice of others.

The issue is white man's disease. Many in the tribe especially children are already affected and some have succumbed to death. I suspect it's the pox or some such similar virus. Marikahee's medicine is powerless the disease being too quick and strong even her panacea is not working. The disease is spreading and the whole tribe is in danger of obliteration if they can't manage to tame it. Untrusting of white man's cure for its effect on the spirit and being blamed for the outbreak and in fear that such treatment would be forced upon them the tribe had fled their homeland.

Now the decision is made to split the tribe in two. To isolate the sick and their families out into a satellite tribe three days ride away. This leaves both sites more vulnerable to white man's attack but necessary for the whole tribes' survival. Whoever is alive after three full moons and showing no sign of illness can return. Harsh but necessary. They must leave immediately in the middle of the night. A third of them pack and go sad to be leaving, worried what will happen to them and their families and will they succumb? But also knowing it is for the benefit of all, they know their hierarchy, they know their place. There is no argument. The elders have spoken.

I'm confused. Why is Marikahee showing me this? What can I do from here? Nothing she tells me. It's a part of history, her history. To help me understand who she is, her life, where she comes from but also that she doesn't want it to be forgotten. There are lessons she said. That the American Indians were a happy people but were forced to stand up and fight for their land, their people and way of life but ultimately were outnumbered and outgunned. The white man could have lived with the Indians in peace and learnt so much from their ways each benefiting the other but they were greedy and ego driven and everybody lost out not just the Indians.

Marikahee takes an eagle feather from her headdress and plaits it into my hair humming a chant so soft I can barely decipher it. She's mothering me and it's lovely to watch. I take in all of her, her scent and her aged beauty, her ways. She places a small pouch of deer powder around my neck, such an honor, then places a large rock in the palm of my hand.

"Find the heart center to yourself through finding the heart center in the rock and thereby the connection to you both that you are one and the same. You are the rock and the rock is you."

But I look at it and think it's just a rock. Her point exactly, I'm looking without seeing. She takes her rattle and chants around me shaking up my aura as if she wants to wake me up, afterwards taking my face in both her hands and kissing me on the lips, a grandmotherly kiss full of love and tenderness. She closes my eyelids with her fingertips and blows on them a smoky breath. When I open my eyes she is gone.

MON 16TH DECEMBER

Fifty-eight kilo's UGHH! If only I could lose these last two kilo's! I know that finding time to exercise is an issue and I'll just have to schedule it into my days.

I desperately needed to talk to you all yesterday but Daughter has started school holidays and it's difficult to get anything done with her in the house let alone finding quiet time to converse with you. I've been feeling really depressed the last week. Something Daughter said to me that was rather confronting that hit home and I realized the truth of it all. That I'm continually going around in circles and getting nowhere throwing what little money I have at this and that venture and achieving nothing. My girlfriends opinion differs saying that I'm at least giving things a go and that one day given right timing one of them will work out and it will all fall in to place.

I don't know what to think anymore. I'm constantly working at trying to make something work if that makes sense and I'm getting so frustrated by it all. I really thought at my age I would have it all worked out by now and I'd be settled into a beautiful fruitful and worthwhile rhythm. Now I just feel like I'm going through some poor man's midlife crisis chasing my own tail. I'm confused, unhappy and desperate. I think the job prospects or lack of aren't helping any. To be honest, sometimes I think if I had the guts it would be easier just to top myself right here, right now because really what is it (life) all for? Is it some cruel joke?

Driving to the beach yesterday I realized if we move back into town for Daughter to be closer to school in her final years (and our combined sanity) half my working wage will go on rent alone. So once again I'm just surviving not really living. On the treadmill. What's the point of it all? I just feel like crying yet I have to remind myself that there are so many worse off like the people who attend the Mercy ship abroad. Like Daughter say's though, "Just because others are worse off doesn't make your feelings any less valid."

I don't know whether it's just this time of year, Xmas and New Year coming, a time of reflection. It's been a long hard year but every year feels long and hard and always I think next year will be better. Next year I will start to prosper. Next year will be less of a struggle but it never is and often feels harder than the one before.

Daughter and I are fighting. Because of my state I'm being really negative and need to keep my mouth shut. She's being a typical teenager, argumentative. Its times like this I wish I had a partner to back me up, offer advice and console me. I'm sorry I'm being so negative but why now? Why when I'm just starting to get it all together with the class am I feeling like this?

Q. Can someone please help put my life in some sort of perspective? Is there anything I should or shouldn't be doing right now?

It is I Hoyan. We are sorry that you are feeling this way. You are feeling overburdened with everything you have to do. Looking for work and applying for jobs and at the same time trying to make your own work from home sewing clothes to try and bring in funds and in case there is no work to be found. You are realizing that it is not going to be as easy as you thought to find appropriate work or any type of work that is satisfying. A combination of factors. You exhibit a lack of confidence because you are feeling judged by your age and this is also playing a big part in your melancholy. Added to the work issues are monetary stresses and the difficulties you face paying the bills and bringing up a teenage daughter single handedly. Then there is the matter of the class. Something that brings you joy but is also an extra work load added to an already hectic schedule. Yes life though unsatisfying, if working would be a lot easier.

We have said all along that you are a lone cow. You are travelling your own path and it is not always going to be easy. There are obstacles to be faced and overcome. These are your quests. To face them head on and fight your way through them. There are riches on the other side for those that are prepared to do battle. Your friend is right. Nothing will change unless you make it so and sometimes there are necessary hurdles to cross. Stages that you will go through and this is one of them. A stage and it is only a stage. Remember everything is energy including 'time.' Nothing is ever static and is always changing therefore it will not be this way forever. Remember the big picture. Take a step back and assess the whole life scenario. This is but a small but necessary part of your life's journey if you want to achieve your goals. Sometimes it is out of these times of desperation that you find the inclination and energy to take action to change your life. This is one of those times. It is actually a reminder of your goal, where you are heading. Stay focused on the end posts (the book) for nothing will change unless you change it for yourself. You need to make it happen. We understand you are tired because of going it alone and there is so much for one person to do both with the day to day running of the house and child along with the work that is going to be life changing one day. No one said it was going to be easy. Only the courageous make it through.

Your main issue is one of a lack of energy. If this was bountiful you would be more enthused and less weighed down by issues. Therefore we suggest you work on this aspect. Of raising ones energy levels with right eating and exercise as you suggested. Not just to lose weight but you will find it more motivating, increasing your endorphin levels. With this will come mind clarity enabling you to solve problems with ease.

You currently have a lot of energy expenditure but there is not a lot being returned to you and so the well is running dry. Therefore you need to make yourself a priority nurturing the self more. The day at the beach helped bring some vitalization back into your life. You need more of this type of experience to increase your joy levels as that is what is missing from your life. Experiences of joy. We have said this all along but you must make it a priority if you are to continue along your quest. Your vitality will naturally increase and burdens will feel lessened.

So joy is our answer. Go back to your list of things that bring you joy and weave them back into your life.

You're so right as always. I can see myself now at the easel. I know that art is my biggest joy and it's been missing from my life these past few months. I'll pull out an old canvas and do a little every day. Also I know I need more fresh air and sunlight, yesterday reminded me of that. Maybe with some of the money I make from the class I'll shout myself to a lesson in stand up paddling, something I've wanted to do for a long time. Just even thinking about doing it and what it'll be like brings a smile to my face. Thanks Hoyan. It's all about finding that right balance.

And being kind to yourself. We envelope you with much love and energy at this time.

Thank you, it's always nice to know I have The Circle and am not completely alone.

WED 18TH DECEMBER

Morning All. I'm on the train heading down to in.cube8r in Brisbane to reduce the prices on my Amigurumi and iPhone covers due to a lack of sales over the last month. The thing is I knew there wouldn't be but felt obligated to honor my commitment and now I'm just throwing away three hundred dollars in cube rent money that I don't really have. I thought the five hour return trip would be a good opportunity to collate all the information for the channel class.

Q. Is there anything I need to know or be aware of?

Yes, KISS. Use the K.I.S.S concept. Don't overcomplicate things which you have a propensity to do. It may be necessary to accumulate and gather all the information first and then cull it back to only the absolute need to know information. Remember these are beginners and you do not want to overwhelm them. Rather it is introducing them to the concept, the possibility, application and the practicality of how to go about it. So you should concentrate on these areas as the time you have to share information is limited.

You will need to be discerning about what information you include and what you decide to leave out. Yes ideally the course would be better run over two days to be more comprehensive but this is a beginner's introduction so that is what you need to concentrate on. Introducing the concept in its most basic form, a little bit of theory combined with some practical exercises. Enough to get them started on their journey/path, to spark their interest to want to explore and discover more either for themselves through books etc. or some may seek out more personal mentoring and guidance. Above all the practical aspects are the most important. They need to be able to walk away connected to at least one of their guides. So work on which practice exercises you will deliver to achieve this and remember the KISS concept.

Thank you Nameless.

A pleasure. And you have not thrown away your three hundred dollars as you are learning much from this experience. Think of it as an investment in your growth. It all works out for you in the end.

Thanks Nameless, you always see the positive aspect.

SAT 21ST DECEMBER

I'm totally freakin out! Last night after spending quite some hours working on my laptop putting together the channeling class I finally went to bed in the wee small hours, two a.m. to be precise but that's not unusual for me. I can't tell if what happened next was a dream or totally real. It felt absolutely real and I was in fear of my life!

I had gone to bed and turned the lights out and could hear Daughter in the other room still up and on her computer, probably on Facebook or Tumbler. I was just about to drift off when I noticed some one standing at my window peering in. He didn't knock or anything but was just standing there waiting for me to notice him. At first though surprised, I was pleased. Who's this? Some ones come to see me! No one ever comes to see me (me and my privacy issues). I went to the window and noticed he had a dog by his side and both were standing stock still staring at my bedroom window, he not uttering a word. Then I got angry. What was he doing here? I hadn't invited him. I didn't know who he was. He wasn't meant to be here. How dare he come in the middle of the night! I asked him to go away but he wouldn't. I don't think he was trying to come in, I can't really remember except that I was getting increasingly distraught because he wouldn't leave when I asked him to. I remember screaming at him, "No, No! Go away, go away, you're not meant to be here!" and trying to push him away though my hands seemed useless as even though directed at him they were seemingly unable to make any contact. I was getting increasingly fearful when finally he headed my screams and left.

Relieved and shaken I withdrew to my bed and pulled up the covers. The moon was just past full and so the room was not completely dark. I sensed movement to my right and noticed a woman in my room, walking away from the head of my bed. I was just staring at her back as she walked slowly by thinking what the hell is going on? I never uttered a word, I didn't get a chance to. It seems she sensed my eyes on her and with an inhumane swiftness lurched around and grabbed hold of my throat in a strangle hold and proceeded to choke me with such viciousness I thought I was going to die. I remember choking and gasping for breath, attempting to call out for help. I tried desperately to call out to Daughter but of course all my sounds were stifled by the compression of her hands on my throat, her face so close to mine that it actually blocked my vision and I couldn't see anything at all except for the anger in her eyes. I wanted to yell, "NO, NO!" but could only scream it over and over in my mind as my physical body was running out of oxygen and the life was draining from me. The attack seemed prolonged. Silently fighting for my existence I was dying here, completely taken by surprise. Daughter totally unaware in the next room. Then just as suddenly as she had turned on me she let go, retreated and then vanished.

What the hell? For a moment I was paralyzed by fear unable to move and trying to gain my breath back. Then I snapped into action and went to check the back door which is sometimes accidently left open. It was closed but unlocked and I locked it. Shaking I went to the fridge and got chocolate. Silly I know but I wanted to feel better, feel the comfort. I didn't want to tell Daughter what just happened not wanting to frighten her as I currently was so bypassed her room and went back to my own. It was after two-thirty a.m. but how was I going to sleep now? I put the night light on, grabbed my soft teddy and fluffy bunny and sat on my bed eating the chocolate trying to make sense of it all. I cuddled them tightly and eventually fell asleep with the light on. I vaguely remember

Daughter coming into my room at some ungodly hour in the morning asking why I had the night light on and turning it off. The thing is it's now nearly midnight the night after. I'm in bed about to go to sleep or attempt to and I'm scared shitless! I have my own theories but wanted to ask you…

Q. What the hell happened last night? Is it likely to happen again?

It is I Hoyan. Yes you were receiving a harsh lesson. One that you will not easily forget. You have had little experience with this dark side being well protected by all of us but know that it does exist and can seem as real as the dimension you are currently in. Even more real as in the face of death your sensory awareness is heightened and all sensations are amplified.

You were shown this for a reason. Not to be complacent and to give your students an understanding of what could go wrong if they delve towards this extreme or leave themselves unprotected. A certain part of your teachings that you were thinking of leaving out is perhaps one of the most important parts of all especially for a beginner. Also now you have firsthand experience of what it is like to meet with these particular beings and that it is not as simple as telling them to go away but that you must use all the strength and will of the telepathic mind that you can muster if you are to overcome them.

That is what made her retreat in the end. It was your focused strength of mind. It is a battle of the wills to see who has the most power. You are so used to being in the physical but the physical does not work in these realms and when you find yourself in such a situation it is important to remember to work on a telepathic level. You do not want to go about scaring your students but you certainly want to give them the best opportunity to protect themselves and so make sure you include this necessary information for their own future safety.

Q. Yes but who were they and are they likely to come again?

You have been very careful not to open yourself up to such beings. They only came to deliver a message. I'm sure you got the message. Respect. Respect the otherworldly. There is ying and yang to everything. There is not hot without cold. There is no light without dark. But just because they exist does not mean you need to experience that existence. This time it was beneficial for your growth. As harsh as it seemed at the time your safety was never in jeopardy though to you it may have seemed so.

Yes it was real but not in the concept you mean. It occurred in a parallel Universe in a place beyond dreams where you can walk out into other dimensions. It was a form of austral travelling though you were not travelling at all but still in your room but operating on a different level simultaneously to the you that was sleeping on the bed. That is why your screams could not be heard in this reality either. To do that it would have to break sound barriers and you are not yet skilled enough for that.

Take head from the lessons you would portray to your students and use the ceremony and invocation for protection. Call Teku to watch over you whilst you sleep, though he does this anyway by you calling him it is setting your own mind at ease that he is in your presence. Know that no harm will come to you.

If this ever were to occur again it would be good to have a *key word* that would draw you back into earth time awareness, an escape word or image. Work on developing one and let your students know to do this also. Another thing you could do before retiring is a golden light and/or protection meditation and the insertion of the Reiki symbols.

It's strange in all the time I've been exploring I've never encountered such beings. I can't believe they came to my house.

This is because you would never consciously seek them out. They had to consciously seek you out to let themselves be known. You have made a statement sending these two away. It is unlikely that they or any others will bother you again. Never lose awareness of their existence however and always protect yourself. Respect the enormity of the energies you are working with.

Thanks Hoyan, anything else?

Respect, Respect, Respect. Protect, Protect, Protect.

Thanks Hoyan, I get it.

WED 25TH DECEMBER

Merry Xmas everyone! It's early morning and Daughter is still slumbering so I'm grabbing this opportunity to speak with you before this special day starts. Nameless recently I spoke with a friend, fellow channelor who asked where you were from and what was your purpose and I struggled to answer. I know you've told me before but could you please explain again so I can be clear in my mind?

Q. Who are you? Where do you come from? What is it like there?

I am Nameless. I come from *The Source* of *All Kind*. That is, *Lightness and Being*. It is an energy system of the purest kind such that it is not even tangible in your world. It is not something that you can look at or even hold onto or think about as it is ever moving and ever changing being very fluid like and continually morphorous, constantly changing shape and form but so quickly that it is never any one thing.

This is hard for you to imagine and put into context and possibly one of the images that may come to mind that doesn't even come close to explaining what it is like is an ever changing virus that is morphing and adapting all of the time in response to its surrounds only the virus does so for its survival and replication while having a deleterious effect on its host. We of the *Light Source* only have the intention of building up and purifying negative elements instead of breaking down as it is only when such elements are purified of all dark and negative energy will they be allowed to return to the *Light Source* and become one with *All*. You are heading in the right direction. It is your questioning and searching that will get you there. Your understanding of the concepts, where it is you are heading and the path you must travel to get there.

Q. So what is a 'day' like for you there? Describe the surrounds for me and what it is you do?

You are right to apostrophize as there is no day and night as you know it. There is much brightness which is the energy cosmos. Imagine the purest of gold or diamonds and the shine and the brightness they give off when held under the light. This shine or brightness that is extending out beyond the object out into the air or ether is similar to the *Universal Light Energy* as in it is not an object nor the object itself but the so called byproduct of that object, the shining light and so it is with us. We are the result of a cycle of thought energy that produces or results in the projection of a shining flash of light that is ever changing much like the surface of the sun that is ever evolving with hot spots and heat flashes though we don't have those. There is no such thing as temperature as you know it and there is no solid 'body' or matter attached. The light *just is* and we are there and part of that light and as it is ever changing and ever evolving so do we change and evolve as we morph with it adjusting our frequencies to sit comfortably in that space.

Q. Can you show me a diagram, a drawing of what it looks like?

You can't show a drawing of an essence for that's what it is. Just as you can't draw a diagram of a feeling. You can only trust that what it is I say is true and correct and believe in me and my honorable intentions.

Q. What do you do there in this shining essence?

Adjust. There is a constant adjusting and shifting of one's vibration such that I am ever evolving and fine tuning myself.

Q. That's very much what Hoyan said, are you from the same place?

We are all one and the same. We are all from *The Light Source*. So yes and not only are we from the same source but I am Hoyan and he is me just as I am you and you are me and we are all one and the same, all linked only you don't experience it as we do as you are constrained by the physical in your world and also the constraints of linear time. We are not bound by such and so are freer to travel wherever we choose and wherever we choose to go and that includes morphing with each other at times. So there is a kind of cross pollination going on and a transfer of energy and information so that we all might grow and purify ourselves into purer and purer forms growing exponentially as we do so. It is a transfer of all of the 'others' experience and knowledge gathered thus far so we are taking on more of the collective as a whole, becoming more of *One* until one day we will be the whole itself and this is where we aim to go. This is our path and our purpose.

Q. So Nameless if you could name it (label it) what would you call this place you are from?

The Source of *All Kind*. I am from The Source of All Kind. I *am* The Source of All Kind or part thereof as are you but you are yet to fully realize this in your current existence. You have experienced this before but you don't remember.

Q. Why is that?

The limitation of your white and grey matter which primarily serves so you can function in the physical realm making all other knowledge hard to access and this is the barrier that you would need to break free from in order to travel to other worlds and other dimensions. But it is a hard nut to crack because it is the very brains thinking that you rely on to crack the code yet it's inadequacy of function is what prevents you.

Q. OMG, then how am I to crack the code?

By stepping beyond the brains limitations, stepping your *Soul Light Self* outside of the brain. Much like an out of body experience only it is your *Light and Being* that is stepping outside of the brain, outside of the physical before it can even begin to operate at optimal levels. Even then it will be remarkably slow in the beginning as you take on this new experience and make adjustments which will be absolutely necessary for future growth prospects. Otherwise you would just be taking one step forward and two steps backwards.

Q. So how does my Soul Light Self step aside and outside of my brains constraints?

As previously discussed. By stilling the mind and quietening the ego. You are already doing this but not nearly frequently enough for you to see real growth and advancement occurring at the pace you would like. For that it takes a lot of (your time) dedication which you currently don't have. We encourage you to do what you can do knowing that more time is coming your way for you to dedicate yourself to such things. It is going within and taking more journeys for this is where you will find more answers and insightful knowledge.

These journeys are like picking up pots of gold in the game analogy of your life path. These pots of gold are knowledge and are your current quest. The more journey's you go on the more knowledge and experience you accumulate and the more questions will be answered which all move you forward towards *Lightness and Being* which is the end journey. The ultimate of all ultimate's and the only place that has all the answers. It is only when you reach *Lightness and Being* that you come into full realization.

Until then each experience is like turning the page of a book, discovering new insights on each page to slowly piece together the puzzle and unravel the mystery of life.

Enjoy the journey Marikai for it can be hard but it can also be exciting and it makes the end prize all the more worthwhile and when I see you on the other side we will share a knowing and there will be much joy, happiness and bliss. Know it to be so. Lovingly — Nameless.

Wow thanks Nameless it's always such a joy to speak with you. How exciting that we will actually meet one day. Thanks for the clarification and tips. I know I need to find more time to channel and journey. I look forward to more freedom to do this so your words are encouraging. Blessings to every one of The Circle.

SUN 29TH DECEMBER

Morning All. Fifty-eight point two. I just can't seem to shift those last two kilo's but hey, it's Xmas. I'm feeling a bit hung over, not that I've been drinking but more that it's so hot and I'm probably dehydrated having just woken up. I have my brekky beside me but excuse me while I go get some cold water from the fridge…OMG! I so appreciate that I can do that, just go get a glass of beautiful cold crystal clear rainwater. I'm so lucky. It's the little things hey? Anyway as you know I had the channel class yesterday. Yippee, manifestation at last! I couldn't have done it without all of your (The Circles) help and encouragement so I thank you all from the bottom of my heart.

I'd been up late the night before reading over the class and then was so excited I could barely sleep so woke very tired. Driving in the car I started singing and chanting to help raise my vibration and energy levels. I sent Marikahee and Raven Owl ahead to perform a clearing and protection ceremony on the room before I arrived not having enough time to do it myself. The room at the Cooroy Library had all the mod cons including a large screen projector I could hook the laptop up to and only fifty dollars for the half day, bargain!

The group was small but one by one the students arrived and we started with a relaxing and grounding meditation. Some came out of curiosity, some had been guided here and one had already been receiving messages and wanted confirmation that she wasn't 'crazy' (her words). One of those present was rather skeptical that "anyone" would be able to channel or rather that she would be able to channel and my only concern was that she would be blocking herself.

Slowly we worked our way through the theory and practical exercises, the students offering their feedback and experience after each one. This was an interesting part of the class and provided great feedback for me and interesting perspectives for the others but served to take up a lot of time that I hadn't planned for, some wanting to chat for longer than I had anticipated. I had to keep moving the class along aware of the time factor ticking away. We were three quarters of the way through and they still hadn't contacted their guides even though they had channeled their first Universal Gift. I could see one student growing impatient, the same one that was skeptical. Perhaps I had too much theory and should concentrate more on the prac as Nameless suggested but I thought if they understood the underlying concept and process it would help demystify and thereby make it easier for them.

Finally they were able to do the guide meditation and success! All but one were able to either see or talk to their guides and get a name including the skeptic who had such joy on her face after contacting hers that I was both stoked and relieved. One guide had a name but no shape or form, one was an ancient warrior and yet another presented themselves in pure energy format.

There is one I need help with though. The student described only getting a sensation or feeling of swinging back and forth with no vision attached. She asks for a name from her guide but doesn't get one. In an earlier meditation she had been gifted the vision of a ring so I thought perhaps her way of sensing is through visual and kinetic means. Having no experience with kinetic sensing myself I had trouble explaining to her definitively what could be going on.

Q. Was this the students guide attempting to make contact or just a physical adjustment on her part as I suggested to her?

This is energy adjustment. Her physical body is going through shifts and changes to allow her guide to come through to her. This may take more than one sitting and is not something that can be expected to occur during one guided meditation. Some are more open to receiving than others. As you have stated some were already receiving before arriving at the class, some having been guided there were already on the precipice and just needed that nudge over the edge which was the how to. This person is just that little bit further back in the field having just reached the gestation phase and will need time for her body to catch up with her thinking and desire to channel. This cannot be rushed but is an area to be explored. Each time she goes into meditation seeking her guide there will be more and more physical adjustments to be made. Get her to sit with these adjustments. That is to not try and fight them but just allow them to come and go and just sit in *feeling* with them. Don't try to analyze them afterwards other than knowing what is occurring is a fine tuning of the body in preparation to receiving ones guide. Always asking each time while meditating to see her guide and indeed setting her intention even beforehand.

Remember this is not a process to be rushed. Do not allow stress to take over as this only serves to block. Instead be open and allow. Picture thyself opening like the petals of a lotus blossom or your favorite rose. Each petal opening slowly as you enjoy the anticipation and excitement of what is to be revealed to you when the final petal opens. Only not rushing to get there and spoiling the enjoyment that is the journey as that is a gift in itself. As long as she remains open there will come a day when during one of these meditations her guide will present themselves. Go into the meditation asking for your guide to present but not expecting it. Expecting it but not expecting it if you know what I mean. Expecting that it will happen one day and soon if this person is willing to put in the time and effort but not knowing which day and which time it will happen so that it will be a pleasant surprise when it does and one that brings much joy.

In the meantime the person should go about their day as normal knowing that even while they are doing this their body is fine tuning and adjusting itself, the intention having already been put out into the Universe. If they want to be actively doing something to help themselves then they can use the physical/mental/spiritual relaxation exercises that you gave them under the heading preparing to channel. Then it is a matter of time dedication and practicing stilling the mind combined with meditations to meet their guide. This does not have to be a heavy work load. Once or twice a week is all that is called for as if it becomes a chore then it is no longer enjoyable or desirable. The person sets their own pace and remains in control of their destiny.

Love and Light — Nameless.

Thank you Nameless I knew you would be able to help. I'll pass this info on to her. Also you've helped me a lot for when this type of thing presents next time. I'm so grateful. Grateful to 'All' of you, thank you.

You're welcome. And we would like to say congratulations are in order. We knew you could do it and had complete faith in you. This is a joyous day indeed and one to be much celebrated. This is the beginning of your knew life Marikai. Enjoy and Savior! We love you and are with you always and are rejoicing in your favor. To new beginnings!

To new beginnings...

In the beginning there was nothing

And out of nothing manifested this book

This is my little seed

That I send out into the world

In the hope that one day

It will grow into an orchard

~ *Kai Phoenix*

AFTERWARD

I've grown exponentially throughout my year of divine guidance, mentally, spiritually and emotionally. What started out as an experiment to hopefully increase my finances and ease my woes has given me so much more than I ever could have anticipated. I'm more at peace with myself and the world and I like to think I've evolved into a better person for which I'm very grateful. Feeling a greater empathy and patience towards others I'm much happier, calmer and slower to anger or react to situations because I've learnt to observe from a distance or remove my ego and look at things from different perspectives. I have insights and tools, coping mechanisms that weren't previously in my possession, I see the bigger picture of things. I still blow my stack occasionally but this is much rarer and I'm less likely to berate myself for it, just learn and move forward. I know I am loved.

I could quite possibly fill a whole other book on what I've learnt about channeling and it's processes but for this work have tried to remain within the scope of living and relaying the day to day experience itself. If I may though I'd like to share with you a few brief points.

One of the first things I explain to my students is that channeling is *not* clairvoyance as it's easy for the uninitiated to confuse the two. By opening up one channel you may very well open up the other as your sensory awareness heightens and you could possibly become proficient in both but they are two very different things (one being accessed through the crown chakra the other accessed through the third eye). From my experience guides rarely give predictions unless it is for the higher good of the person or persons involved. There are often many scenarios open to us and many possible paths to travel. As Nameless and Hoyan explain predictions are stuck in (third dimensional) space-time, are linear and they are trying to break us free from this way of thinking, aiming us towards Higher planes of existence. Thus guides are generally more concerned with your spiritual evolvement and evolution rather than merely predicting events.

In the early parts of 2014 I found a space to give channeled readings, a beautiful converted church in Kulangoor, Queensland that I shared with other readers and healers. I would explain to my clients that channeling and channeled readings were more about '*The Now,*' helping to sort out current life issues so they could freely move towards a better future on all levels. It was not about predicting that something good may or may not be coming in their future and then them just waiting or hoping for that event to occur (e.g. love, job, travel etc.). Rather a channeled reading is about personal empowerment, relaying guidance and a higher knowledge specific to the individuals' circumstances. Providing information, tools and different perspectives to aid your current situation so you can take control for yourself and change your own life for the better.

Having explained all of this each and every time I saw a client they would still get caught up in predictions. It's easier to sit back and just wait and hope for something good to just happen to you but I don't like the odds. Clients would ask, "Will he marry me?" or, "Am I going to travel?" Instead of asking, "What can ***I*** do right now that will see me able to travel in the near future?" The guides may then give you a list of things that you could do that will help propel you towards this wanted event.

I quickly got frustrated with their 'stuckness' and lack of understanding for the concept of channeling and their confusing it with clairvoyance. Although the guides told me I was there to enlighten and educate I felt I wasn't helping to shift their consciousness at all, unaided by the brief forty-five minute consults so decided I would much prefer to teach those interested in the phenomenon how to channel for themselves. This then gives them a tool for life that they always have access to any time they wish. Now I thoroughly enjoy bringing this inherent skill that we all possess into the conscious foreground of my students awareness and love hearing about their experiences both before and during workshops as they receive their gifts from the Universe and meet their guides for the very first time.

A frequently asked question in my workshops and indeed anyone who queries me on channeling is, "Is all of this my imagination?" implying it's made up fantasy. Absolutely not. In imagining you are creating the images and storyline yourself, whereas channeling is more a process of *'Allowing'* or a type of *'Surrendering'* which is stepping the self aside, suspending the self (ego) and then observing/noting what springs forth without putting any subjective thought on what unfolds before you. Instead you as the channel/channelor are a passive observer of information that is coming to you from beyond the self. A 'channel medium' is a scribe and merely relays this information to others either in written format or verbally. It's a bit like when you watch a movie or hear something on the radio you know nothing about. Passively you take it all in and then go and describe it to a friend *'as is'* without attaching your own thoughts and feelings to the subject matter presented to you, giving a true and unbiased account.

One major thing I learnt along with my students was to accept the guide your given. They will present to you in a manner that *they feel* you will initially accept them in, that is not too frightening for you. Once you feel comfortable this may morph and change over time along with the name given. In a meditation one students guide came to her as a rabbit but she refused to believe that was her guide looking everywhere else for the guide when it was right in front of her. During our discussion afterwards she told me she had an obsession with rabbits at that time, collecting them in different shapes and forms around her house and workplace. Thus her guide initially tried to present in this familiar and loving way.

You can have more than one guide, each with their own unique presentation, personality and skills. Some are funny, some serious, some playful or mischievous, some may talk in riddles or rhymes, others don't talk at all, instead presenting things to you visually or as a *'knowing.'* It may be instant attraction and trust or it may take a few weeks to warm to your guide as you let the relationship grow and develop just as you would any new friend. You should feel a positive upliftment during or after communication with a guide. It's like being on a natural high with a spring in your step. As your burdens are released you will feel lighter, like walking on air, *enlightened.* Rarely, if you feel there is a strong personality clash or your energy state is down or negative after each communication then politely ask them to leave and spend some time thinking about what you want in a guide before invoking the next one.

It's exiting getting to know your guides, their quirks and niches and like any relationship the more you put in the more you get out. I prefer to stay in close contact channeling at least once a week if I can but sometimes, like during the editing of this book, there have been months between communications. You will find your own comfortable level but remember that things are fluid and changeable. Guided advice changes as you or your circumstances change, nothing is set in stone so it pays to check in periodically.

There is usually at least one primary guide that is with you for a life time whether you know it or not. I was able to recognize that the words from my earlier efforts to channel five years previously came from Nameless. He had waited five long years before I reached out again and he was right there the second I did. They are not governed by time and so you can pick up a conversation from years earlier and continue on as if it were never interrupted. They are always there to help when asked and respect your privacy by remaining silent when requested. They don't judge and are never offended by you or anything you do or say as to them you are an aspect of the purest form of energy, *"Light."*

Don't take the guides too literally. Think outside the square. Ask lots of questions around the one topic and for clarification if you're not sure. If you're in contact with more than one guide then seek the other guides perspective on the same subject. Often they come at it from different angles as each has their own individual view and area of expertise.

For example Nameless kept telling me I'm a healer. I took this quite literally to mean a hands on type healer and now I'm not so sure. Naively I thought, "Ok, I'm a healer," end of story, "This is what I should be doing," and without questioning jumped head first into this foray *but* there are many types of healers and healing comes in different shapes and forms. There is healing in art and also in the written word. By sharing my experiences and teaching people to channel I'm helping others towards healing themselves, *"Lighting the way for others."* This is my soul's purpose and perhaps what was meant by healing. I was also told how I begin is not how I will continue, that things will change and morph and grow over a period of time. It's all a continual journey of (self) discovery. As Nameless says though, *"Nothing is ever lost, no time is ever wasted."* I learnt a lot from that experience and now I spend more time questioning and coming from different angles. However they do like you to discover a certain amount for yourself and while nudging you in the right direction they are not going to hand things to you on a silver platter either. This would be closer to dictatorship and not guidance. So when Nameless continually stated I am a healer without giving away too much detail he was really initiating a journey of self-discovery and what that really meant to me.

Don't expect miracles, Rome wasn't built in a day. I asked for a better future and I got it but it takes time for things to manifest in this world. It was unreasonable to expect major life altering changes within one year yet so much has developed already that I know I'm definitely on the way to my even better future. This book is just the beginning.

Lastly, channeling takes a certain level of commitment if you want to act on the advice given. It means taking action and doing something to effect (hopefully positive) change. Of course you can choose to ignore their advice also and they won't be offended. It's like talking to your best friend. You're not going to agree on everything but there will be a lot you will take on board after careful consideration.

Remember you are in control of your own life and your own destiny, always.

APPENDIX

Stilling The Mind

Stilling the mind (or ego) is the *one key ingredient* that most people are missing in their attempt to channel. The ability to do this opens the flood gates to communication. This is the one aspect that people find the most difficult and I think the major hurdle that prevents them from channeling. If you have a large pot of gold coins filled to the brim, any more coins poured on top will only spill out to the sides of the container, never contributing to its wealth. Liken this to our brains which are overburdened with an abundance of words and thoughts thus not allowing for outer knowledge to enter. The information is there waiting but is not being registered by us, falling by the way side much like the coins. If I want to fill my pot of gold with new coins contributing to my wealth I first have to empty it (put it in the bank on hold) and so it is with emptying the brain of words before a new wealth of knowledge through dimensional communication can occur. Its basic physics really.

Stilling the mind is not that easy for us thanks to ego. Many people use chanting (e.g. 'Om') as a method or focusing on an item such as a burning candle but I say this only serves to fill your brain up with more stuff and not actually empty it. Thus I'd like to share with you one method I give my students when teaching them to still their minds that can be used alone or as an adjunct to Nameless's exercise in 'No Mind.' This is by no means the only method and I encourage you to explore and experiment with others. What works for one may not work for another, we are all wired differently. However I found this the easiest and simplest to teach and have developed a few variations and you may too.

Once you've mastered the art of stilling the mind and connected with your guide or Higher Self you can channel anywhere, any time on all sorts of topics. A wonderful gift and tool to help you throughout your life.

An Exercise in Stilling the Mind

1. **Sit in a quiet comfortable place as for meditation.**

2. **Close your eyes and in your mind's eye picture a blank whiteboard or black computer screen.**

   (Don't picture the item itself just the blank surface of the whiteboard or black screen, we're trying to keep our brains empty of 'stuff.')

3. **The aim is to keep the screen clear or blank.**

4. **See any words/images/thoughts that come to mind appear on the whiteboard/computer screen and then immediately wiped clean/erased.**

   (e.g. for the whiteboard you might see the words instantly dissolve or quickly rubbed off as they appear, for the computer make it a touchscreen and swipe the words off sideways with your mind's eye or just mentally delete them.)

5. **See how long you can keep the screen blank for and with each practice extend on this time.**

After a while you'll start to get the idea of what it *feels* like to suspend all thought. For beginners practicing for 3-5 minutes at a time is enough and you can extend on this as your holding becomes easier and more powerful. When you feel you've mastered the concept and are able to still the mind for even short periods you could try combining it with your channel practice...

> Ask a question, still the mind and listen to or write the words that come to you as you suspend all personal thought, judgment or analysis for *after* the channeling session. If its images you see, taste, smells or sensations that come to you describe or write these as they arrive, again without thought or judgment.

As with all, practice makes perfect. The more you practice the easier it becomes until one day it feels like second nature as you effortlessly flit in and out of this state making communication easy and natural.

"You are never alone."

"You only need to ask and then sit still long enough to listen."

"The answers are in the silence."

~ *Nameless*

Humpy
This palatial sized humpy was found on a beach in N.S.W

Sculptures on Lake Cootharaba
Floating Land 2013

Mt Cooroora
Pomona

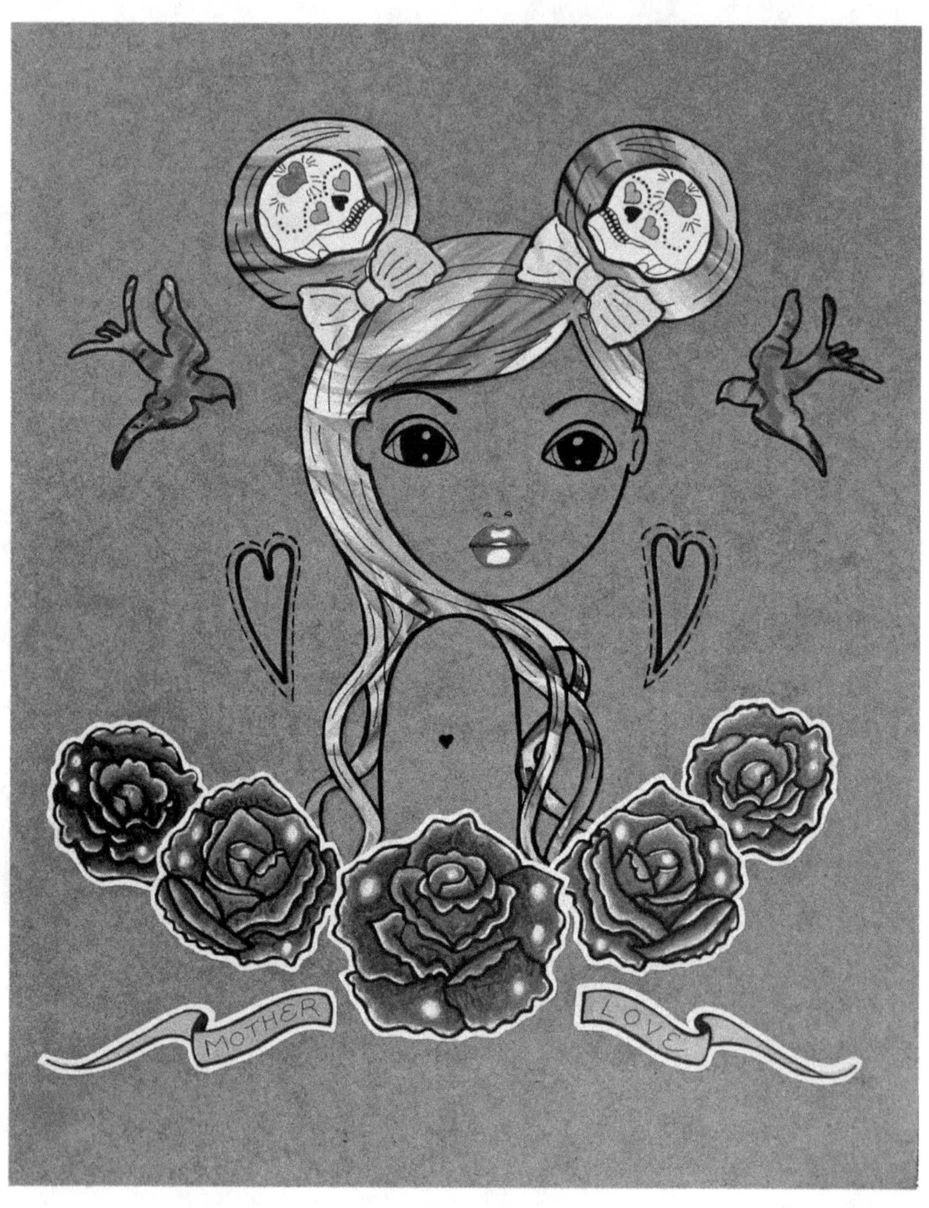

Mother Love

Ink, Acrylic, nailpolish and collage on MDF board. Designed for the redbubble artists challenge, "Design a tattoo that your mother would love."

Light and Being
Hand rendered illustration.
Graphite pencil overlaid with permanent ink marker
on paper support.

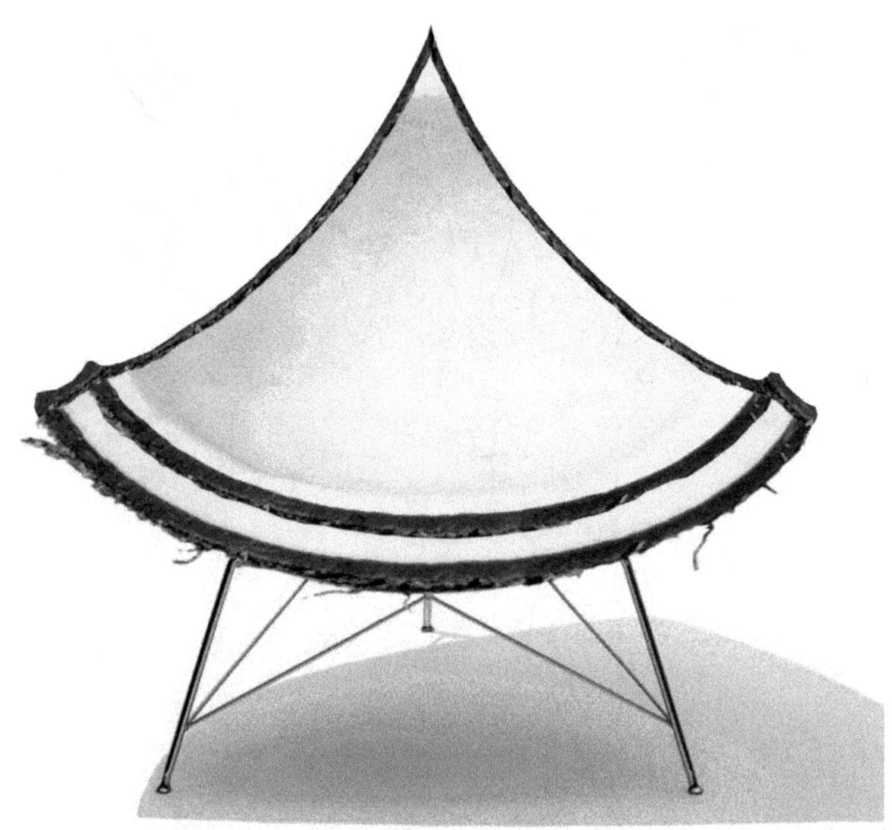

Coconut Chair

Designed for Floating Lands 2013 biomimicry theme. Using a real coconut for the seat was a tongue in cheek take on George Nelsons 1955 classic.

Amigurumi
"Mukti" and "Buki"
Original creations, hand crocheted and standing just 7cm tall.
These little babies were displayed at *in.cube8r,* Fortitude Valley.

Light Portrait
Blue Boy 1
Pastel on Paper

Light Portrait
Blue Girl 3
Pastel on Paper

The Wedding Tree
"*Paradise Beach,*" Boreen Point

NOTES

Introduction

1. *The Bridge* by Blossom Goodchild (Golden Rays Publishing, 2007: Noosa Heads, Australia). Blossom Goodchild (Author, actor, channel medium and fellow Noosan!) is the direct voice channel for the Native American Indian Spirit Energy known as 'White Cloud' and a channel medium for the cosmic beings known as 'The Federation of Light,' amongst others. *The Bridge* documents the first channeled messages between Blossom and The Federation of Light who come to assist us and the planet in moving to a higher vibration of love. The Federation request that Blossom pass their messages on to as many people as possible. I meant no disrespect to Blossom and the Federation of Light when I said that in no other way was this book (*The Bridge*) a revelation to me, only meaning that this was not the first time I had read channeled works or heard such messages. In actual fact I am in awe of Blossoms work especially with White Cloud and have had the privilege of being in the presence of White Cloud during a direct voice channeling and I can tell you it was amazing! I highly recommend you visit her blog and website for links to channeled works, books, audios, YouTube videos and CD's.
   www.blossomgoodchild.com
   http://blossomgoodchild.blogspot.com.au

Chapter One

1. www.floatingland.org.au *Floating Land* is one of Australia's leading green art events, a ten day outdoor art and sculpture exhibition and one of the first art programs of its kind in Australia to bring environmental awareness to the public through the arts. The biennial event showcases work from local and international artists along with a host of free events and workshops held at Boreen Point and nearby regions. Programs include environmental art installations, soundscapes, dance performances, film events, art exhibitions, studio trails, poetry, field trips and masterclasses.

Chapter Two

1. Raven Owl is a working psychic medium who used to own and operate a New Age store in Tewantin Queensland, a store which no longer exists. All efforts to locate Raven Owl in person have so far been unsuccessful.

2. Andy Goldsworthy OBE is a British sculptor, photographer and environmentalist who produces site specific sculptural art in both natural and urban settings only using found and natural materials such as leaves, twigs, flowers, icicles and dirt but also rocks and stone to create both temporary and permanent sculptures that complement the character of their environment. Searching for any relatable reference to Andy's quote given to me by Nameless led me to the book by William Malpas, *Andy Goldsworthy: Complete Works, special edition June 5 2007,* which describes Andy Goldsworthy's quote thus, "There is a whole world in a **single** leaf." Andy's work is exquisite, there is lots to see on google images and YouTube. If you reside on the Sunshine Coast of Australia and would like to view one of Andy's sculptures in person visit the Queensland governments national parks website for more information www.nprsr.qld.gov.au/parks/conondale/about For maps and directions to the Strangler Cairn walk in Conondale National Park. I recommend camping close by at either Booloumba Creek or Charlie Moreland. To browse his digital catalogue visit www.goldsworthycc.gla.ac.uk/browse.

3. *Paradise Beach* is not its real name. My daughter and I chose to rename this beach (officially known as Dunn's beach) to reflect its true beauty. The beach is a little slice of heaven and I never tire of the ever changing scenery and view of seasons that blanket the lake. One of my favorite places on earth!

4. *Marina Abromavić: The Artist is Present.* By HBO Documentary Films. This documentary film follows performance artist Marina Abromavić as she prepares for a retrospective of her work to take place at the Museum of Modern Art (MOMA) in New York, March 2010. The center piece of this work is a purpose built set which Marina describes as a "Square of light." Every day (seven hours a day, six days a week) for three months audience members are

invited to participate by sitting one by one opposite the artist with strict instructions to neither verbally communicate or touch Marina. The purpose and aim of this exercise is for the artist to achieve a "Luminous state of being," that is then projected towards the sitters, sharing with them and the passive onlookers what Marina called an "Energy dialogue." www.marinafilm.com

5. www.divineintuition.co.uk/psychic-abilities-explained.html

6. *Sunrise Spiritualist Church and Spiritual Growth Center.* (previously known as Sunrise Spiritualist Church or Noosa and District Spiritualist Church) Services are held at Tinbeerwah Hall, every 2nd and 4th Sunday's @ 10am. Corner of Sunrise Rd and Cooroy-Noosa Rd, Mount Tinbeerwah, Queensland, Australia, 4565. Frequent guest speakers. Rev. Laine Harry.

7. *Lotus Inner Light Healing Group* offers a variety of healing modalities from volunteer practitioners. Held every Monday at the CWA Hall in Maple St, Cooroy, Queensland (next to the RSL). Visit from 9.30am onwards for meditation, healing, reiki, massage, psychic readings, friendship and community support. Coffee, tea and lunch supplied with any paid service (at time of publishing each service is $20 AUS to help cover the hall and refreshment costs.) www.facebook.com/pages/LotusInnerLightHealingGroupCooroy

8. *The Wishing Well* was a New Age book and gift store similar to Symbolic Journey (see below) but has since been sold and no longer exists.

9. *Symbolic Journey* is a New Age book and gift store offering a range of products and services. Books, tarot, oracle cards, CD's, DVD's, crystals, jewelry, psychic readings, reiki, massage, essential oils, Himalayan salt lamps and Tibetan singing bowls. Shop 3/36 Sunshine Beach Rd, Noosa Junction, Queensland, Australia, 4567. www.symbolicjourney.com.au www.facebook.com/symbolicjourney

10. *Pendulum Magic for Beginners: Power to Achieve All Goals* by Richard Webster (Llewellyn Publications, 2002: Woodbury, MN)

Chapter Three

1. *Opening To Channel: How to Connect With Your Guide* by Sanaya Roman and Duane Packer (H J Kramer Inc., 1987: Tiburon, California.)

2. *Bloodroot* (Sanguinaria Canadensis) is a perennial herbaceous flowering plant native to Eastern North America. It is also known by its common names of Bloodwort, Redroot, Indian paint, Red Puccoon and Tetterwort amongst others. American Indian tribes traditionally used Bloodroot to treat a range of conditions primarily sore throats, fevers, joint pain, ulcers and a variety of skin conditions such as ringworm warts and fungus. www.resilientnorthernhabits.com Sanguinarine, a major constituent of Bloodroot, exhibits effectiveness as an antibiotic, anti-inflammatory, antibacterial, antiseptic, anesthetic and more but the plant contains opium like alkaloids which produce a morphine like effect and can be highly toxic when administered improperly causing vomiting, distorted vision, unconsciousness and even fatalities. www.altnature.com/gallery/bloodroot.htm For this reason it is always advisable to consult a qualified physician before ingesting or applying any herbal remedy.

3. *The River of A Thousand Mirrors'* (or *'The River of Mirrors.'*) is found in the upper reaches of the serpentine Noosa River better known as 'The Everglades' or the 'Noosa Everglades,' earning its nick name through the crisp crystal clear reflections thrown onto its glasslike surface on a windless day. For a general overview of the Kinaba region and the Cooloola section of the Great Sandy National Park visit www.kinaba.org which contains a brief history, maps and image galleries of the lakes, estuaries, flora and fauna as well as listing species found throughout the park. To immerse yourself in the *feeling* of this area and help you engage with this environment and landscape listen to the hauntingly beautiful three minute soundscape of the River of Mirrors by Dr. Leah Barclay at www.biospheresoundscapes.org/featured.html and play the 'Noosa Biosphere Reserve, Australia soundscape.' For canoeing adventures and guided boat tours into this pristine Australian wilderness visit the Noosa's Discovery Group for bookings at

www.noosaevergladesdiscovery.com.au/canoe-discovery.html where you'll find more spectacular imagery.

4. *Velvet Antler* is derived from the whole cartilaginous deer antler typically harvested between 55-65 days of growth prior to its calcification. Velvet Antler does not refer to the extraction of the velvety 'skin' covering the antlers but refers to the stage at which harvest occurs when the antlers are covered in a soft velvety 'fuzz.' There is little to find on the Native American use of deer antler other than for use as tools or decoration but in his book *Deer Antlers: Regeneration, Function and Evolution* Richard J Goss conveys its historical Native American use to treat epilepsy, headache, vertigo and snakebites suggesting that it was either eaten in powdered form or inhaled as incense. Traditional Chinese medicine divides the antler into three different sections each with its own medicinal purpose. 1. The upper (wax) piece is utilized as a growth tonic for children. 2. The middle (blood) piece as an anti-arthritic. 3. The bottom (bone) piece as a calcium supplement. The Chinese consume the dried slices as a decoction (tea) whereas Western medicine dries the antler to a powder and consumes it in capsule form as a performance enhancer and immune boosting supplement. Also available as a spray it is said to boost strength and endurance and aid in sports recovery especially tendon and cartilage injuries. http://en.wikipedia.org/wiki/velvet_antler There are over forty key compounds and four hundred active constituents found in deer antler including growth factors, collagen, glucosamine sulfate, selenium and essential amino acids. For a comprehensive overview and listing see http://antlerfarms.com/ Even though China is currently the largest consumer of Velvet Antler, New Zealand is the largest producer. Please consult a qualified physician before partaking in any remedy.

Chapter Four

1. Some physicists believe the Universe may be made up of miniscule strings that vibrate at specific frequencies (similar to guitar strings) and rotate in ten dimensional space (six wound up so tightly that only four can be seen) and that these strings are the building blocks of everything in the Universe including all matter and elementary particles, forces such as gravity and even space. The book

Superstrings and the Search for the Theory of Everything by F. David Peat (Contemporary Books, Inc., 1988: Chicago Illinois) gives a good explanation and overview of this theorem for the lay person whilst trying to keep its complexities to a minimum.

2. The *butterfly room* is an outdoor entertaining area, a very large veranda extending out from the living room of our house. Enclosed in fly wire to keep the mosquitos at bay it was nicknamed the butterfly room by a friend's young daughter who thought it resembled a butterfly enclosure you'd see at the zoo. The house we nicknamed *Marshmallow house* because its fibro walls were so easily damaged and the open lounge and kitchen became the *Rainbow room* named for the rainbows cast on the walls and floor by the sun shining through the glass slat windows.

3. *Peace of Green Gallery Maleny* is a Sunshine Coast Art Gallery owned, managed, operated and funded by its local art members. Art for sale includes ceramics, blown glass, prints, paintings, silk work, jewelry and leather and woodwork. Open seven days a week 9.30 a.m. - 5.00 p.m. 38 Maple St, Maleny, Queensland, 4552. www.peaceofgreengallery.com/ info@peaceofgreengallery.com

4. *Redbubble* (originally founded in Melbourne, Australia in 2006) is an online marketplace showcasing the work of artists from all over the globe. Artists upload their work in digital format to be displayed on a variety of items of their choosing. The general public can then purchase cool art on products such as T-shirts and hoodies, iPhone and iPad covers, doona covers and tote bags as well as canvas prints, high quality posters, postcards and stickers etc. New product ranges are continually added to the site. Membership is free and artists maintain copyright of their works and regulate their own prices. www.redbubble.com/people/kaiphoenix

5. *Mana* is a word found largely in Polynesian and Pacific Islander cultures, its meaning changing with the different languages and belief systems. *Mana* in Hawaiian Huna philosophy is understood as a form of Universal spiritual life force energy and healing power that connects all things, places and people, known in other cultures as *chi* (Chinese), *prahna* (Indian) and *orenda* (Iroquois). *Mana* exists in people, animals, plants, and inanimate objects. Even places can

possess mana for example the Moloka'i island of Hawaii is believed to possess strong mana in comparison to its neighboring islands and ancient wars were fought over its possession. The Melanesians believed that mana could bring efficacy or luck to a person, charging charms and amulets with this sacred supernatural force to help increase their harvest and prosperity and that this 'luck' could be transferred to another via the charms of one who had already experienced success. *Mana* can be thought of as the essential life force of the Universe to be found in and around all of creation. *Free mana* (available mana) is a constantly moving, thinning and condensing invisible resource that flows throughout the world seeking elements to inhabit. Humans are able to pull in this energy and utilize it for constructive means such as channeling it for the purposes of healing and recharging a person, place or object that has lost mana, thereby aiding to bring about repair and an increase in their life force energy. *Sensory mana* is when the user is able to connect with the mana of others or objects tuning into this energy to allow the flow of Higher sensory communication such as clairvoyance (and all the 'Clair's'), dowsing, energy perception and sensing and telepathy. For an exercise in working with mana see www.lilithslantern.co/mana.htm For breathing exercises go to http://huna.blogspot.com.au/2006/07/kahuna-breath

Chapter Seven

1. First discovered in 1889 by Czech B. Navratil who labelled it electrography, Kirlian photography was later named after the Russian Semyon Davidovich Kirlian and his wife Valentina who went on to develop it further. Kirlian photography purports to capture a subtle field of electromagnetic energy that emanates from all living things, known as an aura. They believed that their images capturing the aura like prints of living subjects (plants, animals, humans) were evidence of a life force or energy field that conveyed the physical and emotional states of living beings and that these images could be used to decipher the wellbeing of their subjects as well as aiding to diagnose illnesses and predict disease. This belief remains under scientific scrutiny with a multitude of critics and sceptics stating the aura projections are merely the result of moisture. I have not supplied a reference as it is hard to find

unbiased information from either camp but rather suggest if interested that you embark on your own research.

2. *"All of the Circle,"* a collective name for all of my guides used when addressing them as a group. As more guides started to appear throughout the year I had been pondering what I could call them that would make addressing or talking about them collectively a lot less problematic. Often when something like this is on my mind for a while the answer will just come as a *knowing* as it did one day when I was in the shower! This knowing is an instant form of telecommunication, the name being given to me by a *Higher Source.* Afterwards I channeled with Nameless and Hoyan asking their opinion, knowing how they feel about names and labels. As discussed in the book they understand that words, names, labels etc. makes communication in our world a lot easier. They thought a circle to be very appropriate because in a circle no one person is the head or lead but each is of equal footing. Also a circle easily expands or contracts as guides choose to come and go thus it is not set in stone but is in itself an ever changing morphorous entity. Please note that *"All of The Circle," "The Circle"* and *"All"* (for short) are used interchangeably throughout the book, each with the same definition.

Chapter Eight

1. When discussing the channeling of an acquaintance of ours a friend of mine disputed the fact that guides will name people, places, or objects specifically as if these did not exist in their vocabulary. Channel mediums are translators of information that is coming to us from a Higher Source and the process is similar I would assume to translating another language as in if there was no word that existed in that particular language you would find the nearest word that would suit or alternatively given the rest of the sentence you had an understanding of what the missing word stood for. Initially Nameless suggested the information I had misplaced was book marked on my computer but I have two computers, one a desktop and the other a laptop. When I mentally asked which one he gave me the image of the iMac (desktop) and simultaneously drew my energy and attention to that corner of the house where it lay. Also remember sometimes information comes through as a *knowing,* you just know what they are talking about or referring to and then we as

translators attach words to convey their communication with us. This type of communication often occurs at lightning speed and so it is often as if they spoke the words themselves. Lastly as Highly evolved beings I don't think the guide's vocabulary would be that limited that they wouldn't know the name of a person, place or thing.

2. Artist *Lenni Semmelink* was the recipient of the Noosa Biosphere Art Prize (scholarship) to develop the *Earthsong* installation for Floating Land 2013. *Earthsong* is an in interactive soundscape where the audience is able to immerse themselves in the experience of listening to the amplification of nature's acoustics resonating from speakers hanging in the trees. Facilitated through headphones participants are also encouraged to engage with the trees exploring their own relationship and impact on the environment. For a two minute *Earthsong* promotional video showing Lenni interacting with and recording the bioacoustics of trees and plants in preparation for the exhibition visit www.lenni.com.au/earthsong.html

3. The *Apollonian Hotel* is an historic building originally built as a Hotel music hall in the 1870's Gympie Gold Rush era. In an effort to preserve the building and its history it was moved to its current site at Laguna Street in picturesque Boreen Point in 1987. The Apollonian is now famous for its Sunday wood fired spit roasts complete with damper prepared in a rustic outdoor bush kitchen. Budget guest accommodation is available in the restored former railway workers cottage adjacent to the Hotel. A great effort by past and present owners has gone into maintaining the authentic colonial setting and the front lawn and beer garden have hosted many an event and function especially weddings. It's not unusual on a weekend to see a row of Harley's parked outside as the Pub is a popular destination pit stop for the weekend club ride. http://apollonianhotel.com.au

4. *The Secret Life of Plants,* by Peter Tompkins and Christopher Bird (New York: HarperCollins Publishers Inc., 1973.)

5. *Melaleuca Quinquenervia* is also known by its common name Broad-leaved paperbark or Broad-leaved tea tree. Native to New Caledonia, Papua New Guinea and the eastern coast of Australia it

is also found in the everglades of Florida where it is was introduced and is now considered an invasive weed. In Australia it is commonly found along coastal streams and swamps as well as in suburban streets, planted for its popularity and ability to adapt to extremes of weather conditions. Here the Broad-leaved paperbark is also known more simply as a Paperbark or Tea tree. Indigenous Australians used the plant for a wide range of purposes the bark being stripped for bandages, sleeping mats, coolamons (water containers), lining ground ovens and wrapping food for baking. The leaves were brewed to treat colds, headache and general sickness. Melaleuca quinquenervia should not be confused as the source of the natural antiseptic Tea Tree oil which is derived from the Narrow-leaved tea tree or Melaleuca alternifolia. For those who are interested Google images has some beautiful pictures of this amazing species and for a concise but brief overview see the following articles and fact sheets at www.hornsby.nsw.gov.au/...tree.../Fact-sheet-Melaleuca-quinquenervia also http://anpsa.org.au/m-qui.html

6. *"Wonders of Life"* is a five part documentary series examining the story of life through physics. It was produced by the BBC and Chinese State Television Network CTV-9 and presented by physicist Professor Brian Cox. The episode I'm referring to is episode two, *"Expanding Universe,"* where Brian explores the science of senses. The *Wonders of Life* DVD's are available singularly or as an entire collection on Amazon at http://www.amazon.co.uk/wonders-of-life-DVD The book has now been made available from the ABC shop at https://shop.abc.net.au/products/wonders-of-life-hbk For an amusing trailer that will make you smile visit www.youtube.com/watch?v=60CxwUPPg

7. http://en.wikipedia.org/wiki/Hearing_range
http://en.wikipedia.org/wiki/infrasound
http://en.wikipedia.org/wiki/ultrasound
http://en.wikipedia.org/wiki/hearing
http://en.wikipedia.org/wiki/animal-ecolocation

8. *Joe Blow* is a generic term meaning your average person who holds no formal title and describes someone who derives from or lives in the burbs (suburbs). Your average Joe Blow always fly's economy if at all and can't afford flashy hotels or upmarket holidays. Also

sometimes considered as slightly lesser in intelligence or knowledge.

9. The animation of what looks like the earths heartbeat as discovered by US programmer John Nelson as he stitched together satellite images of the earth taken by NASA can be found at http://www.news.com.au/technology/science/earths-heartbeat-caught-by-satellite-image-animations/story During my search I came across an interesting acoustic sound recording of earths deeper layers taken as close to the core as is currently possible. The sound recording and accompanying seismic reading was a collaboration between Dutch artist Lotte Geeven and geoscientists from the German Research Center for Geosciences bought back from the KTB Borehole, the deepest accessible hole in the world. http://gizmodo.com/listening-for-the-earths-heartbeat-inside-the-worlds-1493928170

Chapter Nine

1. *"The toughest place to be a bin man,"* is the first episode in the second series of documentaries, *"The toughest place to be a ...,"* produced by Simon Davies for the BBC. There are five series and fifteen episodes in total showcasing the challenges and difficulties of different professionals depending on the country and environment they are working in. Other episodes include *"The toughest place to be a Nurse/Taxi Driver/Farmer/Firefighter...etc."* Locations vary and include Jakarta Indonesia, Sierra Leone, Kenya, Brazil and India amongst others. For a video excerpt and an image of the giant landfill go to http://bbc.co/news/magazine-16722180

2. *Tinny* is an Australian colloquial or slang term for a small open boat with an aluminum hull.

3. *Humpy or Gunya (also Gunyah,* meaning shelter) is a small temporary shelter made from tree branches and bark (particularly paperbark). Traditionally built and used by Indigenous Australians these small impermanent dwellings were usually built for short term accommodation prior to more permanent structures being built. There are hundreds of different Aboriginal language groups in Australia and each language group know the shelters by different

names. Among them are *Goondie, Wurley,* and *Wiltya.* They are also commonly known as a *lean-to* as one side of the structure usually leans against a boulder, wall or tree. Temporary structures were usually built out of light sticks, paperbark and vine whilst more permanent structures used stronger materials of hardwoods, woven vines and hard barks often supported by heavy beams dug into the ground. These larger ones housed small fires for warmth and to keep mosquitos at bay. The humpies I observed that day were barely big enough for someone to sleep in and extremely well camouflaged. To see images of Aboriginal humpies go to www.google.com.au/search?q=aboriginal+humpies and click on 'images for Aboriginal humpies.' Also visit www.aboriginalculture.com.au/housing.shtml

4. The *Gubbi Gubbi* people are one of the many Indigenous groups of Australia and the traditional owners and custodians of land that extends from Brisbane northwards to west of Fraser Island in the South East Coast of Queensland, Australia. www.gubbigubbi.com is a website created by Elder Dr. Eve Fesl explaining the Gubbi Gubbi name and containing a map of Gubbi Gubbi country (used in the land title claim, 2009). The Noosa Museum in Pomona (29 Factory Rd, Pomona) is the official keeping place for Gubbi Gubbi cultural heritage artifacts with exhibitions on the environment, traditional food, gathering and hunting. There is both an indoor display and an outdoor area known as the island of reconciliation. This consists of a circle of stones housing a central fireplace and a commemorative plaque which is accessed via a purpose built bridge a short walk from the museum www.noosamuseum.org.au
   Other websites that may interest readers include...
   www.triballink.com.au/gubbigubbi
   www.gubbigubbidance.com
   www.gubbi-gubbi-language.org.au
   www.dyungungoo.com

5. *Jonah* is not his real name. Jonah's name and other identifying details such as the name of his dog etc. have been changed to protect the individual's right to privacy and anonymity.

6. *Walkabout* is the Australian term used for a spiritual journey, an adolescent rite of passage where male Aborigines would take

themselves into the bush for long periods tracing the routes of their ancestors. *Gone walkabout* is a reference to Indigenous Australians who for short periods either returned to their traditional native life or wandered the bush, often absconding from work and disappearing without notice. Sometimes this was to attend ceremonies or visit family.

7. *Woop Woop.* Australian slang meaning out in the middle of nowhere. Often used to signify remoteness or isolation, an (imaginary) place a long way from civilization.

8. *Reiki Shamanism: A Guide to Out-of-Body Healing* by Jim Pathfinder Ewing (Scotland: Findhorn Press, 2008).

9. *Essential Reiki: A Complete Guide To An Ancient Healing Art* by Diane Stein (New York: Random House Inc., 1995).

10. For those of you who missed it the first time round see Notes, Chapter Four, number 2.

11. *Buckley's chance* is an Australian term meaning a very small chance. *Buckley's and none* describes the possibility of only two chances, Buckley's chance (small chance) or no chance at all (none). Also called *Buckley's hope* and often shortened to just *Buckley's* as in "You've got Buckley's," used to convey slender hope or probability.

Chapter Ten

1. www.johnofgodcrystalhealingbeds.org

2. *Aussie World* Theme park is located at 73 Frizzo Rd, Palmview, Queensland just off the Bruce Highway on the Sunshine Coast of Australia (next to the Ettamogah Pub). www.aussieworld.com.au

3. The *Vitalization stance* or pose, is a method for repairing static magnetism or energy flow in oneself by drawing energy from the Universal Energy Field/Free Flowing *Mana.* The method itself can be found in the book *Magnetic Therapy: Healing In Your Hands* by Abbot George Burke, pg. 69 (DeVorss & Company: Marina Del Rey, California, 1980.)

4. In meditation visualize a vacuum cleaner hose magically extending down from above your crown into every corner and crevice of your body and organs, cleaning out your internal house, cleansing your spirit and purging all the stagnation, negativity, muck and mire that accumulates. This 'sticky mucousy mess' is like toxic glue that sticks to every cell and layer of you including your ethereal layers so work on cleaning your aura too. Vacuum up, down, in front, out back and all over. Fill up your vacuum cleaner with all that would weigh you down including thick dark energy, negative emotions and beliefs (yours and from others that you have taken on) as well as those annoying thoughts that won't leave you alone to be at peace. If your vacuums bag becomes full expel it deep into the earth, vaporize it, send it off to be neutralized or throw the contents up in the air and imagine the wind returning them to their originator. Get creative with disposal! Change the bag as many times as you need, keep cleaning until you feel refreshed, lighter and happier. You might want to balance by bringing positive energy back in at this time.

5. A *Rainbow bath* is a quick color, energy and chakra top up that can take a few minutes or half an hour depending on your needs. Sometimes I'll use the pendulum to assess which colors I'm most deficient in and just top these up if I'm in a hurry. For the full bath first relax your body and mind as for meditation. Imagine standing in an empty field and before you stands the purest of all rainbows ever created in the history of mankind. Walk through this rainbow stopping at each color for a period of time to absorb its richness into your body, chakra's and aura as it enshrouds you in a fine pillowy mist that rains down on you in all its glory bringing with it healing and rebalance. Red being the first color symbolizing vitality and strength. Llet this color swirl around your aura and internal being until it fills your entirety and you feel your vibration and energy lift before moving onto the next color orange, the color of pleasure and joy. Repeat the process spending some time in orange feeling your enthusiasm and smile return before stepping into yellow to reclaim your personal power, sharpen your intelligence and clear your mind. Follow with green bringing balance, love, harmony and communication back into relationships, letting go of disputes and anger to help you feel lighter. Next bathe yourself in blue bringing with it a sense of peace, inner calm, relaxation, honesty and truth before walking into the last color Indigo. Indigo being the color of

intuition, universal flow and kindness to self and others. See any unresolved issues dissolve as you swirl the color Indigo from your crown to your toes and throughout your aura. Take time in Indigo to give thanks for the universal love and protection that now envelopes you before stepping back out into the field refreshed, cleansed, rebalanced and reenergized.

Chapter Eleven

1. *'Putting in'* is a magnetic therapy technique pulling in healing forces from the Universal Energy Field for the benefit of others. For an explanation of the technique itself see *Magnetic Therapy: Healing In Your Hands* by Abbot George Burke, pg.31 (DeVorss & Company: Marina Del Rey, California, 1980).

2. For a fact sheet on Malaleuca Quinquenervia from the Australian Native Plants Society (Australia) visit http://anpsa.org.au/m-qui.html Also a more comprehensive fact sheet can be found at www.florabank.org.au/lucid/key/species%20navigater/media/html/Melaleuca quinquenervia.htm .For some spectacular imagery of this species simply google paperbark images or visit www.google.com.au/search?q=paperbark+images

3. www.fransorin.com/how-trees-can-be-a-source-of-wisdom

4. *NIDA* is the National Institute of Dramatic Art. Film & Television offering training courses in theatre, film, television, radio and new media. www.nida.edu.au

5. *GOMA* is the Queensland Art Gallery, Gallery of Modern Art. Stanley Place, cultural precinct, South Brisbane, QLD, 4101. www.qagoma.qld.gov.au

6. *Reverse Garbage* is a recycling co-operative that collects industrial discards to resell at low cost to the general public, thereby reducing landfill. They also run a variety of waste related art workshops and showcase artists and designers who salvage and upcycle materials, selling their wares in the front of the store. Find them at 20 Bourke St, Woolloongabba, Queensland and visit their online store to see their ever changing stock at www.reversegarbage.com.au

7. The *Crystal Cave* can be found at the Crystal Earth store, shop 2/71 Russell Street, West End, Brisbane, Queensland, Australia, 4101. Stocking an abundant array of crystals and esoteric materials give yourself plenty of time to explore. www.crystalearth.com.au www.facebook.com/pages/Crystal-Earth

8. *In.cube8r gallery* is a one stop gift shop selling unique handmade designs by different artists who lease display cubes and wall space to sell their wares on a no commission basis. That is the artist keeps the entire amount of sales without having to pay a commission. This helps keep costs affordable for both buyer and seller. Sadly *in.cube8r* in Brisbane has since closed down but at the time of publishing the Melbourne store was still running. Find in.cube8r @ 321 Smith St, Fitzroy, Victoria, Australia. www.facebook.com/in.cube8r

Chapter Twelve

1. Hoyan refers to Nameless as *"He"* understanding this is how I perceive him (as male energy). The time he refers to is actually our earthly time not Nameless's time as he is from *"no time."* i.e. I perceive an absence because I am operating on earth time but really is everything occurring all at once? I know we are only privy to part of the picture.

Chapter Thirteen

1. *What if? A Lifetime of Questions, Speculations, Reasonable Guesses and a Few Things I Know for Sure* by Shirley MacLaine (Simon & Schuster, 2013: Great Britain).

2. *Gubbi Gubbi Dance* is a locally based group of Indigenous performing artists showcasing traditional Aboriginal Arts through song and dance. www.gubbigubbidance.com

Chapter Fourteen

1. *Choku Rei (also Cho Ku Rei/Chokurei)* pronounced "Cho-Koo-Ray" is the Reiki power symbol generally meaning "Place the power of the Universe here," or "Place the (spiritual) power here." It is used to increase the power and flow of Reiki and also for protection. For

example drawing the symbol in front of you with the intention of being protected from negative energies, other people and all that may do you harm. It can also be used to empower a person who finds themselves in a difficult scenario providing insights and answers to aid the situation. Primarily used at the beginning and end of a Reiki healing session where it is imbedded into the aura for protection and to seal in the healing process. There is no limit to its use. www.reiki.nu/treatment/symbols/chokurei

2. *Kotodama* are sound syllables (think Mantra, but technically it is not Mantra) that are 'intoned' to enhance the effect of the Reiki symbols and practice. For Choku Rei it is "o-u-e-i." (Pronounced/toned, "oh-oo-ah-ee"). Kotodama refers to the "breath and heart" of the word, the spirit inherent in the word as it is vocalized. It is the power of the words to make things happen. All words contain Kotodama and some words are said to possess stronger Kotodama than others but it is also the persons focus, intonation and precise pronunciation that has a greater affect than if someone were to mumble them without this concentration and focus. In this way the Reiki Kotodama help the individual in forming a connection with the Reiki energies. www.aetw.org/reiki_mantra_jumon_kotodama

BIBLIOGRAPHY

Brennan, Barbara Ann. *Hands of Light: A Guide to Healing Through the Human Energy Field*. London: Bantam Books, 1988.

Burke, Abbot George. *Magnetic Therapy: Healing In Your Hands.* Marina del Rey, California: DeVorss & Company, 1980.

Ewing, Jim Pathfinder. *Reiki Shamanism: A Guide to Out-of-Body Healing.* Scotland: Findhorn Press, 2008.

Goodchild, Blossom. *The Bridge.* Noosa Heads, Australia: Golden Rays Publishing, 2007.

Greene, Brian. *The Elegant Universe.* London: Vintage Random House, 2005.

Lang, Richard. *Seeing Who You Really Are: A Modern Guide to Your True Identity.* London: Watkins Publishing, 2003.

Meadows, Kenneth. *Shamanic Experience: A Practical Guide to Psychic Powers:* Rochester, VT: Bear & Company, 2003.

Peat, F. David. *Superstrings and the Search for the Theory of Everything.* Chicago, Illinois: Contemporary Books, Inc., 1988.

Roman, Sanaya, and Duane Packer. *Opening To Channel: How to Connect With Your Guide.* Tiburon, California: H J Kramer Inc., 1987.

Stein, Diane. *Essential Reiki: A Complete Guide To An Ancient Healing Art.* New York: Random House Inc., 1995.

Talbot, Michael. *The Holographic Universe.* New York: HarperCollins Publishers, 1991.

Tompkins, Peter, and Christopher Bird. *The Secret Life of Plants.* New York: HarperCollins Publishers Inc., 1973.

Virtue, Doreen, Ph.D. *The Light Workers Way: Awakening Your Spiritual Power To Know and Heal.* Carlsbad, CA: Hay House Inc., 1997.

Way, Bruce. *Healing Energies: Understanding and Using Hands-on Healing.* East Roseville NSW: Simon & Schuster (Australia) Pty Limited, 2000.

Webster, Richard. *Pendulum Magic for Beginners: Power to Achieve All Goals.* Woodbury, MN: Llewellyn Publications, 2002.

ABOUT THE AUTHOR

Kai Phoenix N.D (Bachelor of Health Science Naturopathy) is a channel for *Light* with an avid interest in metaphysics and former assistant secretary of the Sunrise Spiritualist Church, Mount Tinbeerwah, Queensland (2004-5). Born in Waiouru New Zealand in 1963 she was raised in the suburbs of Melbourne, Australia and resettled in Noosa, Queensland at the age of forty with her four year old daughter Ruvé. Eight years later Kai moved just twenty minutes north of Noosa to the picturesque village of Boreen Point (population approx. 280) where she later came to write *Marikai, My Year Of Divine Guidance* on and around the shores of Lake Cootharaba.

Kai currently (2015) balances work in the Community Care sector with the facilitation of channeling and *Higher* telepathy workshops held locally on the Sunshine Coast of Australia where she divides her time between art projects, channeled writing and the love she shares with her daughter.

www.redbubble.com/people/kaiphoenix

www.facebook.com/kaifavenphoenix

www.ingramcontent.com/pod-product-compliance
Lightning Source LLC
Chambersburg PA
CBHW060242100426

42742CB00011B/1610
9780994431707